Proving the Value of HR

ROI Case Studies

Second Edition

By Patricia Pulliam Phillips, Ph.D.
and
Jack J. Phillips, Ph.D.

ROI Institute, Inc.
P.O. Box 380637
Birmingham, AL 35238-0637
www.roiinstitute.net

The case studies presented in this book have been previously published in the following publications and are reprinted here with permission.

Chapters 1, 3, 4, 5, and 6
  Phillips, J.J., Stone, R.D., Phillips, P.P., *The Human Resources Scorecard* (Butterworth-Heinemann, Woburn, MA, 2001)

Chapter 2
  Phillips, J.J., *In Action: Volume 2 Measuring Return on Investment* (ASTD, Alexandria, VA, 1997)

Chapters 7 and 8
  Phillips, J.J., Phillips, P.P., *In Action: Volume 3 Measuring Return on Investment* (ASTD, Alexandria, VA, 2001)

Chapter 9
  Phillips, J.J., Phillips, P.P., *In Action: Retaining Your Best Employees* (ASTD, Alexandria, VA, 2002)

Chapters 10 and 11
  Phillips, J.J., Phillips, P.P., *In Action: Measuring Return on Investment in the Public Sector* (ASTD, Alexandria, VA, 2002)

Chapters 12 and 13
  Phillips, J.J., Phillips, P.P., *ROI in Action Casebook* (San Francisco, CA, Pfeiffer, 2008)

Chapter 14
  Phillips, J.J., Phillips, P.P., *ROI at Work: Best Practice Case Studies from the Real World*, (ASTD, Alexandria, VA, 2005)

Chapter 15
  Phillips, J.J., *Return on Investment in Training and Performance Improvement Programs, Second Edition*, (Butterworth-Heinemann, Woburn, MA, 2003)

ISBN-13: 978-0-9790285-3-3
ISBN-10-: 0-9790285-3-1

Printed by EBSCO Media, Birmingham, Alabama, USA.
Edited by Beth Phillips, ROI Institute, Inc.

Table of Contents

ROI Institute, Inc.
P.O. Box 380637
Birmingham, AL 35238-0637
www.roiinstitute.net

Preface

This is a collection of ROI case studies that represents the classic use of the Phillips ROI Methodology™. They represent a variety of applications in the human resources, learning and development, and performance improvement fields. Each case follows the methodology and describes in detail how it was used to show the value of a particular project, program, or initiative.

These case studies have been selected for use in ROI workshops, briefings, and in certification processes. They are designed to be teaching tools. Each case was originally published in another document, either for The American Society for Training and Development (ASTD, Alexandria, VA) or The Society for Human Resource Management (Elsevier Butterworth-Heinemann, - Woburn, MA). Special thanks go to these publishers for allowing us to reprint these useful studies in this special edition for use in our learning process.

Target Audience

This book should interest anyone involved in human resources, learning and development, and performance improvement. The primary audience is practitioners who are struggling to determine the value of programs and to show how programs contribute to the strategic goals of the organization. These practitioners are the ones who request more real-world examples. This same group also expresses concern that there are too many models, methods, strategies, and theories, and too few examples to show if any of them has really made a difference. This publication should satisfy practitioners' needs by providing successful examples of the implementation of comprehensive evaluation processes.

Readers should find this casebook entertaining and engaging. Questions are placed at the end of each case to stimulate additional thought and discussion. One of the most effective ways to maximize the usefulness of this book is through group discussions, using the questions to develop and dissect the issues, techniques, methodologies, and results.

The Cases

The case studies we selected met specific guidelines. Each case study includes data that can be converted to monetary values so that ROI can be calculated. The selected case studies provide a method of isolating the effects of the program. The isolation step is imperative in showing the true value of a program. The methodologies included in the case studies presented in this book are control groups, trend line analysis, forecasting, and participant and manager estimates.

Although there was some attempt to structure cases similarly, they are not identical in style and content. It is important for the reader to experience the programs as they were developed and identify the issues pertinent to each particular setting and situation. The result is a variety of presentations with a variety of styles. Some cases are brief and to the point, outlining precisely what happened and what was achieved. Others provide more detailed background information, including how the need for the program was determined, the personalities involved, and how their backgrounds and biases created a unique situation.

Acknowledgments

We would like to acknowledge the clients who allowed us to publish these case studies. We greatly appreciate the help we have received from these clients as we have worked together in applying this methodology. In addition, we were assisted in the development of some of these cases by Ron Stone (Chapters 4, 6, and 11), Patrick Whalen (Chapter 6), and Dianne Hill (Chapter 1), all of whom have been associated with the ROI Institute.

For a variety of reasons, the clients have elected not to include their names or the names of their organizations. In today's competitive world and in situations where there is an attempt to explore new territory, it is understandable why an organization would choose not to be identified. Identification should not be a critical issue, however. Though some cases are slightly modified, they are based on real-world situations faced by real people.

Suggestions

We welcome your input. If you have ideas or recommendations regarding presentation, case selection, or case quality, please send them to us. Contact us with your comments and suggestions at ROI Institute, P.O. Box 380637, Birmingham, AL 35238-0637, www.roiinstitute.net, info@roiinstitute.net.

Jack and Patti Phillips
ROI Institute, Inc.
March, 2010

Preface to the Second Edition

From the beginning of the ROI Institute, nearly two decades ago, it became obvious to us that our clients had a strong desire to read case studies. Since then, we have developed dozens of case study books to satisfy this growing need. Our clients love them.

The case studies for the first edition of this book were carefully selected to represent some of our best teaching case studies. Consequently the book is used in workshops conducted by the ROI Institute team and our clients. Others use the cases in their own self study approach to understand ROI. Still others just find them interesting and intriguing. Because of this reaction to the first edition, the first printing was exhausted quickly, in less than two years.

With this revised second edition we have added to the value of this case book in three ways:

1. Four new case studies, in the soft skills area, have been added. We have had many requests for additional case studies in this important area.
2. The errors that worked their way into some of the case studies have been removed.
3. Teaching notes have been developed to enhance the use of the case studies in teaching scenarios and self study options. These are available at the ROI Resource Center, www.roiresourcecenter.net.

This new case book is best used with a reference book. When you need more detail on the ROI Methodology, we suggest that this case book be pared with any of the following:

Phillips, Jack .J. and Phillips, Patricia P., *The Value of Learning: How Organizations Capture Value and ROI.* (San Francisco: Pfeiffer, 2007).

Phillips, Jack J., and Schmidt, Lynn, *The Leadership Scorecard.* (Amsterdam: Elsevier Butterworth-Heinemann, 2004).

Phillips, Jack .J. and Phillips, Patricia P., *Proving the Value of HR: How and Why to Measure ROI.* (Alexandria, VA: SHRM, 2005).

Phillips, Jack J., *The Consultants Scorecard, Second Edition.* (New York: McGraw-Hill, 2010).

Phillips, Jack J., *ROI in Training and Performance Improvement Programs, Second Edition.* (Amsterdam: Elsevier Butterworth-Heinemann, 2003).

We want to particularly thank Beth Phillips for her excellent work on this case study book. Although she is new to our team, as Senior Editor, Beth took on this project with determination to make the second edition much better. Because of her meticulous work and excellent editing, this is our best book of case studies. We thank Beth for her contribution and her willingness to tackle a project with a tight time frame.

The ROI Institute team is pleased to provide this book of case studies. We think that you will find it even more useful than the first edition. As always, we welcome your comments, suggestions, and feedback on these case studies and other books. Please address this feedback to Beth Phillips, beth@roiinstute.net, Patti Phillips, patti@roiinstitute.net, or Jack Phillips, jack@roiinstitute.net.

About the Authors

Patti Phillips, Ph.D.

 Dr. Patti Phillips is president and CEO of ROI Institute, Inc., the leading source of ROI competency building, implementation support, networking, and research. She is also co-founder of the ROI Resource Center, a research and publishing firm dedicated to the dissemination of books, articles, research reports and practical resources to support processes of accountability in private, public, and social sector organizations.

After a thirteen-year career in the electrical utility industry, Phillips began her work with the ROI Methodology. Since 1997, she has embraced the ROI process, conducting research on the methodology as well as applying it to a variety of programs. She helps others build capacity in the ROI Methodology through a variety of channels, including the ROI Institute's ROI Certification process.

Patti's academic accomplishments include a Ph.D. in International Development and a Master's degree in Public and Private Management. She has been awarded the ASTD Certified Professional in Learning and Performance (CPLP) designation as well as ISPI's Certified Performance Technologist (CPT) designation. Currently she sits on the board of Cambridge, England-based ABDI, Ltd. She is editor of the ASTD *Handbook of Measuring and Evaluating Training* (2010) and has authored and co-authored a number of publications on the subject of accountability and ROI, including *Beyond Learning Objectives: Develop Measurable Objectives that Link to the Bottom Line* (ASTD, 2008); *The Value of Learning: How Organizations Capture Value and ROI* (Pfeiffer, 2007) and *Show Me the Money: How to Determine ROI in People, Projects, and Programs* (Berrett-Koehler, 2007) and the award winning *The Bottomline on ROI* (CEP Press, ISPI, 2002). Patti can be reached at patti@roiinstitute.net.

Jack J. Phillips, Ph.D.

Dr. Jack Phillips, a world-renowned expert on accountability, measurement, and evaluation, is Chairman of the ROI Institute. Phillips provides consulting services for *Fortune* 500 companies and major global organizations. The author or editor of more than 75 books, Jack conducts workshops and makes conference presentations throughout the world.

His expertise in measurement and evaluation is based on more than 27 years of corporate experience in the aerospace, textile, metals, construction materials, and banking industries. He has served as training and development manager at two Fortune 500 firms, as senior human resource officer at two firms, as president of a regional bank, and as management professor at a major state university.

This background led Jack to develop the ROI Methodology™ a revolutionary process that provides bottom-line figures and accountability for all types of learning, performance improvement, human resource, technology, and public policy programs. Jack regularly consults with clients in manufacturing, service, and government organizations in 52 countries in North and South America, Europe, Africa, Australia, and Asia.

Books most recently authored by Jack Phillips include *Measuring for Success: What CEOs Really Think About Learning Investments* (ROI Institute, ASTD Press, 2010); *ROI in Action Casebook* (Pfeiffer, 2008); *Beyond Learning Objectives: Develop Measurable Objectives That Link to the Bottom Line* (ASTD Press, 2008); *The Value of Learning: How Organizations Capture Value and ROI* (Pfeiffer, 2007); *Show Me the Money* (Berrett-Koehler, 2007); *Proving the Value of Meetings & Events: How and Why to Measure ROI* (ROI Institute, MPI, 2007); *How to Build a Successful Consulting Practice* (McGraw-Hill, 2006); *Investing in Your Company's Human Capital: Strategies to Avoid Spending Too Much or Too Little* (Amacom, 2005); *Return on Investment Basics* (ASTD Press, 2005); *Proving the Value of HR: How and Why to Measure ROI* (SHRM, 2005); *The Leadership Scorecard* (Elsevier Butterworth-Heinemann, 2004); *Managing Employee Retention* (Elsevier Butterworth-Heinemann, 2003); *Return on Investment in Training and Performance Improvement Projects*, 2nd ed. (Elsevier Butterworth-Heinemann, 2003). Jack served as series editor for ASTD's *In Action* casebook series, an ambitious publishing project featuring 30 titles, series editor for Elsevier Butterworth-Heinemann's Improving Human Performance series, and for Pfeiffer's new series on Measurement and Evaluation.

Jack has received several awards for his books and work. The Society for Human Resource Management presented him an award for one of his books and honored a Phillips ROI study with its highest award for creativity. The American Society for Training and Development gave him its highest award, Distinguished Contribution to Workplace Learning and Development, based on his work with ROI. For three years *Meeting News* has named Dr. Phillips one of the 25 most influential people in the Meetings and Events industry, based on his work on ROI for the industry. Jack has undergraduate degrees in electrical engineering, physics, and mathematics; a master's degree in Decision Sciences from Georgia State University; and a Ph.D. in Human Resource Management from the University of Alabama. He has served on the boards of several private businesses—including two NASDAQ companies—and several nonprofits and associations, including the American Society for Training and Development. He can be reached at (205) 678-8101, or by e-mail at jack@roiinstitute.net.

Additional Publications on the ROI Methodology

Measuring for Success: What CEOs Really Think About Learning Investments (ROI Institute, ASTD Press, 2010);

The Consultant's Scorecard: Tracking Results and Bottom-Line Impact of Consulting Projects 2nd Edition (McGraw-Hill, 2010);

Managing Talent Retention: An ROI Approach (Pfeiffer, 2009);

ROI in Action Casebook (Pfeiffer, 2008);

The Measurement and Evaluation Series – ROI Fundamentals 1, Data Collection 2, Isolation of Results 3, Data Conversion 4, Costs and ROI 5, Communication and Implementation 6 (ROI Institute, Pfeiffer, 2008);

The ROI Field Book: Strategies for Implementing ROI in HR and Training (Elsevier Butterworth-Heinemann, 2007);

The Value of Learning: How Organizations Capture Value and ROI (Pfeiffer, 2007);

Show Me the Money: How to Determine ROI in People, Projects, and Programs (Berrett-Koehler, 2007);

Proving the Value of Meetings & Events: How and Why to Measure ROI (ROI Institute, MPI, 2007);

Proving the Value of HR: ROI Case Studies (ROI Institute, 2007);

Proving the Value of HR: How and Why to Measure ROI (SHRM, 2005);

Return on Investment Basics (ASTD Press, 2005);

ROI at Work (ASTD Press, 2005);

The Leadership Scorecard (Elsevier Butterworth-Heinemann, 2004);

Return on Investment in Training and Performance Improvement Projects, 2nd ed. (Elsevier Butterworth-Heinemann, 2003);

The Project Management Scorecard: Measuring the Success of Project Management Solutions (Elsevier Butterworth-Heinemann, 2002);

How to Measure Training Results (McGraw-Hill, 2002);

Measuring ROI in the Public Sector (ASTD Press, 2002);

The Bottom-Line on ROI (CEP Press, 2002);

Measuring Return on Investment: Volume 3 (ASTD, 2001);

The Human Resources Scorecard: Measuring Return on Investment (Elsevier Butterworth-Heinemann, 2001);

Measuring Return on Investment: Volume 2 (ASTD Press, 1997);

Accountability in Human Resource Management (Gulf Publishing, 1996);

Handbook of Training Evaluation and Measuring Methods, 3rd ed. (Elsevier Butterworth-Heinemann, 1997).

How to Use this Casebook

These cases present a variety of approaches to evaluating human resources, learning and development, and performance improvement training programs. The cases focus on evaluation at the ultimate level—return on investment (ROI). Collectively, the cases offer a wide range of settings, methods, techniques, strategies, and approaches and represent manufacturing, service, and governmental organizations. Target groups for the programs vary from all employees to managers to technical specialists. As a group, these cases represent a rich source of information about the strategies of some of the best practitioners, consultants, and researchers in the field.

Each case does not necessarily represent the ideal approach for the specific situation. In every case it is possible to identify areas that might benefit from refinement to improvement. That is part of the learning process—to build on the work of others. Although the implementation processes are contextual, the methods and techniques can be used in other organizations.

Table 1 represents basic descriptions of the cases in the order in which they appear in the book. This table can serve as a quick reference for readers who want to examine the implementation approach for a particular type of program, audience, or industry.

Using the Cases

There are several ways to use this book. It will be helpful to anyone who wants to see real-life examples of the return on investment of specific programs. The authors recommend the following four uses:

1. This book will be useful to professionals as a basic reference of practical applications of measurement and evaluation. A reader can analyze and dissect each of the cases to develop an understanding of the issues, approaches, and, most of all, possible refinements or improvements.
2. This book will be useful in group discussions in which interested individuals can react to the material, offer different perspectives, and draw conclusions about approaches and techniques. The questions at the end of each case can serve as a beginning point for lively and entertaining discussion.
3. This book will serve as a supplement to other textbooks. It

provides the extra dimensions of real-life cases that show the outcomes of human resources, learning and development, and performance improvement programs.

4. Finally, this book will be extremely valuable for managers who do
not have primary human resources, learning and development, or
performance improvement responsibility. These managers provide support and assistance to the staff, and it is helpful for them
to understand the results that their programs can yield.

It is important to remember that each organization and its programs
are unique. What works well for one, may not work well for another, even
if they are in similar settings.

Follow-Up
Space limitations necessitated that some cases be shorter than the
authors would have liked. Some information concerning background,
assumptions, strategies, and results had to be omitted. If additional information on a case is needed, we are pleased for you to contact us directly
at jack@roiinstitute.net or patti@roiinstitute.net.

Table 1. Overview of Case Studies.

Case	Industry	Program	Target Audience
Healthcare Organization	Healthcare	Sexual Harassment Prevention	First-and-Second Level Supervisors, Managers, All Employees
Canadian Valve Company	Manufacturing	New Employee Training	Machine Operators
Midwest Electric, Inc.	Electric Utility	Stress Management	All Employees
National Steel	Manufacturing	Safety Incentives	Operating Employees
Imperial National Bank	Financial Services	Executive Leadership Development	Top Executives, High-Potential Leaders
United Petroleum International	Oil Refinery	eLearning	Sales Engineers, Sales Managers
Cracker Box	Restaurant	Performance Management Training	Store Manager Trainees
Retail Merchandise Company	Retail Stores	Basic Selling Skills	Sales Associates
Southeast Corridor Bank	Financial Services	Skills-Based Pay	Branch Employees
Federal Information Agency	Public Sector – Federal	Internal MS Degree Program	Technical Specialists
Metro Transit Authority	Transportation	Absenteeism Reduction	Bus Drivers
TechnoTel Corp.	Telecom	Meeting Management	Project Managers
Nations Hotel Corp.	Hospitality	Business Coaching	Executives
Global Car Rental	Transportation	Leadership Development	First Level Managers
Linear Network Systems	Technology	Leadership Development	First Level Managers

CHAPTER

Measuring ROI in Sexual Harassment Prevention

Healthcare Inc.

Most organizations have sexual harassment prevention programs, but few are subjected to accountability up to and including a return-on-investment (ROI) analysis. In the setting in this case, a large healthcare chain conducted a sexual harassment prevention workshop involving first-level managers and supervisors. Workshops were followed by meetings with all employees, conducted by the same managers and supervisors. In all, seventeen workshops were presented, and the monetary impact was developed. Several unique issues are involved in this case, including the techniques to isolate the effects of training and convert data to monetary values. The analysis used a traditional ROI model and yielded significant and impressive results that surprised the evaluation team and senior managers.

Background

Healthcare Inc. (HI) is a regional provider of a variety of healthcare services through a chain of hospitals, HMOs, and clinics. HI has grown steadily in the last few years and has earned a reputation as an aggressive and financially sound company. HI is publicly owned, with an aggressive management team poised for additional growth.

The healthcare industry in the USA continues to operate in a state of tremendous transformation and transition. The concern about healthcare costs, the threat of additional government regulation, and the implementation of new technology and healthcare

This case was prepared to serve as a basis for discussion rather than an illustration of either effective or ineffective administrative and management practices. All names, dates, places, and organizations have been disguised at the request of the author or organization.

delivery systems are radically transforming the healthcare field. HI is attempting to take advantage of these challenges and carve out a significant market share in its regional area of operation.

Events Leading to Program

In the USA, sexual harassment continues to grow as an important and significant employee relations issue. Sexual harassment claims throughout the USA and in the healthcare industry continue to grow, sparked in part by increased public awareness of the issue and the willingness of the victims to report harassment complaints. HI has experienced an increasing number of sexual harassment complaints, with a significant number of them converting to charges and lawsuits. The company record was considered excessive by executives and represented a persistent and irritating problem. In addition, HI was experiencing an unusually high level of turnover, which may have been linked to sexual harassment.

Senior management, concerned about the stigma of continued sexual harassment complaints and the increasing cost of defending the company against claims, instructed the HR vice president to take corrective and preventive action to significantly reduce complaints and ultimately rid the workplace of any signs of harassment. The HR vice president instructed the HRD staff to develop a workshop for employees or managers or both, but only if a lack of understanding and knowledge of the issue existed.

In response to the request, the HRD staff conducted interviews with the entire EEO and affirmative action staff in which the magnitude of the problem and the potential causes were explored. Most of the staff indicated that there seemed to be a significant lack of understanding of the company's policy on sexual harassment and what actually constituted inappropriate or illegal behavior. In addition, the complaints for the last year were examined for issues and patterns. Exit interviews of terminating employees for the last year were reviewed to see if there was a linkage to sexual harassment. Approximately 11 percent of terminating employees identified sexual harassment as a factor in their decision to leave HI. Because of the request to proceed with this program, the HRD staff members did not conduct a full-scale needs assessment. Instead, they augmented the input from the EEO/AA staff with the exit interviews conducted with ten randomly selected first-level supervisors to explore the level of understanding of the policy, inappropriate and illegal behavior, and the perceived causes of the increased complaint activity.

From an analysis of complaints, the typical person accused of sexual harassment was a supervisor and male. The typical victim of harassment was non-supervisory and female. The analysis also revealed that the type of sexual harassment typically experienced at HI was in the category, defined by the EEOC as "an individual making unwelcome sexual advances or other verbal or physical conduct of a sexual nature with the purpose of, or that creates the effect of, unreasonably interfering with an individual's work performance or creating an intimidating, hostile, or offensive working environment." This type of harassment should be minimized by developing a clear understanding of HI's policy regarding harassment and by teaching managers to identify illegal and inappropriate activity. As part of HI's policy, supervisors and managers were required to conduct a limited investigation of informal complaints and to discuss issues as they surfaced.

The Program: Design, Development, and Implementation

Armed with input from ten interviews and with detailed input from the EEO/AA staff, the major causes of the problem were identified. There was an apparent lack of understanding of (1) the company's sexual harassment policy and (2) what constituted inappropriate and illegal behavior. In addition, there was an apparent insensitivity to the issue. As a result, a one-day sexual harassment prevention workshop was designed for all first- and second-level supervisors and managers. The program had the following objectives. After attending this program, participants should be able to:

- Understand and administer the company's policy on sexual harassment
- Identify inappropriate and illegal behavior related to sexual harassment
- Investigate and discuss sexual harassment issues
- Conduct a meeting with all direct reports to discuss policy and expected behavior
- Ensure that the workplace is free from sexual harassment
- Reduce the number of sexual harassment complaints

Because of the implications of this issue, it was important for the information to be discussed with all employees so that there would not be any misunderstanding about the policy or inappropriate behavior. Each supervisor was asked to conduct a meeting with his or her direct employees to discuss this topic.

The program design was typical of HI programs, using a combination of purchased and internally-developed materials. The one-day program was implemented and conducted during a 45-day period, with 17 sessions involving 655 managers. HR managers and coordinators served as program facilitators.

Why ROI?

HR/HRD programs usually targeted for an ROI calculation are those perceived to be adding significant value to the company, closely linked to the organizational goals and strategic objectives. Then, the ROI calculation is pursued to confirm the added value, and based on the results of the ROI analysis, these programs may be enhanced, redesigned, or eliminated altogether if the ROI is negative. The sexual harassment prevention program is different. If the ROI analysis yields a negative value, the program would not be discontinued. It might be altered for future sessions but only if the behavior changes were not occurring at Level 3.

At HI, this program was chosen for an ROI calculation for two reasons. First, the HR and HRD departments were interested in the accountability of all programs, including sexual harassment programs. Second, a positive ROI would clearly show management that these types of programs, which are preventive in nature, can significantly impact the bottom line when implemented throughout the organization and supported by management.

Data Collection

Figure 1 shows the completed data collection plan for the sexual harassment training program. A pre/post-test was administered to measure knowledge of HI's sexual harassment policy and of inappropriate and illegal behavior. The 20-item questionnaire was evenly split on policy and behavior issues.

Figure 1. Evaluation Plan: Data Collection.

Program: Preventing Sexual Harassment   **Responsibility:** _____   **Date:** _____

Level	Program Objective(s)	Evaluation Method	Timing	Responsibilities
I. Reaction, Satisfaction and Planned Actions	• Obtain a positive reaction to program and materials • Obtain input for suggestions for improving program • Identify planned actions	• Reaction questionnaire	• End of session	• Facilitator
II. Learning	• Knowledge of policy on sexual harassment • Knowledge of inappropriate and illegal behavior • Skills to investigate and discuss sexual harassment	• Pre/post-test • Skill practices	• Beginning of session • End of session • During session	• Facilitator
III. Job Application	• Administer policy • Conduct meeting with employees • Ensure that workplace is free of sexual harassment	• Self-assessment questionnaire (1) • Complete and submit meeting record • Employee Survey (25% sample)	• 6 months after program • 1 month after program • 6 months after program	• Program evaluator • HRIS staff • Employee communication
IV. Business Results	• Reduce internal complaints • Reduce external complaints • Reduce employee turnover	• Performance monitoring • Self-assessment questionnaire (1)	• Monthly for 1 year before and after program • 6 months after program	• Program evaluator

(1) Same Questionnaire

Measuring ROI in Sexual Harassment Prevention **5**

To measure the success of program application, three data collection methods were used. First, a meeting record was required of each supervisor and manager to document the actual meeting with employees, recording the time, duration, topics, and participants. Although, this form did not address the quality of the meeting, it provided evidence that the meeting was conducted.

The second data collection method was a survey of the non-supervisory employees, the typical target group for harassment activity. Although the entire team could have been surveyed, it was felt that it was more important to examine behavior change from the perspective of those who were more likely to be victims of harassment. The survey was planned for administration six months after the program was completed. It provided post-program data only and therefore each questionnaire had to be worded to capture change since the training was conducted. The 15-item survey examined specific behavior changes and environmental changes related to harassment activity, including actions that might be considered inappropriate or offensive. Figure 2 shows some typical questions.

Figure 2. Sample of Questions.

	Strongly Disagree	Disagree	Neutral	Agree	Strongly Agree
I have noticed less offensive language at work.	☐	☐	☐	☐	☐
I am certain that the company will take swift action against those who are found guilty of sexual harassment.	☐	☐	☐	☐	☐

The third data collection method was a self-assessment questionnaire completed by supervisors and managers. This questionnaire captured actions, behavior change, and results linked to the program. Although there were a variety of other data collection possibilities, including focus groups, interviews, and third party observation, it was felt that, given the time and cost considerations, these three methods provided sufficient data to capture behavior change and show that the program had succeeded.

Business results measures included several items. Initially, it was planned that internal complaints, lodged formally with the HR division, would be monitored along with external charges filed with various agencies (primarily the EEOC). Because of the lag time between changes in behavior and a reduction in complaints, data would be collected for one year after the program and compared with data from one year before the program to determine specific improvements. Also, as alternative information, litigated complaints would be tracked along with the direct costs, including legal fees, settlements, and losses. In addition, because of the perceived link between a hostile work environment and turnover, annual employee turnover would be examined for the same time period.

ROI Analysis

To develop the ROI calculation, several other issues needed to be addressed to plan for the Level 5 evaluation. The specific method(s) to isolate the effects of the program from other influences would have to be selected and implemented. The various ways in which data are converted to monetary values would need to be pinpointed. Each specific program cost element would have to be identified along with other issues that might influence the reduction in complaints and litigation expenses. Finally, intangible benefits expected from the program needed to be itemized and the communication targets established.

ROI Analysis Plan

Figure 3 shows the completed document for the ROI analysis plan. Because of the relatively short timeframe required to implement the program and the desire from top management to implement it throughout the organization quickly, a control group arrangement was not feasible. However, because historical data are available for all complaint measures, a trend-line analysis was initially planned. Complaint activity would be projected based on 12 months of data prior to the program. Actual performance would be compared with the projected value, and the difference would reflect the actual impact of the program on that measure. In addition to

Figure 3. Evaluation Strategy: ROI Analysis.

Program: Preventing Sexual Harassment   **Responsibility:** _____   **Date:** _____

Data Items	Methods of Isolating the Effects of the Program	Methods of Converting Data	Cost Categories	Intangible Benefits	Other Influences/Issues	Commnication Targets
Formal internal complaints of sexual harassment	• Trendline analysis • Participant estimation	• Historical costs with estimation from EEO/AA staff	• Needs assessment • Program development/ acquisition • Coordination/ facilitation time • Program materials • Food/ refreshments • Facilities • Participant salaries and benefits • Evaluation	• Job satisfaction • Absenteeism • Stress reduction • Image of HI • Recruiting	• Several initiatives to reduce turnover were implemented during this time period	• All employees (condensed info.) • Senior executives (summary of report with detailed backup)
External complaints of sexual harassment	• Trendline analysis • Participant estimation	• Historical costs with estimation from EEO/AA staff			• Must not duplicate benefits from both internal and external complaints	• All supervisors and manager (brief report)
Employee turnover	• Forecasting using percent of turnover related to sexual harassment	• External studies within industry				• All HR/RD staff (full report)

trend-line analysis, participants' estimation was planned to compare with trend-line data. In this type of situation, supervisors and managers (participants) are asked to indicate the extent to which the program influenced the changes in the number of complaints.

For turnover, trend-line analysis could not be used because of the other initiatives implemented to reduce turnover. Therefore, a type of forecasting was used in which the percentage of turnover related to sexual harassment is developed for the 12-month period prior to the program The same percentage is developed for the post-program period.

In regard to converting the data to monetary values, the cost of complaints would be derived both from historical data, when available, and from estimates for other factors, such as the actual time used for harassment complaints. The estimates would be developed with input from the EEO/AA staff. For turnover, industry data would be used because HI had not calculated the actual cost of turnover for any employee groups. The specific cost items, intangible benefits, other influences, and communication targets were all identified and are presented in Figure 3.

Reaction and Learning Data

A typical end-of-program questionnaire was used to capture reaction data. Overall, the participants reacted positively to the program and perceived it to be timely and useful. A composite rating of 4.11 out of a possible 5 was achieved. The vast majority of the participants (93 percent) provided a list of action items planned as a result of the program.

For a Level 2 evaluation, the pre-program test scores averaged 51 and the post-program scores averaged 84, representing a dramatic increase of 65 percent. These results were significant and exceeded the expectations of the program developers. Two important points were underscored with the Level 2 measures. First, the low scores on pre-program testing provided evidence that the program was necessary. The participants did not understand the organization's policy, nor did they recognize what constituted inappropriate and illegal behavior. Second, the dramatic improvement in scores provided assurance that the content of the program was appropriate for both key issues, as the participants learned much about policy and behavior. As part of the Level 2 evaluation, participants were involved in skill practices for issues involving administering policy.

On-the-Job Application

One of the initial actions required of participants was to conduct a meeting with his/her employees to discuss sexual harassment issues, review HI's policy on sexual harassment, and discuss what constitutes inappropriate and illegal behavior. Handouts and visual aids were provided to each supervisor and manager to assist with the meeting. A meeting record form had to be completed and submitted to the HR department as evidence that the meeting was conducted. The time of the meeting, the duration, the participants by name, and the specific topics covered were noted on the form. Within one month of the program, 82 percent of the participants had completed the meeting record.

Ultimately, 96 percent completed it. Some managers did not conduct meetings because they did not have direct reports.

Six months after the program was conducted, an anonymous survey was conducted with a 25 percent sample of non-supervisory employees. A total of 1,720 surveys were distributed, and 1,100 were returned for a response rate of 64 percent. The survey yielded an average score of 4.1 on a scale of 1 to 5. The rating represents the extent to which the behavior had changed in the six months since the program was conducted. Overall, the survey results indicated that significant behavior change had occurred and the work environment was largely free of harassment.

A follow-up questionnaire was administered directly to all participants six months after the program was conducted. A total of 571 questionnaires were returned, representing a response rate of 87 percent. The questionnaire probed the extent to which program materials were used and specific behavior changes had been realized. In addition, participants estimated the amount of improvement in sexual harassment complaints that was directly attributable to this program. Although the input from participants (managers and supervisors) may be biased, significant changes were reported. With regard to actions completed, 92 percent reported that some actions were completed, while 68 percent reported that all actions were completed.

Business Impact

Figure 4 shows the complaint and turnover data for one year prior to the program and one year after the program. In the six-month follow-up questionnaire, participants were provided the six-month averages from before and after the program and were asked to estimate the percent of improvement actually caused by this program. The average percentages from all participants are included in the right column. The results also show the turnover rate for the non-supervisory employees for the 12 months preceding the program and for the 12 months after the program.

Figure 4. Complaint and Turnover Data.

Business Performance Measure	One Year Prior to Program	One Year After Program	Factor for Isolating the Effects of the Program
Internal Complaints	55	35	74%
External Charges	24	14	62%
Litigated Complaints	10	6	51%
Legal Fees and Expenses	$632,000	$481,000	
Settlement/Losses	$450,000	$125,000	
Total Cost of Sexual Harassment Prevention, Investigation, and Defense*	$1,655,000	$852,000	
Turnover (Non-Supervisory) Annualized	24.2%	19.9%	

* Includes legal fees, settlement/losses, portion of EEO/AA staff assigned to sexual harassment, management time for this activity, printed materials, and miscellaneous expenses.

Figure 5 shows a plot of the formal internal complaints of sexual harassment 12 months prior to the program and 12 months after the program. Prior to the program, there was an upward trend of complaints and senior managers felt this would continue if they took no action to improve the situation. Also, no other initiatives were undertaken to focus attention on sexual harassment. The magnitude of the program, involving 17 training sessions with 655 managers and meetings with all employees, focused significant attention on the issue. Therefore, it was felt that the trend-line analysis might be an effective tool for isolating the effects of the training.

Figure 5. Formal Internal Complaints of Sexual Harassment.

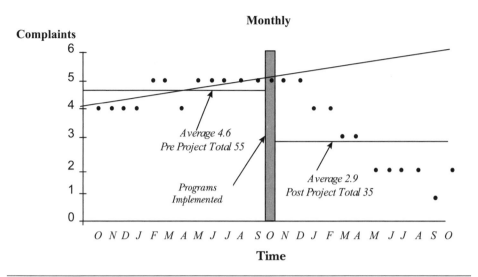

The turnover rate showed a dramatic improvement during this same timeframe. However, because of the serious problem with turnover, other initiatives were undertaken to help reduce the departure rate of employees. Recruiting processes were enhanced, entry-level salaries were increased, and more effective selection techniques were employed during the same time period. All these actions were initiated to develop a better match between the employees and the culture at HI. Therefore, the trend-line forecast for the turnover rate would be accurate because of the influence of these factors on the turnover rate.

To estimate the percent of turnover reduction directly related to this program, a special version of the forecasting process was considered. During the needs assessment, the exit interview files were reviewed for evidence of sexual harassment as a factor in the decision to leave. In these cases, 11 percent of the actual turnovers had mentioned sexual harassment. Employees are often reluctant to indicate the presence of sexual harassment, although this issue may be the reason for their departure. Therefore, it was felt that this 11 percent figure was a conservative estimate of the number of terminations related to a hostile work environment. A 12-month review of exit interviews, on a post-program basis, revealed that only 3 percent of the interviewees mentioned sexual harassment or a hostile work environment as a reason for their departure. The percent of employees leaving because of sexual harassment dropped from 11 to 3 percent of terminations. The target group for the turnover reduction was non-supervisory employees, which represented an average of 6,844 on a post-program basis and 6,651 on a pre-program basis. For the 12-month period after the program, the employment levels at HI averaged 7,540, including 655 for the target group for training and 41 senior managers who did not participate directly in the training program. The average non-supervisory salary for the post-program period was $27,850, and for the pre-program period, it was $26,541. Several industry studies on the cost of turnover were briefly discussed, which showed ranges from 110 percent to 150 percent of annual salaries. The evaluation team felt that 75 percent of annual salaries would be a conservative estimate.

Program Costs

Program costs are fully loaded and include the cost of the needs assessment ($9,000), design and development ($15,000), and evaluation ($31,000). The needs assessment cost was an estimate based on the direct time and expenses involved in the process. The development costs were low because of the availability of materials for purchase. The evaluation costs include an estimate of all internal and external costs associated with the follow-up evaluation, including the ROI. Participants' salaries and benefits were included, although it was not HI's policy to include salaries and benefits as a training expense for a one-day program for supervisors and managers.

Figure 6 shows the salary profile of participating supervisors and managers. The time necessary for program coordination was estimated along with the time for facilitator preparation and delivery. When considering the average salaries plus benefits for these individuals, a value of $9,600 was estimated. Travel and lodging for coordination and facilitation was a minor factor, estimated at $1,520. Program materials cost $12 per participant, and food and refreshments during the workshop cost $30 per participant. The estimated value of the conference rooms used for the program was $150 per day.

Figure 6. Salaries and Benefits of Participants.

Management Level	Number Participating in Program	Salary Midpoint Value
7	41	$32,500
8	435	43,600
9	121	54,300
10	58	66,700

Employee benefits costs as a percent of payroll = 39%.
Managers work an average of 47 weeks per year.

Monetary Benefits from Program

Figure 7 shows the calculation for the monetary benefits from the sexual harassment program. For the reduction of complaints, the value could be based on reducing internal complaints, external charges, or litigated complaints, but not all three. The value for each measure is shown in the exhibit. The values are developed by taking the total cost of sexual harassment prevention, investigation, and defense from Figure 4 and dividing it by each of these three measures. The total value of the reduction for each measure (indicated in Figure 4) was developed, leaving the decision of which measure to use. Because of the interest in tracking internal complaints, the evaluation team decided to use it as the unit of improvement in the analysis. Therefore, the value of one internal complaint was placed at $24,343. If one complaint could be avoided, HI would save that amount. The lower value is used to be conservative. Another approach is to examine the total cost of sexual harassment, including prevention, investigation, and defense, and use a value equal to the reduction in cost. However, because there is a lag between measures of complaints and actual losses and legal expenses, the reduction illustrated in Exhibit 3 may not reflect the actual cost savings.

Figure 7. Monetary Benefits from Program.

Complaint Reduction		
	Pre-Program	**Post-Program**
Average Cost of Internal Complaint	$30,090	$24,343
Average Cost of External Complaint	$68,958	$60,857
Average Cost of Litigated Complaint	$165,500	$142,000

> Unit of Improvement = One Internal Complaint
> Value of One Internal Complaint = $24,343
> Total Improvement: 55 − 35 = 20
> Improvement Related to Program: 20 × 74% = 14.8
> Value of Improvement = 14.8 × $24,343 = $360,276

Turnover Reduction
Unit of Improvement = One Turnover Statistic (Termination)
Turnover Pre-Program = 6,651 x 24.2% = 1,610
Turnover, Pre-Program, Related to Hostile Environment: 1,610 x 11% = 177
Turnover, Post-Program: 6,844 x 19.9% = 1,362
Turnover Post-Program Related to Hostile Environment: 1,362 x 3% = 41
Improvement Related to Program: 177 − 41 = 136
Cost of One Turnover: 75% of Annual Salary = $27,850 x .75 = $20,887
Value of Improvement: 136 x $20,887 = $2,840,632

Although the total improvement is 20 internal complaints, the improvement related directly to the program is 74 percent of that figure, or 14.8 complaints. The 74 percent is an estimate from the supervisors and managers taken directly from the questionnaire, as they were asked to indicate the extent to which the reduction in complaints was related directly to the program and the confidence of the estimate. The value of the improvement is $360,276. Figure 7 shows these calculations.

The value for the turnover reduction was developed in a similar manner. The unit of improvement is one turnover statistic. The 24.2 percent turnover rate represents 1,610 employees who, before the program, left voluntarily or were forced to leave because of performance. According to the exit interviews, 11 percent of those were related to sexual harassment. Therefore, 177 terminations were related to sexual harassment. On a post-program basis, the 19.9 percent turnover represents 1,362 employees. Post-program exit interviews revealed that 3 percent were related to a hostile work environment. Therefore, 41 employees left because of sexual harassment. The improvement related directly to the program is 136 terminations, a significant number when the cost of turnover is included. Although there was sufficient evidence to use the annual salary as a cost of turnover, to be conservative the team used 75 percent of the annual salaries, representing $20,887 as a cost of one turnover statistic. The 136 yielded a staggering $2,840,632 as the savings generated by the reduction in turnover that was caused by sexual harassment.

Figure 5, presented earlier, shows the trend-line projections for the internal complaint data. The trend, established prior to the program, was projected for the evaluation period. As the projection shows, the impact of the program is even more dramatic than illustrated in the above calculations because of the upward trend of the data. Instead of a value of 14.8 (20 x 74%), a value of 32 could be used in the analysis. Because the impact is more conservative using the participants' estimates, this figure was used in the analysis. Therefore, the actual calculations represent an understatement of actual performance.

Program Cost

Figure 8 shows the detail of the program cost categories. Most of the cost items were straightforward and taken from actual cost statements or from estimates given by those closely involved in the process. Participants' salaries and benefits were developed using midpoint values for the managers in each classification. The managers' midpoint salary data were converted to a daily rate by dividing by 235 (the number of days actually worked), and this was multiplied by the number of managers at that grade level attending the program. Participants' salaries and benefits greatly overshadow the other cost elements.

Figure 8. Program Costs.

Needs Assessment (Estimated Cost of Time)	$ 9,000
Program Development/Acquisition	15,000
Program Coordination/Facilitation Time	9,600
Travel and Lodging for Facilitation and Coordinators	1,520
Program Materials (655 @ $12)	7,860
Food/Refreshments (655 @ $30)	19,650
Facilities (17 @ $150)	2,550
Participant Salaries and Benefits ($130,797 x 1.39)	181,807
Evaluation	31,000
	$277,987

ROI Calculation

Figure 9 shows the benefit/cost ratio and ROI calculations for these values. Benefits based entirely on complaint reduction and turnover reduction are used in the benefits/costs ratio to yield 11.5:1. Therefore, for each $1 spent on the program, $11.50 was returned. The ROI calculation, which uses net benefits, shows a return of 1,052 percent, an impressive and staggering amount.

Figure 9. ROI Calculation.

$$BCR = \frac{Benefits}{Costs} = \frac{\$360,276 + \$2,840,632}{\$277,987} = \frac{\$3,200,908}{\$277,987} = 11.5:1$$

$$ROI = \frac{Net\ Benefits}{Costs} = \frac{\$3,200,908 - \$277,987}{\$277,987} = 1,052\%$$

Questions for Discussion

1. Was the needs assessment appropriate for this situation? Please explain.
2. Should this program be evaluated at Levels 4 and 5? If so, what specific measures should be used for Level 4 data?
3. What specific method(s) should be used to isolate the effects of the program?
4. What are the most appropriate ways to convert the Level 4 data to monetary values?
5. Critique the Level 2 and Level 3 results. Was the employee survey necessary? Explain.
6. Which Level 4 complaint measure is most appropriate? Why?
7. Project the trend-line for internal complaints and estimate the impact of the program on the number of complaints. Use the average of the last three months for comparison.
8. Is the ROI lower or higher than you expected? Please comment.
9. Do you consider this estimate realistic?
10. How could this process be improved?
11. How would you present these data to management? To all employees?

Forecasting ROI for Machine Operator Training

Canadian Valve Company

Before funds can be allocated for major training programs, management sometimes needs information on the forecasted return-on-investment (ROI). In this case, which involves the training of machine operators, the proposed program included significant capital expenditures and the creation of a training facility. Prior to pursuing the project, an ROI was developed using a small-scale pilot effort. The ROI was developed using methods typically reserved for postprogram evaluation. The results of the process can apply to almost any type of setting in which a major training expenditure is under consideration.

Background

Canadian Valve Company (CVC) has enjoyed a long and profitable history as a family-owned business, serving the international industrial valve market. CVC machines, polishes, and assembles valves to be shipped to the worldwide market from several strategically located plants. The company has enjoyed tremendous growth in recent years, much of it in foreign markets.

The company's growth and persistent employee turnover have always left a critical need for new machine operators. Unfortunately, the skilled labor market was unable to adequately supply trained machine operators, and CVC had to develop its own training program. Machine operators work various equipment including lathes, drill presses, and

This case was prepared to serve as a basis for discussion rather than to illustrate either effective or ineffective administrative and management practices. All names, dates, places, and organizations have been disguised at the request of the author or organization.

milling machines. New employees recruited for the machining area were usually untrained, inexperienced operators who received on-the-job training by their supervisors using the regular production equipment. This approach had created problems because new trainees were not productive during initial employment, and production machines were virtually out of service during training. Production management considered the traditional on-the-job training methods not very effective, and the training time to prepare new operators appeared excessive. In addition, the problems of high scrap and excessive machine downtime were often by-products of ineffective initial training provided to new employees. Too often a new machine operator, in the midst of frustration, left the company and became a turnover statistic.

The production division, led by Bob Merkle, was concerned about the approach to training and wanted some changes. The human resources manager, Jim Gates, thought that a separate area for training was needed along with a comprehensive training program. In an initial conversation, Merkle concluded that a structured training program taught by an experienced instructor away from the pressures of production should reduce costs, increase productivity, and improve the training process. Jim Gates saw an excellent opportunity to make a significant impact with training, and he wanted to use the resources of the Ontario Training and Adjustment Board (OTAB).

Jim Gates and the Opportunity

A 10-year employee with Canadian Valve, Jim Gates had worked in production before taking on the job of human resource development manager. He understood the company's business and was anxious to help the company solve problems. He had earned an excellent reputation for producing effective programs and saw the comprehensive program to train new machine operators as an excellent opportunity to show the benefits of training and boost his own career opportunities at CVC. He was becoming convinced that if there was any area of training and development in which a cost-benefit analysis could be forecasted, it would be with the machine operator training and he was very interested in pursuing this project.

Bob Merkle and the Challenge

A task-oriented production manager with an engineering degree, Bob Merkle joined CVC as a management trainee 20 years earlier and progressed to vice president of production. Most of his job assignments were in the production area. He was very concerned about the bottom line and took great pride in his cost-control methods and strategies to improve efficiency.

In all his years in production, Merkle was never completely convinced that training was worth the time and effort. He had supported it primarily because the president had a strong commitment to training and development. Although his employees had always participated in programs, both on and off the job, he was skeptical of the results they produced. He felt training was best accomplished on the job by the immediate supervisor.

In recent months, however, his own production supervisors had complained about the approach to training new machine operators and the problems that new recruits created for the various departments. The production supervisors wanted to hire experienced operators and often could not understand why they were not available. The employment office had tried unsuccessfully to find experienced machine operators, using a variety of recruiting strategies. The production departments had to settle with unstructured on-the-job training with inexperienced operators.

Gates had initially approached Bob Merkle about the idea of a separate training area utilizing off-the-job training. On a pilot basis, they borrowed a production machine from one department and prepared it for training. A relief supervisor was assigned the task of training new recruits. Gates and the supervisors were pleased with the experimental effort and the reaction from the union was positive. Consequently, they took the proposal to Merkle to consider establishing a comprehensive training program.

The Project

After listening to the initial proposal from Gates, Merkle seemed to be interested in pursuing the process. Finally he said to Gates, "Jim, prepare a detailed analysis of the savings that this new approach to training would generate. Contact the Ontario Training and Adjustment Board to see if funding assistance is available to help with this type of program. Be sure to include a labor representative on your team. Calculate the benefits of this approach in terms of an expected return-on-investment. Based on the analysis we will go forward with it." Merkle knew the president would support the project if the payback were sufficient.

Gates was pleased with the assignment and added, "This is an excellent project. We know we can deliver a top-notch training program that we all can be proud of, and one that will bring significant improvements. With the help OTAB, we will complete the task and have the full proposal in two weeks." Gates assembled a task force to work on the project.

A major issue in developing the program was the question of where the training should take place. The task force concluded that training should take place out of the production environment where the trainee could learn under the close supervision of a professional instructor who was experienced with all the machines. As a result, Gates explored the possibility of locating a separate area in a remote section of the main production area. In his view, this assignment had three major tasks:

1. Develop a complete training plan detailing the type of training program duration, training outlines, training structure, and training organization.
2. Design a preliminary layout of the area planned for training and determine how to procure machines for training.
3. Estimate the expected benefits and costs for the proposed program.

Although challenging, the tasks were feasible and could be completed in about two weeks. Gates was very excited about this opportunity.

John McIntosh

Gates contacted John McIntosh, a consultant for the Ontario Skills Development Office (OSDO), who was assigned to a local college near Canadian Valve's main location. McIntosh provides training and development consulting services to local clients from this location. Having worked in a variety of training and manufacturing companies before joining the OSDO program, he is always eager to help his clients with training plans. Because of the sheer number of clients, however, he was limited with the amount of time he could spend with them to develop a cost-benefit analysis (CBA).

Program Benefits

Although small in scale, the experimental pilot project revealed surprising results. Trainees were able to reach target levels of productivity much faster than expected, and their error rates were much lower than anticipated. In addition, the trainees seemed to be more satisfied with their jobs. In a brief meeting with McIntosh, Gates and his staff identified several areas for potential cost savings. Most of these were developed after an analysis of the performance of the employees in the pilot training program when compared to the performance of the employees who had not participated in the training. Gates and McIntosh decided that they would drive the project evaluation with several important performance improvement measures. Other benefits could be identified as additional reasons for moving forward with the project. They expected improvements in productivity, scrap rates, safety, and maintenance expense. Other benefits were not so obvious. Previously, trainees had become frustrated when supervisors did not have time to work with them on a one-on-one basis to develop skills. The frustration led to a turnover statistic. The following performance measurements were isolated:

- Reduction in time to reach a standard proficiency level (training time)
- Improvement in the scrap rate for new employees
- Improvement in the employee safety record (first-aid injuries)
- Reduction in equipment maintenance expense
- Reduction in turnover of new employees

These tangible benefits were to be used in the analysis. Gates and McIntosh could see other benefits. Low tolerance production could be performed in the training area as practice work for the trainees. Limited small-scale research and development projects could also be performed there. Although these benefits would be monitored, there would be no attempt to place a monetary value on them. They would be listed as intangible benefits.

Employees in training make mistakes and sometimes do not meet with friendly responses from their supervisors, so they were always frustrated during their initial stages of employment. This training program, if implemented properly, should improve employee attitudes and morale. Another benefit was improved absenteeism. When employees are frustrated and having difficulty on a job, they sometimes remove themselves from the frustration and take a day off. The anxiety or frustration may cause problems, leaving employees thinking they are actually sick when they are not. Finally, another advantage is a reduction in training responsibility for supervisors. With an influx of new employees in the shop, many supervisors have complained that they do not have time to train them. Consequently, they neglect other duties. This new approach to training should free supervisors to perform what they do best—plan and coordinate the work of machine operators and keep them motivated. Because of the difficulty of measuring these additional intangible benefits, Gates decided not to use them in calculations of cost savings. Instead, he would rely on the improvements in the five tangible measurement factors listed earlier.

Converting Data to Values

One of the most difficult tasks in completing an ROI evaluation is estimating the expected benefits from the program. This calculation is more difficult to do than a postprogram evaluation where the results can be compared to a before-and-after situation. With this assignment, Gates had to estimate the benefits, relying on two sources of information. First, the pilot program, which was conducted earlier, presented some measurable improvements, and this information was used in each of the five tangible benefit areas. As part of the analysis of the pilot results, Gates asked the relief supervisor, who was responsible for the training, and his department manager if there had been other actors that contributed to the results. The answer was negative.

Next, Gates and McIntosh consulted with production supervisors who were involved in early discussions of the concept of the program. In a focus group format, they discussed the benefits of the new approach to training and provided estimates of the extent of improvements that could be achieved. When combined, these two approaches formed the basis for estimating the potential improvements that would be relayed directly to the new approach to training.

Training Time

As a standard practice, supervisors recorded the production shortfall with new employees until they reached the standard rate for a machine. These losses were essentially lost production as a result of trainees taking time allowed to learn to operate a machine at a standard rate. Company records indicated that more than $65,000 was charged to trainee losses in the machining areas during the previous years. The pilot program showed a 64 percent reduction, and the supervisors estimated that trainee losses could be reduced by 50 percent with a structured training program in a separate area. The lower value was used, resulting in a projected savings of $33,000. (Note that all dollars are in Canadian funds).

Machining Scrap

Although many factors contribute to machining scrap, one of the biggest factors is lack of training with new and inexperienced operators. The supervisors estimated that there could be at least a 10 percent reduction in total scrap costs with the new training program. To be conservative, the lower value was used. In machining areas the annual cost of scrap was $450,000 for all product lines. A 10 percent reduction results in a $45,000 savings. This figure was significant because the potential for scrap reduction was high. Management felt that the estimate was conservative.

Turnover

The turnover rate in the machining area was eight employees per month. Because of the smaller numbers of employees involved in the pilot program, turnover reduction data were inconclusive. The supervisors felt that a significant percentage of this turnover was directly related to ineffective or insufficient training, or both, and they estimated that a new approach to training could reduce this turnover rate by at least 30 percent. This value was used in the analysis. The turnover of eight employees per month translates into 96 employees per year. The estimated cost to recruit and train a new employee was $4,000, representing a total annual cost of $384,000. A 30 percent savings is $115,200.

This estimate was considered conservative. The $4,000 cost to recruit, employ, and train a new employee includes unproductive time in the first week of employment. On the average, new employees who left the company during the training program worked longer than one week. Therefore, the cost to the company was probably greater than $4,000 because some lost production occurred after the first week.

Safety

Most of the accidents in the machining area were not lost-time injuries, but were first aid injuries that were treated in the company's medical facility. First-aid injuries were used in the analysis. The pilot program reflected a 25 percent reduction. The supervisors estimated that accidents could be reduced by 30 percent with an effective training program that emphasized safety practices. The number of first-aid injuries in the machining area was averaging 86 per year with the majority of them involving new employees. The total cost in a year for these accidents (including outside medical costs, workers' compensation, and first aid) was $57,000. The 25 percent value was used, resulting in an annual cost savings of $14,250.

Maintenance Expense

Effective training of new employees should result in less maintenance required on production machines. A part of the current, unscheduled machine downtime is caused by new employees improperly operating equipment during their training period. The pilot program showed a dramatic reduction of 45 percent. However, the supervisors estimated that the unscheduled maintenance expense could be reduced by 10 percent each year with the implementation of the training program. The lower value was used. The annual unscheduled maintenance costs for the machining areas were $975,000. The annual savings would be $97,500. This estimate was considered to be very conservative.

Savings Summary

The total projected annual savings are as follows:

		Pilot Results ($)	Supervisor Estimate ($)
Training time		41,600	33,000 ✓
Machining scrap		76,500	45,000 ✓
Turnover		N/A	115,200 ✓
Accidents		14,290	14,250 ✓
Maintenance expense		438,750	97,500 ✓
	Total	571,100	304,950

The values with the check (✓) were used in the benefits calculation, resulting in a total of $304,950. To ensure that top management bought into the process, Gates and McIntosh reviewed the benefits analysis and the assumptions, including the logic, with all the supervisors and the managers in the machining area. Collectively, they felt the estimates were conservative and supported the projected cost savings.

Program Costs

The cost for the proposed program involved the acquisition of the necessary equipment, the salaries and expenses of two instructors, and the additional administrative overhead expenses connected with the training program. The most efficient approach was to utilize space in a remote, currently unused part of the plant. A nominal rent of $10,000 per year was to be charged to the project. The initial program development cost was estimated to be $15,000. This amount was spread over two years. The equipment cost was less than expected. Most of the equipment planned for the new facility was surplus equipment from the production line that was modified and reconditioned for use in training. The total equipment cost was estimated to be $95,000. This figure included $7,000 initial installation expenses. The cost included the equipment for staffing two cubicles for the instructors and providing them with various training aids, including overhead projectors. This investment was prorated over a five-year period.

The salaries of two instructors plus benefits and expenses were estimated to be $80,000 per year. The overhead costs, which include normal maintenance, were estimated to be $15,000 each year.

The total annualized costs are as follows:

Equipment (prorated)	$19,000
Space (rental)	10,000
Program development (prorated)	7,500
Instructors	80,00
Maintenance	15,000
	$131,500

Although there may be other costs, Gates and McIntosh thought that these were the most significant costs and covered what would be necessary in the proposal. As with the benefits, cost figures were reviewed with production managers as well as the finance and accounting staff to ensure that there was complete support for the numbers. With minor adjustments, they were ready to move forward and calculate the return.

As part of the funding assistance available from OTAB, a reimbursement of one-third of the development costs and instructor costs was available. However, to ensure that the costs are fully loaded, this reimbursement was not considered in the analysis.

Calculating the Expected Return

A comparison of the costs with the savings yields the following calculations. The benefit-cost ratio (BCR) is:

$$\text{BCR} = \frac{304{,}950}{131{,}500} = 2.32$$

The first-year net savings are as follows:

Annual gross savings	$304,950
Less program costs	131,950
Net savings	173,450

The expected ROI for the first year is

$$ROI = \frac{173,450}{131,500} \times 100 = 132\%$$

The investment in the equipment and the program development spread over several years (five years and two years, respectively). This approach assumes a useful life of five years for the building, equipment, and program development.

This estimate of BCR and ROI seemed to be a little high but was expected in this case. Gates attributed high value of this ratio to the following reasons:

- The equipment costs were low, using the salvage value plus costs for reconditioning. New equipment would cost much more but have a longer useful life.
- There was no additional investment in a new facility, which would have added significantly to the start-up costs.
- However, several items make a case for the BCR and the ROI to be undervalued: The cost savings were probably understated because the lower value was used when two values were available. Pilot program results were usually greater.
- The reimbursement of a portion of the costs from OTAB was not considered in the analysis. Thus, the actual project costs are overstated.
- The potential monetary benefits from the intangible measures could add to the cost savings.

Presentation

With calculations developed, the project was ready for presentation. The training program details had been designed with input from production supervisors and the training staff. Both Gates and McIntosh contributed to the final arrangement for the proposal. The engineering department assisted in the layout and work flow. Gates set up a meeting with Merkle and the production managers and presented the proposal in the following order:

- Program design
- Equipment procurement and layout
- Program benefits
- Costs
- Expected return-on-investment and cost-benefit analysis
- Intangible benefits

Although there were a few questions, the methodology, assumptions, and calculation were fully supported. The managers were particularly impressed with the conservative approach used in the analysis and the involvement of the supervisors. The project was approved in the meeting.

As Gates left the meeting, he felt a great sense of accomplishment in demonstrating the potential benefits of training on a forecasted basis. He knew that now the challenge was up to his group to show that the project would realize the benefits forecasted. He would use a comprehensive measurement system to track the performance measures used to estimate cost savings and would report on results in six months.

Questions for Discussion

1. How credible is the process? Explain.
2. Without the information from the pilot program, could the ROI be forecasted? Explain.
3. How would you critique the methods used in converting data to monetary values?
4. An important part of any ROI calculation is to account for other factors, which may influence output measures? How is this issue addressed in this case?
5. Are the projected costs for the program reasonable? Explain.
6. How realistic are the values for BCR and ROI. Explain.
7. How helpful is the role of OTAB in this process?
8. How important are the intangible benefits? Could other intangible benefits be identified? Should they be converted to monetary benefits?

CHAPTER

Measuring ROI in Stress Management

Midwest Electric Inc.

This case study begins by describing how the needs for a stress management program were determined and how an organization development solution was evaluated through ROI. The comprehensive approach includes the use of the StressMap® to measure learning, as well as the use of control groups to isolate the effects of the program. A description of how the ROI was measured is included. The specific forms, issues, and processes make this a practical case study for organizations interested in a comprehensive, balanced approach to evaluation.

Background

Midwest Electric Inc. (MEI) is a growing electric utility serving several midwestern states. Since deregulation of the industry, MEI has been on a course of diversification and growth. Through a series of acquisitions, MEI has moved outside its traditional operating areas and into several related businesses.

MEI had been experiencing significant workplace changes as it transformed from a bureaucratic, sluggish organization into a lean, competitive force in the marketplace. These changes placed tremendous pressure on employees to develop multiple skills and perform additional work. Employees, working in teams, had to constantly strive to reduce costs, maintain excellent quality, boost productivity,

This case was prepared to serve as a basis for discussion rather than an illustration of either effective or ineffective administrative and management practices. All names, dates, places, and organizations have been disguised at the request of the author or organization.

and generate new and efficient ways to supply customers and improve service.

As with many industries in a deregulated environment, MEI detected symptoms of employee stress. The safety and health function in the company suggested that employee stress lowered productivity and reduced employee effectiveness. Stress was also considered a significant employee health risk. Research had shown that high levels of stress were commonplace in many work groups and that organizations were taking steps to help employees and work groups reduce stress in a variety of ways. The vice president of human resources at MEI asked the safety and health department, with the help of the training department, to develop a program for work groups to help them alleviate stressful situations and deal more productively and effectively with job-induced stress.

Needs Assessment

Because of its size and sophisticated human resource systems, MEI had an extensive database on employee-related measures. MEI prided itself as being one of the leaders in the industry in human resources issues. Needs assessments had been routinely conducted at MEI, and the HR vice president was willing to allow sufficient time for an adequate needs assessment before proceeding with the stress management program.

The overall purpose of the needs assessment was to identify the causes of a perceived problem. The needs assessment would:

- Confirm that a problem did exist and provide an assessment of the actual impact of this problem
- Uncover potential causes of the problem within the work unit, company, and environment
- Provide insight into potential rememdies to correct the problem

The sources of data for the needs assessment included company records, external research, team members, team leaders, and managers. The assessment began with a review of external research that identified the factors usually related to high stress and the consequences of high stress in work groups. The consequences uncovered specific measures that could be identified at MEI.

This external research led to a review of several key data items in company records, including attitude surveys, medical claims, employee assistance plan (EAP) use, safety and health records, and exit interviews. The attitude survey data represented the results from the previous year and were reviewed for low scores on the specific questions that could yield stress-related symptoms. Medical claims were analyzed by codes to identify the extent of those related to stress-induced illnesses. EAP data were reviewed to determine the extent to which employees were using provisions and services of the plan perceived to be stress-related. Safety records were reviewed to determine if specific accidents were stress-related or if causes of accidents could be traced to high levels of stress. In each of the above areas, the data were compared with data from the previous year to determine whether stress-related measures were changing. Also, where available, data were compared with expected norms from the external research. Finally, exit interviews for the previous six months were analyzed to determine the extent to which the stress-related situations were factors in an employee's decision to voluntarily leave MEI.

During MEI's needs assessment process, a small sample of employees (10 team members) was interviewed to discuss their work-life situations and to uncover symptoms of stress at work. Also, a small group of managers (five) was interviewed with the same purpose. To provide more detail about this input, a 10 percent sample of employees received a questionnaire to explore the same issues. MEI had 22,550 employees with 18,220 non-supervisory team members.

Summary of Findings

The needs assessment process uncovered several significant findings:

- There was evidence of high levels of stress in work groups, caused by MEI's deregulation, restructuring, and job changes – in essence, the change in the nature of work-induced, high levels of stress in most work groups.
- Stress had led to a deterioration in several performance measures, including medical costs, short-term disability, withdrawals (absenteeism, turnover), and job satisfaction.

- Employees were often not fully aware of stress factors and the effect stress had on them and their work.
- Employees had inadequate skills for coping with stress and adjusting to, managing, and eliminating highly stressful situations.
- Managers had more insight into the causes of stress but did not have the skills or mechanisms to deal with most stressful situations.

Program Planning and Design

Several inherent factors about work groups and data at MEI influenced the program and its subsequent evaluation. MEI was organized around teams, and groups were not usually identical. However, many teams had similar performance measures. The HR database was rich with a variety of measures and with data about employees and work unit factors. Because of the team environment and the important role of the team leader/manager, the program to reduce stress needed to involve the management group in a proactive way. Any efforts to reduce stress needed to shift much of the responsibility to participants and therefore reduce the amount of time off the job. Job pressures in the deregulated environment provided fewer off-the-job opportunities for meeting and development activities.

Program Design

Although several approaches could have feasibly satisfied this need, four issues surfaced that influenced program design:

- A skills and knowledge deficiency existed, and some type of learning event was necessary.
- Several stress management programs were commercially available, which could prevent developing a new program from scratch.
- Managers needed to be involved in the process to the greatest extent possible.
- Because of the concerns about time away from the job, the actual classroom/formal meeting activities needed to be limited to one or two days.

With this in mind, the program outlined in Figure 1 was designed to meet this important need.

Figure 1. Stress Management for Intact Work Teams.

Departments or work groups of 10 or more people who are committed to improving the satisfaction and effectiveness of their teams will benefit by this more comprehensive approach to stress. The process uses the StressMap® tool as the starting point.

Managers and representative employees will participate in focus groups to identify work satisfiers and distressors and then will collaborate on alleviating systemic sources of stress.

What Group Members Will Learn
- How to identify sources of stress and their personal response to them
- That individuals have the ability to make a difference in their lives
- How to take the first steps to enhance personal health and overall performance
- How to access resources, internally and externally, to help teach personal goals

What the Group/Manager Will Learn
- Group profile of sources of stress and response patterns
- Additional information about sources of both work distress and work satisfaction obtained through focus groups and themes identified when possible
- New stress reduction skills specific to the needs of the group
- Development of recommendations for next steps to improve work satisfaction and productivity

Highlights
- Through completion of a comprehensive self-assessment tool called StressMap®, individuals will be able to immediately score themselves on 21 stress scales dealing with work and home life, as well as learn about their preferred coping styles and the thinking and feeling patterns that impact their ability to manage stress. Anonymous copies of each member's StressMap® will be compiled to create a group score.
- A 3–4 hour StressMap® debriefing session designed to help individuals better interpret their scores will be followed by a four-hour module suited to the needs of the group (such as situation mastery, changing habits, creating climate for agreement). Total of one day.

Precourse Requirements
- Management commitment to the process is essential. Employees will complete the StressMap® tool and submit a confidential copy.

Length and Format
- Lead time of three to four weeks minimum for preparation and communication
- Consultant on-site 1-1/2 days
- Initial follow-up one to two weeks later on-site or by phone to senior management (Subsequent follow-up on impact of the initiative to occur as negotiated with three to four hours of telephone follow-up included).

Cost
- Approximately $XXXX (plus taxes) US per group of 8 to 25; $XX US per set of materials. Travel and living expenses for consultant are additional.

Why ROI?

HR programs usually targeted for a Level 5 ROI evaluation are those perceived to be adding significant value to the company, and closely linked to the organizational goals and strategic objectives. The evaluation is then pursued to confirm the added value. Based on the results of the analysis, these programs may be enhanced, redesigned, or eliminated if the results are insufficient. Stress management can be different. If the results are inadequate, the program may not be discontinued but may be altered for future sessions, particularly if behavior changes are not identified in the Level 3 evaluation.

At MEI, the stress management program was chosen for an ROI evaluation for two reasons. First, the HR department was interested in the accountability of all programs, including stress management. Second, positive results would clearly show management that these types of programs, which are preventive in nature, could significantly contribute to the bottom line when implemented and supported by management.

Because the program could have been expensive if applied to the entire company, it was decided to try it on a limited basis to determine its success and then to either adjust the program, discontinue the program, or expand the program to other areas in MEI. The evaluation methodology provided the best information to make that decision.

Data Collection Plan

Figure 2 shows the data collection plan for the stress management program. Broad objectives were established for Levels 1, 2, 3, and 4 data collection. The data collection plan was comprehensive but necessary to meet all of requirements at each of the four levels of data collection. The timing and responsibilities were detailed. For measuring learning, three tools were used. The StressMap® was one measure of learning in the awareness category. Completion of the StressMap® provided insight into stress factors and stress signals. In addition, built into the one-day program was an end-of-course self-assessment to measure learning. Finally, the facilitator had a brief checklist to indicate the extent of learning for the group.

At Level 3 data collection, the completion of the 21-day plan provided some evidence that the participants had changed behavior to

Figure 2. Data Collection Plan.

Program: Stress Management for Intact Groups   Responsibility: _____   Date: _____

Level	Broad Program Objective(s)	Data Collection Method	Timing of Data Collection	Responsibilities for Data Collection
I Reaction, Satisfaction, and Planned Actions	• Positive Reaction • Suggestions for Improvements • Planned Action	• Standard Questionnaire • 21-Day Action Plan	• End of 1-Day Course • End of Course	• Facilitator • Facilitator
II Learning	• Personal Stress Awareness • Coping Strategies • Stress Reduction Skills	• StressMap® • Self-Assessment • Facilitator Assessment	• Prior to Course • End of Course • End of Course	• Facilitator • Facilitator • Facilitator
III Application	• Change Behavior to Reduce Stress • Develop Group Action Plan and Communicate to Group • Access Internal/External Resources • Application of Skills/Knowledge	• Completion of 21-Day Plan • Conference Call • Follow-Up Session • Review Records • Follow-Up Questionnaire	• 21 Days After Course • 21 Days After Course • 1-2 Weeks After 1-Day Course • 6 Months After Course • 6 Months After Course	• No Report • Facilitator • Facilitator/Manager • Program Coordinator • External Consultant
IV Business Impact	• Reduce Medical Care Costs • Reduce Absenteeism • Reduce Turnover • Increase Productivity • Increase Job Satisfaction	• Group Records • Group Records • Group Records • Group Records • Follow-Up Questionnaire	• 6 Months After Course • 6 Months After Course • 6 Months After Course • 6 Months After Course • 6 Months After Course	• Program Coordinator • Program Coordinator • Program Coordinator • Program Coordinator • External Consultant

reduce stress. A conference call was planned with the facilitator, team manager, and the team 21 days after the course. This provided a review of issues and addressed any concerns or barriers to further implementation. A follow-up session was planned with the team, co-facilitated by the manager and facilitator, approximately one to two weeks after the one-day program, to discuss changes in behavior and to address barriers. To determine the extent to which the participants were using internal or external resources to address stress-related problems, records of those requests were scheduled to be reviewed for approximately six months. Finally, a detailed follow-up questionnaire was planned for six months after the program to collect both Levels 3 and 4 data. This questionnaire was intended to capture sustained behavior changes, indicate barriers to improvement, and identify impact measures for both groups and individuals.

Group records were expected to reveal changes in medical costs, absenteeism, turnover, and productivity six months after the program. In addition, increased job satisfaction was to be determined from the follow-up questionnaire, which would be administered six months after the program (the same questionnaire described earlier).

ROI Analysis Plan

Figure 3 shows the ROI analysis plan. For most data items, the method to isolate the effects of the program would be obtained in a control group arrangement in which the performance of the group involved in the program would be compared with the performance of a carefully-matched companion control group. In addition, for most of the data items, trend-line analysis was scheduled for use. Historical data were projected in a trend and compared with the actual data to determine the impact of the program.

The methods of converting data involved a variety of approaches, including tabulating direct costs, using standard values, using external data, and securing estimates from a variety of target audiences. The cost categories represented fully-loaded costs for the program. Expected intangible benefits from the program were based on the experience of other organizations and other stress reduction programs. The communication target audience consisted of six key groups ranging from corporate and business unit managers to participants and their immediate supervisors.

Figure 3. Evaluation Strategy: ROI Analysis.

Program: Stress Management for Intact Groups   Responsibility: _____   Date: _____

Data Items (Usually Level 4)	Methods of Isolating the Effects of the Program	Methods of Converting Data	Cost Categories	Intangible Benefits	Other Influences/Issues	Communication Targets
Medical Health Care Costs—Preventable Claims	• Control Group Arrangement • Treadline Analysis	• Direct Costs	• Needs Assessment • Program Development	• Improved Communication • Time Savings	• Match Groups Appropriately • Limit Communications with Control Group	• Program Participants • Intact Team/Manager
Absenteeism	• Control Group Arrangement • Treadline Analysis	• Supervisor Estimation • Standard Value	• Program Materials • Participant Salaries/Benefits	• Fewer Conflicts • Teamwork	• Check for Team-Building Initiatives During Program	• Senior Manager/Management in Business Units
Employee Turnover	• Control Group • Treadline Analysis	• External Study—Cost of Turnover in High Tech Industry • Management Review	• Participant Travel (if applicable) • Facilitator • Meeting Facilities (Room, Food, Beverages)	• Improvement in Problem Solving	• Monitor Restructuring Activities During Program	• Training and Education Staff • Safety and Health Staff
Employee Job Satisfaction	• Control Group Arrangement • Management Estimation	• Management Estimation	• Program Coordinator • Training and Education Overhead		• 6 Grtoups Will Be Monitored	• Senior Corporate Management
Employee/Group Productivity	• Control Group Arrangement • Treadline Analysis	• Standard Values • Management Estimation	• Evaluation Costs			• Prospective Team Leaders

Management Involvement

Management involvement was a key issue from the beginning and was integrated throughout the design of the program. The manager served as the team leader for the program, although a facilitator provided assistance and conducted a one-day workshop.

Figure 4 illustrates the tool used for identifying initial problems as the work group began using the stress management program. With this brief questionnaire, the manager identified specific problem areas and provided appropriate comments and details. This exercise allowed program planning to focus on the problems and provided guidance to the facilitator and the team.

**Figure 4. Manager Input: Potential Area for Improvement
Stress Reduction for Intact Work Teams.**

Before you begin the stress reduction program for your team, it is important to capture specific concerns that you have about your work group. Some of these concerns may be stress related and therefore may be used to help structure specific goals and objectives for your team. For each of the following potential areas of improvement, please check all that apply to your group. Add others if appropriate. Next to the item, provide specific comments to detail your concerns and indicate if you think this concern may be related to excessive stress.

• Employee Turnover. Comments:

_____

_____

• Employee Absenteeism. Comments:

_____

_____

• Employee Complaints. Comments:

_____

_____

• Morale/Job Satisfaction. Comments:

_____

_____

- Conflicts with the Team. Comments:

  _____

  _____

- Productivity. Comments:

  _____

  _____

- Quality. Comments:

  _____

  _____

- Customer Satisfaction. Comments:

  _____

  _____

- Customer Service. Comments:

  _____

  _____

- Work Backlog. Comments:

  _____

  _____

- Delays. Comments:

  _____

  _____

- Other Areas. List and Provide Comments:

  _____

  _____

Figure 5 illustrates manager responsibility and involvement for the process. This handout, provided directly to the managers, details 12 specific areas of responsibility and involvement for the managers. Collectively, initial planning, program design, and detailing of responsibilities pushed the manager into a higher-profile position in the program.

Figure 5. Manager Responsibility and Involvement
Stress Management for Intact Work Teams.

With the team approach, the team manager should:

1. Have a discussion with the facilitator to share reasons for interest in stress reduction and the desired outcome of the program. Gain a greater understanding of the StressMap® and the OD approach. Discuss recent changes in the work group and identify any known stressors. This meeting could be held with the senior manager or the senior management team.
2. Identify any additional work group members for the consultant to call to gather preliminary information.
3. Appoint a project coordinator, preferably an individual with good organizing and influencing skills, who is respected by the work group.
4. Send out a letter with a personal endorsement and signature, inviting the group to participate in the program.
5. Allocate eight hours of work time per employee for completion of StressMap® and attendance at a StressMap® debriefing and customized course.
6. Schedule a focus group after discussing desired group composition with the facilitator. Ideal size is 10 to 22 participants. The manager should not attend.
7. Attend the workshop and ensure that direct reports attend.
8. Participate in the follow-up meeting held after the last workshop, either in person or by conference call. Other participants to include are the HR representative for your area, the Safety and Health representative for your area, and your management team. The facilitator will provide feedback about the group issues and make recommendations of actions to take to reduce work stress or increase work satisfaction.
9. Commit to an action plan to reduce workplace distress and/or increase workplace satisfaction after thoughtfully considering feedback.
10. Communicate the action plan to your work group.
11. Schedule and participate in a 21-day follow-up call with the consultant and your work group.
12. Work with your team (managers, HR, safety and health, facilitator) to evaluate the success of the action plan and determine the next steps.

Control Group Arrangement

The appropriateness of control groups was reviewed in this setting. If a stress reduction program was needed, it would be appropriate and ethical to withhold the program for certain groups while the experiment was being conducted. It was concluded that this approach was appropriate because the impact of the planned program was in question. Although it was clear that stress-induced problems existed at MEI, there was no guarantee that this program would correct them. Six control groups were planned. The control group arrangement was diligently pursued because it represented the best approach to isolating the effects of the program, if the groups could be matched.

Several criteria were available for group selection. Figure 6 shows the data collection instrument used to identify groups for a control group arrangement. At the first cut, only those groups that had the same measures were considered (that is, at least 75 percent of the measures were common in the group). This action provided an opportunity to compare performance in the six months preceding the program.

Next, only groups in the same function code were used. At MEI, all groups were assigned a code depending on the type of work, such as finance and accounting or engineering. Therefore, each experimental group had to be in the same code as the matched control group. It was also required that all six groups span at least three different codes.

Two other variables were used in the matching process: group size and tenure. The number of employees in the groups had to be within a 20 percent spread, and the average tenure had to be within a two-year range. At MEI, as with many other utilities, there was a high average tenure rate.

Although other variables could have been used to make the match, these five were considered the most influential in the outcome. In summary, the following criteria were used to select the two sets of groups:

- Same measures of performance
- Similar performance in the previous six months
- Same function code
- Similar size
- Similar tenure

The six pairs of groups represented a total level of employment of 138 team members and six managers for the experimental groups, and 132 team members and six managers for the control groups.

Figure 6. Manager Input: Group Measures and Characteristics Stress Management for Intact Work Teams.

To measure the progress of your team, a brief profile of performance measures for employees and your work group is needed. This information will be helpful to determine the feasibility of using your group in a pilot study to measure the impact of the stress management program. Changes in performance measures will be monitored for six months after the program.

Listed below are several categories of measures for your work group. Check the appropriate category and please indicate the specific measure under the description. In addition, indicate if it is a group measure or an individual measure. If other measures are available in other categories, please include them under "Other."

Key Performance Measures   Dept_____

Performance Category	Measure	Description of Measure	Group Measure	Individual Measure
Productivity	1.		☐	☐
	2.		☐	☐
Efficiency	3.		☐	☐
	4.		☐	☐
Quality	5.		☐	☐
	6.		☐	☐
Response Time	7.		☐	☐
	8.		☐	☐
Cost Control/ Budgets	9.		☐	☐
	10.		☐	☐
Customer Satisfaction	11.		☐	☐
	12.		☐	☐
Absenteeism	13.		☐	☐
Turnover	14.		☐	☐
Morale/ Job Satisfaction	15.		☐	☐
	16.		☐	☐
Other (please specify)	17.		☐	☐
	18.		☐	☐
	19.		☐	☐
	20.		☐	☐

Group Characteristics

Average tenure for group _____ years   Group function code _____
Average job grade for group _____   Average age _____
Number in group _____   Average educational level _____

Program Results

Questionnaire Response

A follow-up questionnaire, Figure 7, served as the primary data collection instrument for participants. A similar, slightly modified instrument was used with the managers. In all, 73 percent of the participants returned the questionnaire. This excellent response rate was caused, in part, by a variety of actions taken to ensure an appropriate response rate. Some of the most important actions were:

- The team manager distributed the questionnaire and encouraged participants to return it to the external consulting firm. The manager also provided a follow-up reminder.
- A full explanation of how the evaluation data would be used was provided to participants.
- The questionnaire was reviewed during the follow-up session.
- Two types of incentives were used.
- Participants were promised a copy of the questionnaire results.

Figure 7. Stress Management for Intact Work Teams Impact Questionnaire.

Check one: ☐ Team Member ☐ Team Leader/Manager

1. Listed below are the objectives of the stress management program. After reflecting on this program, please indicate the degree of success in meeting the objectives.

OBJECTIVES	Failed	Limited Success	Generally Successful	Completely Successful
PERSONAL				
• Identify sources of stress in work, personal, and family worlds				
• Apply coping strategies to manage stressful situations				
• Understand to what degree stress is hampering your health and performance				
• Take steps to enhance personal health and overall performance				
• Access internal and external resources to help reach personal goals				

GROUP

- Identify sources of stress for group

- Identify sources of distress and satisfaction

- Apply skills to manage and reduce stress in work group

- Develop action plan to improve work group effectiveness

- Improve effectiveness and efficiency measures for work group

_____

_____

_____

2. Did you develop and implement a 21-day action plan?
   Yes ☐ No ☐
   If yes, please describe the success of the plan. If not, explain why. _____
   _____

3. Please rate, on a scale of 1–5, the relevance of each of the program elements to your job, with (1) indicating no relevance, and (5) indicating very relevant.

   _____ StressMap® Instrument   _____ Action Planning
   _____ Group Discussion   _____ Program Content

4. Please indicate the degree of success in applying the following skills and behaviors as a result of your participation in the stress management program.

Figure 7. *(continued)*

	1 No	2 Little	3 Some	4 Significant	5 Very Much	No Opportunity To Use Skills
a) Selecting containable behavior for change						
b) Identifying measures of behavior						
c) Taking full responsibility for your actions						
d) Selecting a buddy to help you change behavior						
e) Identifying and removing barriers to changing behavior						
f) Identifying and using enablers to help change behavior						
g) Staying on track with the 21-day action plan						
h) Applying coping strategies to manage stressful situations						
i) Using control effectively						
j) Knowing when to let go						
k) Responding effectively to conflict						
l) Creating a positive climate						
m) Acknowledging a complaint properly						
n) Reframing problems						
o) Using stress talk strategies						

5. List (3) behaviors or skills you have used most as a result of the stress management program.

_____

_____

6. When did you first use one of the skills from the program?

_____ During the program

_____ Day(s) after the program (indicate number)

_____ Week(s) after the program (indicate number)

7. Indicate the types of relationships in which you have used the skills.

☐ Coworkers
☐ Manager or supervisor
☐ MEI employee in another function
☐ Spouse
☐ Child
☐ Friend
☐ Other (list): _____

PERSONAL CHANGES

8. What has changed about your on-the-job behavior as a result of this program? (positive attitude, fewer conflicts, better organized, fewer outbursts of anger, etc.)

_____

_____

_____

Figure 7. (continued)

9. Recognizing the changes in your own behavior and perceptions, please identify any specific personal accomplishments/improvements that you can link to this program. (time savings, project completion, fewer mistakes, etc.)

_____

_____

10. What specific value in U.S. dollars can be attributed to the above accomplishments/improvements? Although this is a difficult question, try to think of specific ways in which the above improvements can be converted to monetary units. Use one year of data. Along with the monetary value, please indicate the basis of your calculation.

$ _____

Basis _____

_____

11. What level of confidence do you place in the above estimations? (0% = No Confidence, 100% = Certainty) _____ %

12. Other factors often influence improvements in performance. Please indicate the percent of the above improvement that is related directly to this program. _____ %

Please explain. _____

_____

GROUP CHANGES

13. What has changed about your work group as a result of your group's participation in this program? (interactions, cooperation, commitment, problem solving, creativity, etc.)

_____

_____

_____

_____

14. Please identify any specific group accomplishments/improvements that you can link to the program. (project completion, response times, innovative approaches)

_____

_____

_____

15. What specific value in U.S. dollars can be attributed to the above accomplishments/improvements? Although this is a difficult question, try to think of specific ways in which the above improvements can be converted to monetary units. Use one year of values. Along with the monetary value, please indicate the basis of your calculation.

$ _____

Basis _____

_____

_____

16. What level of confidence do you place in the above estimations? (0% = No Confidence, 100% = Certainty) _____ %

Figure 7. *(continued)*

17. Other factors often influence improvements in performance. Please indicate the percent of the above improvement that is related directly to this program. _____ %

_____

_____

18. Do you think this program represented a good investment for MEI?

Yes ☐   No ☐

Please explain. _____

_____

_____

19. What barriers, if any, have you encountered that have prevented you from using skills or knowledge gained in this program? Check all that apply. Please explain, if possible.

☐ Not enough time
☐ Work environment does not support it
☐ Management does not support it
☐ Information is not useful (comments)
☐ Other _____

_____

_____

20. Which of the following best describes the actions of your manager during the stress management program?

☐ Very little discussion or reference to the program
☐ Casual mention of program with few specifics
☐ Discussed details of program in terms of content, issues, concerns, etc.
☐ Discussed how the program could be applied to work group
☐ Set goals for changes/improvements
☐ Provided ongoing feedback about the action plan
☐ Provided encouragement and support to help change behavior
☐ Other (comments) . . _____

21. For each of the areas below, indicate the extent to which you think this program has influenced these measures in your work group.

	No Influence	Some Influence	Moderate Influence	Significant Influence	Very Much Influence
a) Productivity					
b) Efficiency					
c) Quality					
d) Response Time					
e) Cost Control					
f) Customer Service					
g) Customer Satisfaction					
h) Employee Turnover					
i) Absenteeism					
j) Employee Satisfaction					
k) Healthcare Costs					
l) Safety and Health Costs					

Figure 7. *(continued)*

Please cite specific examples or provide more details.

_____

_____

_____

22. What specific suggestions do you have for improving the stress management program? Please specify.

☐ Content
☐ Duration
☐ Presentation
☐ Other

23. Other comments:

_____

_____

_____

Application Data

The application of the program was considered an outstanding success with 92 percent of the participants completing their 21-day action plan. A conference call at the end of the 21 days showed positive feedback and much enthusiasm for the progress made. The follow-up session also demonstrated success because most of the participants had indicated changes in behavior.

The most comprehensive application data came from the six-month questionnaire administered to participants and managers. The following skills and behaviors were reported as achieving significant success:

- Taking full responsibility for one's actions
- Identifying or removing barriers to change behavior
- Applying coping strategies to manage stressful situations
- Responding effectively to conflict
- Creating a positive climate
- Acknowledging a complaint properly

Coworkers were the most frequently cited group in which relationships had improved through use of the skills, with 95 percent indicating application improvement with this group.

Barriers

Information collected throughout the process, including the two follow-up questionnaires, indicated few barriers to implementing the process. The two most frequently listed barriers were:

- There is not enough time
- The work environment does not support the process

Management Support

Manager support seemed quite effective. The most frequently listed behaviors of managers were:

- Managers set goals for change and improvement
- Managers discussed how the program could apply to the work group

Impact Data

The program had significant impact with regard to both perceptions and actual values. On Figure 7, the follow-up questionnaire, 90 percent of the participants perceived this program as a good investment for MEI. In addition, participants perceived that this program had a significantly influenced:

- Employee satisfaction
- Absenteeism
- Turnover
- Healthcare cost
- Safety and health cost

This assessment appears to support the actual improvement data, outlined below. For each measure below, only the team data were collected and presented. Because managers were not the target of the program, manager performance data were not included. An average of months five and six, instead of the sixth month, was used consistently for the post-program data analysis to eliminate the spike effect.

Healthcare Costs. Healthcare costs for employees were categorized by diagnostic code. It was a simple process to track the cost of stress-induced illnesses. Although few differences were shown in the first three months after the program began, by months five and six, an average difference of $120 per employee per month was identified. This was apparently caused by the lack of stress-related incidents and the subsequent medical costs resulting from the stress. It was believed that this amount would be an appropriate improvement to use. The trend-line projection of healthcare costs was inconclusive because of the variability of the medical care costs prior to the program. A consistent trend could not be identified.

Absenteeism. There was significant difference of absenteeism in the two groups. The average absenteeism for the control group for months five and six was 4.65 percent. The absenteeism rate for the groups involved in the program was 3.2 percent. Employees worked an average of 220 days. The trend-line analysis appeared to support the absenteeism reduction. Because no other issues were identified that could have influenced absenteeism during this time period, the trend-line analysis provided an accurate estimate of the impact.

Turnover. Although turnover at MEI was traditionally low, in the past two years it had increased because of significant changes in the workplace. A turnover reduction was identified using the differences in the control group and experimental group. The control group had an average annual turnover rate of 19.2 percent for months five and six. The experimental group had an average of 14.1 percent for the same two months. As with absenteeism, the trend-line analysis supported the turnover reduction.

Productivity. Control group differences showed no significant improvement in productivity. Of all the measures collected, the productivity measure was the most difficult to match between the two groups, which may account for the inconclusive results. Also, the trend-line differences showed some slight improvement, but not enough to develop an actual value for productivity changes.

Job Satisfaction. Because of the timing difference in collecting attitude survey data, complete job satisfaction data were not available. Participants did provide input about the extent to which they felt the program actually influenced job satisfaction. The results were positive, with a significant influence rating for that variable. Because of the subjective nature of job satisfaction and the difficulties with measurement, a value was not assigned to job satisfaction.

Monetary Values

The determination of monetary benefits for the program was developed using the methods outlined in the ROI analysis plan. The medical costs were converted directly. A $120 per month savings yielded a $198,720 annual benefit. A standard value had routinely been used at MEI to reflect the cost of an absence. This value was 1.25 times the average daily wage rate. For the experimental group, the average wage rate was $123 per day. This yielded an annual improvement value of $67,684. For employee turnover, several turnover cost studies were available, which revealed a value of 85 percent of annual base pay. As expected, senior managers felt this cost of turnover was slightly overstated and preferred to use a value of 70 percent, yielding an annual benefit of $157,553. No values were used for productivity or job satisfaction. The total annual benefit of the stress management program was $423,957. Table 1 reflects the total economic benefits of the program.

The medical costs were converted directly. A $120 per month savings yielded a $198,720 annual benefit. Other values are as follows:

Unit Value for an Absence

$123 x 1.25 = $153.75

Unit Value for Turnover

$31,980 x 70% = $22,386

Improvement for Absenteeism
138 employees x 220 workdays x 1.45% x $153.75 = $67,684

Table 1. Annual Monetary Benefits for 138 Participants.

	Monthly Difference	Unit Value	Annual Improvement Value
Medical Costs	$120	-	$198,720
Absenteeism	1.45%	$153.75	$ 67,684
Turnover	5.1% (annualized)	$22,386	$157,553
TOTAL			**$423,957**

Improvement for Turnover

138 employees x 5.1% x $22,386 = $157,553

No values were used for productivity or job satisfaction.

Intangible Benefits
Several intangible benefits were identified in the study and confirmed by actual input from participants and questionnaires. The following benefits were pinpointed:

- Employee satisfaction
- Teamwork
- Improved relationships with family and friends
- Time savings
- Improved image in the company
- Fewer conflicts

No attempt was made to place monetary values on any of the intangibles.

Program Costs

Calculating the costs of the stress management program also followed the categories outlined in the evaluation plan. For needs assessment, all the costs were fully allocated to the six groups. Although the needs assessment was necessary, the total cost of needs assessment, $16,500, was included. All program development costs were estimated at $95 per participant, or $4,800. The program could have possibly been spread through other parts of the organization, and then the cost would ultimately have been prorated across all the sessions. However, the costs were low because the materials were readily available for most of the effort, and the total development cost was used.

The salaries for the team members averaged $31,980, while the six team managers had average salaries of $49,140. The benefits factor for MEI was 37 percent for both groups. Although the program took a little more than one day of staff time, one day of program was considered sufficient for the cost. The total salary cost was $24,108. The participants' travel cost ($38 per participant) was low because the programs were conducted in the area. The facilitator cost, program coordination cost, and training and development overhead costs were estimated to be $10,800. The meeting room facilities, food, and refreshments averaged $22 per participant, for a total of $3,968. Evaluation costs were $22,320. It was decided that all the evaluation costs would be allocated to these six groups. This determination was extremely conservative because the evaluation costs could be prorated if the program was implemented over other areas.

Table 2 details the stress management program costs.

These costs were considered fully loaded with no proration, except for needs assessment. Additional time could have been used for participants' off-the-job activities. However, it was concluded one day should be sufficient (for the one-day program).

Table 2. Program Costs.

Cost Category	Total Cost
Needs Assessment	$16,500
Program Development	$4,800
Program Materials (144 x $95)	$13,680
Participant Salaries/Benefits Based on 1 day 138 x $123 x 1.37 and 6 x 189 x 1.37	$24,108
Travel and Lodging 144 x 38	$5,472
Facilitation, Coordination, T&D Overhead	$10,800
Meeting Room, Food, and Refreshments 144 x 22	$3,168
Evaluation Costs	$22,320
TOTAL	**$100,848**

Results: ROI

Based on the given monetary benefits and costs, the return on investment and the benefits/costs ratio are shown below.

$$\text{BCR} = \frac{\$423,957}{\$100,848} = 4.20$$

$$\text{ROI} = \frac{\$423,957 - \$100,848}{\$100,848} = 320\%$$

Although this number is considered quite large, it is still conservative because of the following assumptions and adjustments:

- Only first-year values were used. The program should actually have second- and third-year benefits.
- Control group differences were used in analysis, which is often the most effective way to isolate the effects of the program. These differences were also confirmed with the trend-line analysis.
- The participants provided additional monetary benefits, detailed on the questionnaires. Although these benefits could have been added to the total numbers, they were not included because only 23 participants of the 144 supplied values for those questions.
- The costs are fully loaded.

When considering these adjustments, the value should represent a realistic value calculation for the actual return on investment.

Communication Strategies

Because of the importance of sharing the analysis results, a communication strategy was developed. Table 3 outlines this strategy. Three separate documents were developed to communicate with the different target groups in a variety of ways.

Table 3. Communication Strategies.

Communication Document	Communication Target	Distribution
Complete report with appendices (75 pages)	• Training and Education Staff • Safety and Health Staff • Intact Team Manager	Distributed and discussed in a special meeting
Executive Summary (8 pages)	• Senior Management in the Business Units • Senior Corporate Management	Distributed and discussed in routine meeting
General interest overview and summary without the actual ROI calculation (10 pages)	• Program Participants	Mailed with letter
Brochure highlighting program, objectives, and specific results	• Prospective Team Leaders	Included with other program descriptions

Policy and Practice Implications

Because of the significance of the study and the information, two issues became policy. Whenever programs are considered that involve large groups of employees or a significant investment of funds, a detailed needs assessment should be conducted to ensure the proper program is developed. Also, an ROI study should be conducted for a small group of programs to measure the impact before complete implementation. In essence, this influenced the policy and practice on needs assessment, pilot program evaluation, and the number of impact studies developed.

Questions for Discussion

1. What is the purpose of the needs assessment?
2. What specific sources of data should be used?
3. Critique the data collection plan.
4. What other methods could be used to isolate the effects of the program?
5. Critique the methods to convert data to monetary values.
6. Are the costs fully loaded? Explain.
7. Is the ROI value realistic? Explain.
8. Critique the communication strategy.

CHAPTER **4**

Measuring ROI in a Safety Incentive Program

National Steel

This case addresses measuring the effectiveness of an incentive program designed to influence employee behavior and to reduce accidents in a manufacturing environment. Although top executives were concerned about the safety and well-being of employees, they also wanted to reduce the cost of accidents. The cost of accidents was reaching the point that it was an obstacle to the company becoming a low-cost provider of products in a competitive industry. This case demonstrates that an evaluation of an HR program can be implemented with minimal resources. It also demonstrates that although some programs may achieve a return on investment, it is sometimes best to communicate the ROI results to a limited audience.

Background

National Steel is a large manufacturing operation with divisions in the southeastern, southwestern, and midwestern United States. Each division has multiple plants. The company also has several foreign plants in operation and two others in the construction phase. The plants produce steel products such as bar stock and plate steel. They also fabricate specialized fasteners used in the commercial building industry. The nature of National's manufacturing business requires that safety always receives a top priority with management and the work force. The concern for employee safety is a significant

This case was prepared to serve as a basis for discussion rather than an illustration of either effective or ineffective administrative and management practices. All names, dates, places, and organizations have been disguised at the request of the author or organization.

issue. Additionally, domestic and foreign competition is a major factor in National's strategy to become a low-cost producer.

The company had always been concerned about the human element of a safe work environment, but economic issues were now a significant concern being driven by the cost of accidents. The company had long had a group, the Central Safety Committee, in place to continually review safety issues, direct accident investigations, and establish policy and best practices. The committee was made up of a senior line officer (who served as the sponsor), one line manager, two foremen, six members of the work force, the corporate manager of safety, and the VP of HR.

A Performance Problem

The committee had recently informed the senior management of National Steel that the midwestern division of the company was experiencing unacceptable accident frequency rates, accident severity rates, and total accident costs. For a two-year period, these costs had been in the $400,000 to $500,000 range, annually—much too high for the Central Safety Committee and management to accept.

The Needs Assessment

The safety manager was directed to meet with managers and employees in the three plants of the midwestern division to seek causes of the problem and to work with the division manager to implement the appropriate solutions. A team of HR specialists completed the assignment. The team also analyzed the cost and types of accidents. The team of specialists concluded:

- Employees' safety habits were inconsistent, and they were not focusing enough attention on safety.
- Employees knew and understood safety guidelines and practices; therefore, training was not an issue.
- A significant number of accidents and accident-related costs involved injuries of a questionable nature.
- Some type of monetary incentive would likely influence employee behavior.
- Peer pressure could possibly be used to help employees focus on safety practices and on the need to avoid the costs of seeing a physician when it was unnecessary.

The Solution

As a result of the assessment, the team recommended that the division implement a group-based safety incentive plan at the three plants. A monetary incentive had been successful in another division during previous years. The division manager reviewed the details of the plan and even helped craft some of the components. He accepted the recommendations and agreed to sponsor the implementation. The two objectives of the recommended plan were:

1. Reduce the annual accident frequency rate from a level of 60 to a much lower level of approximately 20, or less.
2. Reduce the annual disabling accident frequency rate from a level of 18 to 0.

The Measure of Success

The HR team expressed the need to track certain measures on a continual basis. Once the incentive plan's objectives were established, the team identified the specific data needed to analyze safety performance. The measures identified were:

- Number of medical treatment cases
- Number of lost-time accidents
- Number of lost-time days
- Accident costs
- Hours worked
- Incentive costs

The team decided that data should be collected monthly. Because the data collection system had been in place before the implementation of the safety incentive plan, no additional data collection procedures were needed. The same system was also used by the HR specialists when the Central Safety Committee asked them to review the problem and make recommendations. Management was also interested in a payback for the incentive program. Although accident reduction and severity were major concerns, there was also a need to achieve low-cost provider goals. Management requested to see figures that demonstrated that the benefits from the plan exceeded the costs of implementation. The team members concluded that they could use the same tracking system to determine the return on investment.

The Incentive Plan

The incentive plan consisted of a cash award of $75, after taxes, to each employee in the plant for every six months the plant worked without a medical treatment case. A medical treatment case was defined as an accident that could not be treated by plant first-aid and, therefore, needed the attention of a physician. Each plant had a work force of about 120 employees. A team effort at each plant was important because the actions of one employee could impact the safety of another. Peer pressure was necessary to keep employees focused and to remind them to avoid unnecessary physician costs. Therefore, the award was paid at each of the three plants independently. An award was not paid unless the entire plant completed a six-month period without a medical treatment case. When a medical treatment case occurred, a new six-month period began.

Implementation of the Incentive Plan

The plant managers implemented the plan at the beginning of the new year so results could easily be monitored and compared with performance in previous years. Each plant manager announced the plan to employees and distributed the guidelines for payout. The managers communicated the details of the plan and answered questions during the regular monthly safety meeting at each plant. Thorough communication ensured that each employee clearly understood how the plan functioned and what the group had to accomplish to receive an award.

Cost Monitoring

Two groups of costs were monitored: the total accident costs, and the incentive compensation costs. Total accident costs were monitored prior to the safety incentive plan as part of collecting routine safety performance data. The additional costs related directly to incentive compensation were also tabulated. Because the $75 cash was provided after taxes, the cost to the division was approximately $97.50 per employee for each six-month period completed without a medical treatment case. Additional administration costs were minimal because the data used in analysis were already collected prior to the new plan and because the time required to administer the plan and calculate the award was almost negligible. No additional staff was needed, and no overtime for existing staff could be directly attributed to the plan. However, a conservative estimate of $1,600 per year of plan administration costs was used in the tabulation of incentive costs.

Data Collection and Analysis

In addition to the two-year data history, data were collected during a two-year period after the plan implementation to provide an adequate before-and-after comparison. Medical treatment injuries, lost-time injuries, accident frequency rates, and accident costs were all monitored to show the contribution of the safety incentive plan. The data shown in Table 1 document the accident costs for the four-year period. The data reveal significant reductions in accident costs for the two-year period after the implementation of the plan.

When comparing the average of Years 3 and 4 (after the incentive plan) with the Years 1 and 2 average (before the incentive plan), the accident frequency was reduced by 68 percent, while the disabling accident frequency was reduced by 74 percent. The annual cost of accidents (averaging the two years before and the two years after the incentive plan) dropped from $523,244 to $18,701, producing a significant savings of $504,543.

Table 1. Accident Costs and Frequency for All 3 Plants.

	Year 1 Before Plan	Year 2 Before Plan	Year 3 After Plan	Year 4 After Plan
Accident Frequency	61.2	58.8	19.6	18.4
Disabling Frequency	17.4	18.9	5.7	3.8
Medical Treatment Injuries	121	111	19	17
Lost-Time Injuries	23	21	6.8	5.2
Actual Cost of Accidents	$468,360	$578,128	$18,058	$19,343

The objective of the plan to reduce the annual accident frequency rate to less than 20 was met with a post-plan average of 19. The objective of reducing the annual disabling accident frequency rate from 18 to 0 was not achieved. Although the average after two years dropped significantly from 18.15 annually to 4.75 annually, this was still short of the target. Both calculations are shown below.

BEFORE INCENTIVE PLAN   AFTER INCENTIVE PLAN

Accident Frequency 61.2 + 58.8 = 120   19.6 + 18.4 = 38

Annual Average (÷ 2) = 60 ANNUALLY   = 19 ANNUALLY
Annual Improvmt. 60 − 19 = 41
% Accident Improvmt. 41 ÷ 60 = 68%

BEFORE INCENTIVE PLAN   AFTER INCENTIVE PLAN

Disabling Frequency 17.4 + 18.9 = 36.3   5.7 + 3.8 = 9.5
Annual Average (÷ 2) = 18.15 ANNUALLY   = 4.75 ANNUALLY
Annual Improvmt. 18.15 − 4.75 = 13.4
% Disabling Improvmt. 13.4 ÷ 18.15 = 74%

These impressive results demonstrated a positive business impact. The incentive plan resulted in a safer work environment, fewer accidents, and fewer disabling accidents. Although these results improved the overall safety program considerably, the issue of cost savings remained unanswered. Did the incentive plan bring greater monetary benefits than the cost incurred to implement and administer it? Table 2 details the additional cost issues. There was also the issue of how much the incentive plan influenced improvement in the measures when compared with other actions that may have influenced improvements.

Table 2. The Contribution of the Safety Incentive Plan for All 3 Plants.

	Year 1 Before Plan	Year 2 Before Plan	Year 3 After Plan	Year 4 After Plan
Needs Assessment Costs (spread)	—	—	$1,200	$1,200
Plan's Annual Administration and Evaluation Costs	—	—	$1,600	$1,600
Safety Incentive Plan Payout Costs	—	—	$58,013	$80,730
Actual Cost of Accidents	$468,360	$578,128	$18,058	$19,343
Total Cost of Accidents and Prevention	$468,360	$578,128	$78,871	$102,873

Plan implemented beginning in Year 3

The needs assessment cost of $2,400 consisted of capturing the time and travel expenses for the HR team to conduct 20 interviews with plant operations and management staff and to develop recommendations. The cost to administer the incentive plan was $1,600 annually. The cost of the incentive plan payout must be captured and included in the total cost of accident prevention. Payout is determined by calculating the amount of incentive awards paid to employees in Years 3 and 4. Table 3 provides a breakdown of the payout.

Table 3. The Safety Incentive Plan Payout.

Plant 1 Payout, Year 3:	115 employees × $97.50 × 1 PAYOUT = $11,213
Plant 2 Payout, Year 3:	122 employees × $97.50 × 2 PAYOUTS = $23,790
Plant 3 Payout, Year 3:	118 employees × $97.50 × 2 PAYOUTS = $23,010
	Total Payout, Year 3 $58,013
Plant 1 Payout, Year 4:	115 employees × $97.50 × 2 PAYOUTS = $22,425
Plant 2 Payout, Year 4:	122 employees × $97.50 × 2 PAYOUTS = $23,790
Plant 3 Payout, Year 4:	118 employees × $97.50 × 3 PAYOUTS = $34,515
	Total Payout, Year 4 $80,730
	Total Payout, Years 3 and 4 $138,743

Data Interpretation and Conclusion

The contribution of the safety incentive plan was determined by adding the accident and administrative costs for Years 3 and 4 to the safety incentive plan payout costs and then comparing this total with the accident costs of Years 1 and 2. As Table 2 shows, the total costs were reduced significantly. Accident costs from Years 1 and 2 (see Table 2) totaled $1,046,488, for an average of $523,244 annually. Accident and prevention costs for Years 3 and 4 totaled $181,744, for an average of $90,872 annually. This was an annual improvement of $432,372.

The Central Safety Committee discussed the issue of isolating the effects of the safety incentive plan. As a group, committee members decided the incentive plan should be credited for most of the improvement. They felt that it was the incentive plan that influenced a new safety awareness and caused peer pressure to work. After much debate, they accepted an estimate from the in-house expert, the safety manager, using data from an industry trade group that presented convincing evidence that management's attention to safe work habits had been shown to reduce the cost of accidents by 20 percent. Before these data were presented, the improvement was going to be attributed entirely to the incentive plan because no other factors that could have influenced safety performance during this period had been identified. Also, the safety record at the other two divisions showed no improvement during the same time period.

Calculating the Return on Investment

To determine the return on investment, the costs and monetary benefits of the incentive plan were needed. The annual cost of incentive payouts (two-year average of $69,372) added to annual administration costs ($1,200 plus $1,600) provided a total incentive plan cost of $72,172. The benefits were calculated starting with the annual monetary benefits of $432,372. Because the Central Safety Committee accepted the suggestion of the safety manager—that management attention played a role in influencing the improvement (20 percent)—then an adjustment had to be made. Therefore, 80 percent of $432,372 resulted in an estimated impact of $345,898. The ROI became:

$$\text{ROI} = \frac{\text{Net Benefits}}{\text{Costs}} = \frac{\$345,898 - \$72,172}{\$72,172} = 3.79 \times 100 = 379\%$$

Communication of Results

The results of the safety incentive plan were communicated to a variety of target audiences to show the contribution of the plan. First, the division president summarized the results in a monthly report to the chief executive officer of the corporation. The focal point was on the reduction in accident frequency and severity, the reduction in costs, the improvement in safety awareness, and the return on investment for the incentive plan.

The HR department presented the results in its monthly report to all middle and upper division management with the same focus that was presented to the CEO. Return on investment information was reserved for the eyes of management because it was felt that employees might misunderstand this as being the focus of plant safety.

The results were presented to all plant employees through the monthly Safety Newsletter. This communication focused on the reduction in medical treatment injuries, as well as improvements in lost-time accidents, disabling accidents, and accident frequency. It also recognized employees for their accomplishments, as did all the communication.

Finally, the results were communicated to all division employees through the division newsletter. This communication focused on the same issues presented to plant employees. Communications were positive and increased the awareness of the need for the continuation of the incentive plan.

Questions for Discussion

1. What questions would you have asked during the needs assessment?
2. Should reaction, learning, and application data be collected and presented?
3. What are your thoughts about the way the Central Safety Committee decided to isolate the effects of the safety incentive plan?
4. What other alternatives could have been explored to isolate the effects?
5. Would you have sought approval to collect additional data from employees during the follow-up evaluation regarding what caused the improvements? Why would you want

additional data? How would you have justified the cost of this additional work?

6. Were there additional costs that should have been included? Should the cost of communication be included?

7. How would you have communicated the results differently?

8. How credible is this study?

CHAPTER **5**

Measuring ROI in Executive Leadership Development

Imperial National Bank

This case shows the monetary impact of a leadership development program using an action learning process. The projected cost of the program was the driving force in this evaluation and underscores the complexity of measuring the impact of leadership development. More importantly, this case shows how changes in program design can significantly increase the actual return on investment.

Background

As with many large global organizations in a competitive industry, Imperial National Bank (INB)—a large, multi-service bank operating in 14 states—recognized that it needed effective leaders. As a result, a comprehensive leadership development program was developed. The program followed a learning-while-earning model, whereby high-potential leaders worked together on selected high-priority business issues with access to just-in-time coaching, advice from senior executives, and a faculty of subject-matter experts. The program structure combined class time and project work.

A process called action reflection learning (ARL) was the principal vehicle used in the leadership development program to assist in learning new approaches to behavioral change and perceptions. The process helped participants associate learning with making things

This case was prepared to serve as a basis for discussion rather than an illustration of either effective or ineffective administrative and management practices. All names, dates, places, and organizations have been disguised at the request of the author or organization.

happen in real time. ARL confronted participants with challenges and risks, had them search for information, and had them complete tasks that were outside their regular scope of activities. In essence, ARL took advantage of the fact that when learning is linked to action on real issues, in which there are real consequences and risks, adults are more motivated to learn.

Three critical success factors were identified that needed to be fully operational and executed for the program to achieve the desired success:

- A significant amount of time needed to be invested by the management committee, clients, and participants.
- Real projects that were enterprise-wide and strategic needed to be developed.
- Influential participants needed to be selected based on performance and future potential.

These factors capture the most important issues surrounding this program.

Initiation of the Leadership Development Program

Around the globe, there is a need for more accountability and evaluation in leadership development. In accordance with this need, the director of INB's learning and development function initiated an evaluation of the leadership program. A leading international consulting firm that focuses on measuring the return on investment in human resources programs, was called in as an external consultant to direct the evaluation. The firm, ROI Institute, was not involved in the design, development, or delivery of this program, therefore ensuring an independent evaluation.

The leadership program was deemed an ideal candidate for ROI evaluation for several reasons:

The program was INB's first attempt to integrate traditional leadership development with on-the-job, real-life projects, designed to add significant value to the organization.

- The program targeted a critical audience at INB—future leaders.
- The vision for the program had been developed and refined at the highest levels of the organization.

- On a per-participant basis, the program was perhaps the most expensive program undertaken at INB. It was also the most visible.
- The program was designed to focus on important projects that represented real-life situations and involved key operational and strategic issues.

Several issues apparent at the beginning of the study, however, had the potential to influence the ability to develop a specific ROI:

- Initially, the program was not designed to deliver a measurable business impact. Therefore, key performance measures were not linked to the program, and specific objectives were not developed to improve measurable performance.
- Although the projects were included to add value to INB, the nature of some of the projects made this task difficult. Also, the requirements for developing the projects did not include a process for capturing monetary value.
- Data collection systems had not been developed and refined to link with the leadership development program. Performance data were scattered throughout the company and, in some cases, not readily available.
- The intangible benefits from this program were expected to be significant and long term, providing non-monetary values that might exceed the monetary benefits.

Even with the presence of the above difficulties, there was a desire to measure ROI, using the most credible processes. Through the implementation of a comprehensive data collection and analysis process spanning a time period of September to June, this evaluation took place, using the ROI process model described throughout this book.

Data Collection Plan

An effective evaluation must be carefully planned with appropriate timing established and responsibilities defined. Table 1 shows the data collection plan for this evaluation. The data collection plan was initially developed and approved by the support team with additional adjustments made during the program to ensure that appropriate input was obtained from all individuals. Although the amount

Table 1. Data Collection Plan.

Level	Broad Program Objective(s)	Data Collection Method	Timing of Data Collection	Responsibilities for Data Collection
I Reaction, Satisfaction	• Favorable reaction from participants, teams and observers • Suggestions for improvement	• Questionnaire from participants (1) • Follow-up questionnaire from participants (2) • Interviews with participants (5) • Observation • Interviews with sponsors (3) • Follow-up questionnaire from manager (4)	• End of each session and end of program • 60–90 days after end of program • 60–90 days after end of program • Daily • 60–90 days after end of program • 60–90 days after end of program	• PRO • PRO • PRO • Manager • PRO • PRO
II Learning	• Enhance knowledge and skills in fourteen areas	• Observation • Questionnaire from participants (1) • Values technology instrument • Executive success profile • Follow-up questionnaire from participants (2)	• Daily • End of each session and end of program • During program • During program • 60–90 days after end of program	• Manager • PRO • Facilitators • Facilitators • PRO

III Application	• Use of skills and knowledge • Frequency of skill use • Interaction with management and policy committee	• Observation • Follow-up questionnaire from participants (2) • Follow-up questionnaire from manager (4) • Interviews with participants (5) • Interviews with sponsors	• During program • 60–90 days after end of program • 60–90 days after end of program • 60–90 days after end of program • 60–90 days after end of program	• Managers • PRO • PRO • PRO • PRO
IV Business Impact	• Benefits from research, recommendations made by project teams, and resulting savings and/or earnings • Improvement in business impact measures as each participant applies skills in business unit • Enhanced quality of executive talent pool	• Financial performance indicators from project presentations • Interviews with participants (5) • Follow-up questionnaire from participants (2) • Follow-up questionnaire from manager (4) • HR records	• 60–90 days after end of program • 60–90 days after end of program • 60–90 days after end of program • 60–90 days after end of program • 3 years after end of program	• Program Director • PRO • PRO • PRO • PRO

(1) Same questionnaire, (2) Same questionnaire, (3) Same questionnaire, (4) Same interview, (5) Same interview

of data collected might be considered excessive and the multiple methods might provide duplication and overlap, this was considered a necessity because of the importance of the program, the cost of the program in both time and money, and the target audience involved.

Timing of Data Collection

The timing of collection was critical. End-of-program questionnaires were collected at the end of each session and at the end of the program. Reaction data was also collected from a variety of individuals at the program's completion. Learning data was collected during the session and during on-the job observations.

The most critical timing issue to address was data collection for application and impact. Although a leadership development program is designed to have a long-term impact, the specific improvements from programs are difficult to capture if assessed years after the program is completed. Although the connection may exist, it is difficult for the participants and participants' managers to make the connection between a training program and specific improvement. In addition, for longer periods of time, additional variables will influence business measures, therefore complicating the cause-and-effect relationship between training and improvement.

The timing of data collection was complicated because senior management wanted the evaluation completed before making a decision about the implementation of future programs. Ideally, the application and impact data should be captured within six months to one year after a program is completed. Following this schedule would push the data collection and completion of the evaluation beyond the requested timeframe desired to make decisions about a second program.

The spacing of the sessions further complicated the timing of the study. The first session was held in September and the last in February. The time needed to apply skills learned in the first session would place the evaluation in the spring. For the last session, the follow-up would normally be in the fall. Therefore, a period of 60 to 90 days from the last session was selected to allow enough time for application.

End-of-Program Feedback

An essential part of any evaluation is the typical feedback

obtained at the end of a training program. A modified version of the standard questionnaire used by the learning and development department captured feedback at the end of each session. This feedback was tabulated and provided to the external consultants, as well as the training support team. Adjustments were routinely made using this feedback data.

Observation

An important part of evaluation was provided by the research component of the program. An expert in action reflection learning research provided observation throughout the program. Although most of the observation occurred during sessions and captured actual learning, some observation took place in work settings as part of an executive shadow program. The results of these observations were provided as feedback to program faculty, the training support team, and program participants. Although results of this research are included in this case as part of the total assessment and evaluation, it is important to note that this research was not designed to serve as program assessment and evaluation.

Questionnaire from Participants

One of the most important data collection methods was the detailed follow-up questionnaire completed by participants in the time frame of 60 to 90 days from the end of the last session. During the third session, participants were briefed about the plans for the questionnaire, and the general topics were discussed. Participants were also reminded about the questionnaire at the last session, and a final reminder was sent approximately one month after the last session. This reminder came directly from the training director, encouraging them to take appropriate notes of details that could be reported in the questionnaires. As of mid-June, the participant response rate was 73 percent, representing 16 of the 22 participants. In addition, questionnaire responses were thorough and served as a valuable data source. The questionnaire focused on application and impact data (Levels 3 and 4).

Interviews with Participants

To supplement input from questionnaires, interviews were conducted with each participant. Lasting approximately 1 to 1.5 hours, each interview explored individual application and impact topics. Additional probing was used to uncover business impact applications and to gain further insight into skill applications, barriers, concerns, and important issues surrounding the success of the program. These interviews were conducted within 60 to 90 days after the last session.

Questionnaires for Managers

To gain the perspective of participants' managers, a questionnaire was sent directly to them within the timeframe of 60 to 90 days from the end of the program. The managers of participants were involved early in the process when participants were selected. They often had to make adjustments in the business units while participants attended sessions and worked on the project. Manager input was considered important, as their support was necessary for success. As of mid-June, 46 percent of managers had returned the questionnaire.

Interview with Sponsors

Because senior managers' involvement in this program was significant, their interest was high, and therefore, their influence was critical to its success. Interviews with these project sponsors provided a wealth of candid input about the success of the program, as well as the concerns from the unique perspective of these key executives.

Questionnaire from the Support Team

To provide additional input from other members critical to the success of the program, a customized questionnaire was distributed to the external consultants and the training support team. Their input focused on reaction to the program, assessment of success, and suggestions for improvement.

Performance Monitoring

Capturing specific data from business impact applications and project evaluation required collecting data from the business records of the organization. This was a factor only in those areas in which impact was identified or on which the projects had a direct influence.

Project Review

To capture the potential value of the projects, the status was explored with each project owner to determine the extent of implementation and the prospects for future implementations. In some cases, the project review went a step further by placing an actual value on the projects.

Summary

Collectively, these data collection methods yielded a tremendous amount of data, far exceeding expectations. The different perspectives and types of data ensured a thorough assessment of the program and provided a backdrop for insightful recommendations for making improvements.

Reaction and Learning

Table 2 shows how the data were integrated for analysis and reporting along the four levels of evaluation, as well as the cost of the program. Data on reaction to the program and relevant learning that took place was obtained through end-of-session feedback, interviews with participants, and questionnaires from participants. Questionnaires from managers of participants and faculty/support teams, as well as interviews with sponsors, provided additional reaction data while research provided additional data on relevant learning.

Reaction

The data collected throughout the first leadership development program indicated both high and low points during the program. The participant overall mean score indicated a decline in the value of the sessions. Also, as the participants progressed through the program, a number of issues arose. These issues centered on [1] progress of project team work, [2] lack of time, [3] external presenters/content (2 of 4), and [4] team dynamics.

The components that contributed the most to the participant learning using a five-point scale were: [1] project work (4.6), [2] cross-functional team work (4.6), and [3] being involved in strategic issues at INB (4.5). The components that contributed the least were external resources (2.8) and feedback instruments (3.4).

Table 2. Data Integration.

	Level 1 Reaction to Program	Level 2 Learning: Skills, Knowledge, Changes in Perception	Level 3 Application Implementation and Use on the job	Level 4 Impact in Business Unit	Costs
End of Session Feedback	X	X			
Research		X	X		
Interviews with Participants	X	X	X	X	X
Questionnaires from Participants	X	X	X	X	
Questionnaires from Managers of Participants	X		X	X	
Interviews with Sponsors	X				
Questionnaires for Faculty/Support Team	X				
Company Records				X	X

Barriers/Concerns   ROI

Therefore, the areas that were sources of frustration during the program were also the areas that contributed the most to the learning—the project work and team dynamics.

Learning

Learning was examined in significant detail as part of the research component for the program. The major findings from the research program are contained in Table 3.

Table 3. Major Findings from Research Project Measures of Learning.

Learning:
- Learning was "managed" by the participants through the use of several "filters."
- Learning was impacted by the existing culture of the organization.
- Executive learning included cognitive re-framing, as well as information transfer and skill development.

Team Skill Development:
- Development was affected by executive role and position.
- Skill development was affected by cultural norms and values.
- Skill development was affected by project focus.
- Development was affected by interaction with learning coaches.

Projects:
- Projects were affected by team and individual sponsorship.
- Projects were affected by program schedule and design.
- Projects were affected by interaction among teams and by interaction as a group.

Application

Application of Skills, Knowledge, and Behavior

Although the leadership development program was not designed to develop a number of skills to produce immediate on-the-job results, specific areas were addressed that had immediate application potential. The questionnaire response from participants showed significant changes in behavior in several important skill areas. Not surprisingly, "reflection and dialogue" showed the most significant change, followed closely by "thinking strategically" and "communicating effectively." This mirrored, to a certain extent, the results obtained from participant interviews and manager questionnaires. "Using market research and data analysis" showed the least change, principally because it was not developed much in the program, although it was part of the original plan. Surprisingly, "planning personal development" did not show the extent of the transfer to the job as anticipated.

Ironically, the manager questionnaire input provided a more positive assessment of behavior change, particularly with "applying power and influence" and "managing small work groups."

Action Reflection Learning Approach

The action reflection learning approach (ARL) was at the core of the learning process in the sessions. Although the reaction for most of the elements of ARL was positive, there was concern about the overall success of some of the initiatives. The questionnaire responses from participants revealed that the most successful elements of ARL were the abilities to "engage in cross-functional work teams" and "learn from your own experience." The least successful appeared to be "associate learning with making things happen in real time."

Business Impact

Linkage with Key Measures

To achieve results, participants needed to realize a connection or linkage between the application of acquired knowledge and skills and changes in key business measures. According to input from participants and other groups, the strongest linkage occurred with employee satisfaction and customer satisfaction. Building effective leadership skills often improves employee satisfaction while improving the relationship with customers. In addition, the projects contributed significantly to this connection. The weakest linkage with key business measures and this program appeared to be with productivity, revenue generation, profits, cost control, and customer response time. These were some of INB's most important business measures. This assessment was to be expected, unless the program had had mechanisms to provide a connection to these key business variables.

Specific Impact from Individual Projects

Although the team projects were expected to add significant value to INB, it was anticipated that individual participants would undertake specific improvements in their work settings. Participants were asked to identify these improvements, where possible.

Usually when this type of improvement data is desired from a leadership development program, individual business action plans are developed to guide the application of the new skills and report the results. This process of capturing values from individual plans is much more difficult when the action plans have not been developed, as was the case with the leadership development program. Because the team projects were developed for the program, the program designers were not interested in requiring action plans for individual application. Therefore, there was no formal planning for the use of individual skills and no mechanism in place for capturing specific improvements.

In the follow-up questionnaire, participants were asked to explore business results with a series of impact questions, which provided an opportunity to offer details about the specific impact. As anticipated, only a small number of participants were able to place values on the questionnaire. Four participants provided values. Two are reported in Table 4, which identifies the specific impact derived from the program.

Table 4. Impact of Individual Projects from Questionnaires.

Description of Project	Monetary Impact	Basis/Time Frame	Contribution Factor	Confidence of Values	Comments
1. This project involves the delivery strategy for the customer-centric enterprise. Combining both business and technology strategies, the project involves a combination of: • Identification, profiling, and delivery of the customer to the most appropriate and cost-effective resource. • Enhancement of the customer-employee interaction through effective real time delivery of meaningful customer intelligence to the specialists. • Collection measurement and reporting on the customer experience and behaviors.	$3,625,000 annually	The utilization of call-by-call intelligent network routing will provide load balancing and optimization across the entire organization. The industry estimates 10% to 15% efficiency in the areas of staffing resources and telecommunications expenses. A conservative estimate of 5% for INB would provide the following annual benefit based on current assumptions: • Agent efficiency based on 2,000 agents @ $30K annual salary with a 5% gain would provide a benefit of $3,000,000 annually. • Telecommunication costs based on 100,000,000 minutes annually at 7.5 cents per	25%	75%	This is an extensive project, which was initiated directly from the program. However, due to other factors and influences that may have brought this project forward in the future, only 25% of the improvement is credited to the program. A more detailed document, including a proposal that was presented to the executive group, is available.

		minute with a 5% gain would provide a benefit of $375,000 annually. • The use of shared equipment at the network level and the repositioning of equipment to provide efficiencies is estimated at a 5% gain on a $5,000,000 annual capital budget resulting in a benefit of $250,000 annually.		
2. This project involves designed strategic development and implementation planning to turn INB into a more customer-centric organization.	$20,000,000	When the customer-centric organization is successfully implemented, a 10% impact on customer loyalty, at a minimum, should be realized. A 1-point improvement on any of the loyalty measures is estimated to deliver 30¢ per month, per customer. This produces a $20,000,000 improvement.	The program moved this project ahead by one year. Thus one year of results can be attributed to this program.	This is only one element of the customer-centric Implementation but affects all of the bank. This is being driven by an individual who participated in the program, and the estimates are based only on one element of the project within the scope of that individual.
			N/A	

In an effort to capture additional input about business impact, the same series of questions was asked of the participants during the one-on-one interviews whenever there was an opportunity to explore business results. This questioning yielded 11 more instances in which value may be linked to the program. These projects, without monetary values, are listed in Table 5.

Collectively, these values do not appear reliable at this stage. However, this attempt to find specific individual project results related to the program is essential to the evaluation. At the outset, it was concluded that this would be a difficult exercise and that it would be unlikely to generate a tremendous amount of specific and reliable data. Although several individual projects were identified, the values were not used in the ROI calculation.

Turnover Prevention/Reduction

Perhaps an unexpected benefit linked to the leadership development program was staff turnover prevention. The program caused several of the participants to examine their careers and gain a renewed respect for INB. Suddenly, they realized that the company valued them as executives, was interested in their careers, and more important, was interested in developing critical skills for additional responsibilities. In essence, this program strengthened the bond between the employee and the company, increasing loyalty and commitment. For example, four individuals indicated that this program prevented or probably prevented them from leaving the company within the next couple of years.

Project Results

The team projects were an integral part of the program from the design and delivery perspective and turned out to be the most significant and meaningful part of the process from the participant viewpoint. Without exception, the reaction to the projects was extremely favorable. Participants saw them as frustrating and stressful, but rewarding. Eighty percent of the participants considered the project successful or very successful.

There was, however, some debate and concern about the purpose of the projects. All stakeholders felt that the projects served as excellent learning activities and that even if the recommendations were never implemented, they learned much about themselves, their

Table 5. Individual Projects from Interviews.

Type of Contribution	Brief Description of Improvement
1. Department Initiative	One participant used the communication skills and action-reflection learning skills in an off-site meeting to plan improvements for the department. In this meeting, 14 initiatives were generated from the group using skills taken directly from the leadership development program. This participant estimated that typically in this type of meeting, only five initiatives would have surfaced. However, using a different approach with new skills, 14 initiatives surfaced. Therefore, nine initiatives can be credited with the leadership development program.
2. New Product	Two participants are teaming to develop a project for small business. This is a Web-based product and the value is generated because the bank will actually provide the service instead of another contractor. Without the leadership development program connection and collaboration, an external resource would have been used instead of the bank.
3. New Customers	One participant has obtained a new customer in the USA as a result of the networking from the leadership development program. The new customer is providing a direct benefit to the bank.
4. Partnership	One participant is building a partnership to share resources, referrals and technology as well as assets with another important and often competing part of the organization.
5. Tool Application	One participant has used the strategic planning process on a particular project for which he/she is responsible. This improved process is adding direct benefits.

team, the bank, and the particular topic as a result of the project development and presentation. However, almost all participants indicated that the projects represented real issues that need to be resolved and were concerned that they be implemented.

An important part of the leadership development program design was to use the processes and principles of action reflection learning as participants developed their projects and identified recommendations. Participants gave mixed responses about using ARL as an important and successful part of project success. Some felt ARL was not important to project success.

Program Costs

A fully-loaded cost profile was used in this study. Table 6 shows the listing of cost elements considered in this analysis.

All costs for the program were absorbed by the training department with the exception of some project-related costs incurred by the team members. The fees charged by the consultants and hotels are actual. The remainder of the costs is aggregated estimates (that is, salary and benefits were calculated by number of participants $\times$ average salary $\times$ benefit factor $\times$ number of hours).

Although there is often some debate as to whether participant salaries and benefits should be included in the cost of the program, in reality the participants were not replaced while they attended this program. Therefore, the company did not experience a replacement cost. However, employees are compensated for being on the job every day, and they are expected to make a contribution roughly equal to their compensation. If they are removed from the job for a week, or four weeks in the case of the leadership development program, then the company has lost their contribution for that period of time. To be fully loaded with costs and also be conservative, this value was estimated and included in the overall cost profile.

The issue of prorating costs was an important consideration. In this case, it was reasonably certain that a second session would be conducted. The design and development expenses of $580,657 could therefore be prorated over two sessions. Therefore, in the actual ROI calculation, half of this number was used to arrive at the total value. This left a total program cost of $2,019,598 to include in the analysis. On a participant basis, this was $91,800, or $22,950 for each week of formal sessions. Although this was expensive, it was still close to a rough benchmark of weekly costs of several senior executive leadership programs.

Table 6. Leadership Development Program Costs.

Design/Development	
External Consultants	$525,330
Training Department	$28,785
Management Committee	$26,542
Delivery	
Conference Facilities	$142,554
(Hotel)	
Consultants/External	$812,110
Training Department Salaries & Benefits	$15,283
(For Direct Work with the Program)	
Training Department Travel Expenses	$37,500
Management Committee (Time)	$75,470
Project Costs ($25,000 x 4)	$100,000
Participant Salaries & Benefits (Class Sessions)	$84,564
(Average Daily Salary x Benefits Factor x Number	
of Program Days)	
Participant Salaries and Benefits (Project Work)	
Travel & Lodging for Participants	$117,353
Cost of Materials	$100,938
(Handouts, Purchased Materials)	$6,872
Research and Evaluation	
Research	$110,750
Evaluation	$125,875
Total Costs	**$2,309,926**

ROI Analysis

When developing the ROI, two important issues had to be addressed: (1) isolating the effects of the program, and (2) converting data to monetary values. The role of the participants was extremely critical because the participants provided data on actual improvements, isolated the effects of the program on the improvements, and in some cases converted data to actual monetary values. Although there are many other approaches to isolate the effects of the program and a variety of techniques to convert data to monetary values, several issues prevented the use of a majority of other approaches and techniques:

- The timing of the decision to measure the ROI eliminated some of the possibilities. The decision to measure the impact was made after the program had begun, and it was too late to influence the design and to use more objective approaches to isolating the effects of the program.
- The nature of leadership development eliminated many other techniques. The application and ultimate impact is an individual process, and the improvements must come from the participants themselves—who may all influence different performance improvement measures. This situation makes it difficult to link the program to any finite set of performance measures.
- The vast number of business units represented and the nature of their issues, challenges, and performance measures made the process difficult to link to any small number of applications.

Challenges in Developing ROI for the Leadership Development Program

Several challenges were encountered as the return on investment was developed for the program:

- There was a lack of data tied to specific improvements from each individual. Part of this was caused by lack of design initiatives around the requirement and the focus on achieving results.
- There was concern about the nature and scope of the projects and the ability to implement their recommendations. A different type of project with specific guidelines for capturing value would have made the ROI values of projects much easier to capture.
- The timing issue hampered the ROI analysis. The need to have the evaluation study completed soon after the last session of the program so a decision could be made to proceed or adjust the

program led to an earlier-than-desired analysis of the actual impact.

• The nature of this program, in terms of its soft skills and the focus on learning without the implications of the impact of what was being learned, made the program more difficult to evaluate at this level.

Collectively, these problems represented critical challenges that had to be overcome to a certain extent to develop values. The result was a less-than-optimum value.

ROI Calculations

The ROI calculations had several components, as illustrated in Figure 1. For the first component, project value, two approaches were considered. The first was to develop the value of a project based on the equivalent value as if a consulting firm had developed the project. This resulted in a value of $2,050,000 and was the most credible way of placing a value on the projects at such an early time-frame. The second approach was to place a value on a project at the actual value of an implementation. This value is difficult to develop, but it is estimated to be in the hundreds of millions of dollars. The first approach was used to calculate a project value.

Figure 1. Business impact categories.

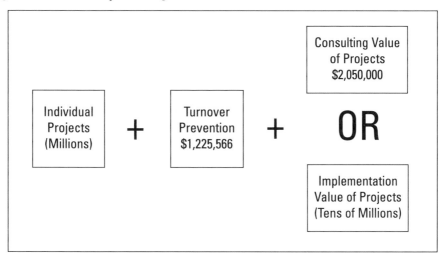

The second component involved the value of the individual projects undertaken by the participants, collected anonymously using questionnaires and confidential interviews. It was too early to develop a precise value at the time of evaluation. Therefore, individual project values, estimated to be in the millions, were not used in the ROI analysis. Finally, the last component was the prevention of turnover. The program conclusively prevented several turnover statistics. Although the exact number will never be known, it was conservative to forecast that four could be attributed to this program, yielding a value of $1,225,566.

The conservative ROI calculation is as follows:

$$ROI = \frac{\text{Net Benefits}}{\text{Program Costs}}$$

$$= \frac{(\$2,050,000 + \$1,225,566) - \$2,019,598}{\$2,019,598} = 62\%$$

If the value of the other blocks in Figure 1 had been included, the value would have been much larger.

Up-Front Emphasis: A Key to ROI Success

The application of the ROI Process model is much more effective when programs are designed to have a specific business impact on the organization. Unfortunately for INB's leadership development program, the decision to calculate an ROI was made after the program was implemented. The original objectives of the programs did not reflect a bottom-line contribution. Therefore, the process of calculating the ROI became a much more difficult issue.

Intangible Benefits

Perhaps the most important results of the leadership development program were the intangible benefits, both short and long term. By definition, these benefits were not converted to monetary value for use in the ROI calculation. They were not measured precisely and are subjective, but still important. Most leadership development programs have been evaluated through perceived or actual intangible benefits. The main intangible benefits reported were as follows:

- Without exception, each participant considered networking a positive and important outcome. The individuals developed close relationships and, more important, they came to understand each other's perspectives, viewpoints, issues, concerns, and problems.
- Participants now take a more enterprise view of their jobs, their decisions, and the challenges facing INB. They have a much greater appreciation for the other functions and their relationship to the whole.
- Participants are reducing, and sometimes removing, silos that have developed within INB. Participants now see each other as contributors who have the bank's interest at the forefront.
- Participants reported that their decision-making capability was greatly enhanced through this program. They are using many of the communication techniques to build the proper rapport with the staff so that they will have free-flowing ideas and input into the decision-making process.
- A surprising intangible benefit was increased loyalty to INB as a result of participation in the leadership program. Participation in this program left many participants with the desire and determination to remain with INB and continue to make a contribution.
- Through the project teams and other team-related exercises, including those involving the larger group of 22, the participants gained a much greater appreciation for the advantages of teamwork and team building. Many of them are using teams to a greater extent in their own work, and they are encouraging teams to be used in other aspects of the bank.
- Some rated this program as a significant personal development experience.
- One of the important objectives of this program was the development of an executive talent pool of capable leaders who would be available for future key positions. Some participants think the program did not help build the talent pool, while others feel they are more capable to take on increased

responsibility. Two things are certain: Participants understand the enterprise view and are better prepared for a potential promotion, and they know the areas that need improvement to continue to sharpen their skills and enhance their ability for future promotions.

Results

The major objectives of the program were met, although not completely successful. Participants rated the most success with the objectives that related to participants taking an enterprise view and acting on synergies within the INB business areas. The least success was achieved with the objective characterized as "participants are prepared to assume senior leadership roles that become vacant or are created based on market needs."

Two major goals were established for the program, and the program was less than successful in meeting these goals. There was more success with the goal to increase the capability of leaders to be high-performing, cross-functional executives. Less success was realized with helping INB become more competitive by tackling and resolving major organizational projects.

There was general agreement about the achievement level for the critical success factors. Less success was attained on the first factor ("a significant amount of time must be invested by the management committee, clients, and participants") because participants did not perceive that, on the whole, the executive and management committee invested significant time in the program. The most success was realized with the second factor, "real projects must be developed that are enterprise-wide and strategic." The success achieved in the third factor, "influential participants must be selected based on performance and future potential," however, was mixed. The selection of the participants was an issue of much concern and debate. It was generally assumed that the participants were high-potential executives with the ability to move into key senior management positions. In reality, most participants think this did not occur. The selection criteria was not followed consistently across both major operational units or within those units.

There was general agreement about the success of major outcomes both from the organizational perspective and the individual perspective. There were mixed results in terms of the outcomes of enhancing the quality of executive talent and on the outcome of research and recommendations for solutions to key strategic issues. There was general agreement that success was realized with management committee interaction with high potential leaders. Generally, the individuals felt that the outcomes related directly to them faired much better. There was consistent agreement that they were exposed to a broader range of INB businesses and to establishing networks across business lines. There was less agreement relative to building skills in systems and strategic thinking, communication, and building high-performance teams. There were varied results identified for reaching accelerated personal and leadership development.

Frequently, a program is only as successful as the support provided to ensure that it functions efficiently, effectively, and achieves its desired goals. The overall support was rated quite good, with some specific issues raising concerns. Learning coaches were rated effective, as was executive support. In the interviews, most indicated that executive support improved during the program and was at its peak toward the end during the presentations. There was a perception of a "wait and see" attitude. The mentor role was misunderstood and not appreciated and most felt it was not effective. The clients generally received good remarks, although the results were mixed for certain individuals. The clients were often referred to as sponsors and met with the individual teams to help develop the projects. The faculty received good ratings; the subject-matter experts, however, did not receive favorable ratings. Although some were outstanding, others were considered extremely ineffective. The support provided by the program director was rated as somewhat effective.

There was expectation that the program would be one of the most significant personal development experiences encountered by the participants. However, most participants disagreed, and only 27 percent rated the experience as very effective. In the interviews, almost every participant indicated that he or she had experienced a more effective leadership and personal development program.

Overall, the success versus the plans was mixed, with several areas requiring adjustments in the future.

Questions for Discussion

1. Discuss why intangible benefits were perhaps the most important results of the leadership program.
2. How might the background of this organization have affected the program?
3. If you had been in charge of this program, would you have done anything differently?
4. What is the role of the supplier in this type of evaluation?
5. Critique the data collection plan.
6. Critique the method to isolate the program.
7. Critique the approach to costing the program.
8. How many years should the benefits be monitored? Explain.
9. Is the ROI realistic? Explain.
10. What role could ROI forecasting play in this evaluation?
11. Choose another case presented in this book—similar in some way to this one—and compare and contrast it with this case. Specifically, decide why the different situations called for different approaches.

CHAPTER

Measuring ROI in an e-Learning Sales Program

United Petroleum International

This case addresses measuring the effectiveness and return on investment of an eLearning solution in an international sales environment. This can be especially challenging when management wants the program to pay for itself in the first year. This case demonstrates that, with a proper needs assessment and support from the organization, a well-designed training program can influence business measures significantly. The program contribution to sales and other business measures are determined by using one or more methods to isolate the effects of the program. The $500,000 projected price tag of the training was a key factor in management's decision to support an impact study to determine the return on investment.

Background

United Petroleum International (UPI) is an international organization headquartered in the southwestern United States. UPI operates several refineries and engages in the sales and service of petroleum products worldwide. UPI has approximately 17,500 employees. International sales of petroleum products have plummeted during the last three quarters, and the outlook shows this trend will continue.

Increased competition abroad and a diminishing quality of sales relationships with customers/prospects were determined to be the major reasons for the lack of performance. The results from quarterly customer satisfaction surveys revealed specific areas of low performance. The executive vice president (EVP) of international sales asked for an assessment of the performance improvement needs of the UPI International Sales Organization (ISO). International Sales has 117 sales engineers and eight sales managers. They are supported by 50 administrative employees who maintain the customer/prospect database, develop sales quotes for the sales engineers, maintain pricing and inventory lists, and provide HR services.

A senior representative from corporate HR and two of UPI's internal consultants teamed with an external consultant from The ROI Institute to implement the Performance Assessment and Analysis Process™ to identify problems, opportunities, and solutions in ISO. The report provided to the EVP identified overall findings, performance gaps, and recommended solutions. At the end of the presentation, the EVP agreed to fund an intense improvement effort, including sales training and restructuring of the ISO incentive pay plan, which was no longer competitive in the changing markets. Funding was also made available for The ROI Institute to design and implement a comprehensive evaluation system to determine business impact and return on investment. The EVP was particularly interested in knowing the ROI for the program. A business objective was established to improve three business measures. Measures to be tracked were identified as sales, monthly closing ratios, and customer satisfaction. Because measurement is an inherent component of the process, the methods and timing were designed and put into place. Baseline data were collected from UPI's performance records.

Designing and Implementing the Solutions

The HR department worked with the design team to design and implement a more appropriate and competitive incentive plan. This new incentive plan was designed after a review of several models and an analysis of application to UPI's markets. The plan was approved and scheduled for implementation in June.

The second solution, addressing the skill and knowledge needs within the sales force, was more difficult to design and implement. Client workload, time constraints, and the scattered locations of the sales engineers were impediments to implementing traditional instructor-led training. Electronic learning methods were considered a viable alternative. A plus for this delivery method at ISO was that all sales engineers had electronic online and CD capabilities on their laptop computers. Another plus was that the flexibility of the electronic delivery method allowed it to be available at any time of the day. This flexibility is attractive to participants who are compensated principally through incentive pay and who desire to spend their available time making customer contacts. The decision was made that the 117 sales engineers and eight sales managers would receive an electronically-delivered interactive sales training process to improve their skills and effectively achieve the business objectives. During the performance analysis, it was discovered that the corporate HR group had identified sales competencies from a previous project and had already begun developing a curriculum. Much of this in-work product served as an important input for the new initiative and greatly assisted the on-time completion of the project.

The design called for a more focused training effort, paying specific attention to the sales relationships engaged by sales engineers and allowing for significant practice of the required skills. The training had to present numerous job scenarios and challenges currently being encountered in the marketplace. The EVP of International Sales assigned the training project to the manager of sales training, who subsequently established a project team to provide the coordination, design, and development of this project.

Several modules were developed with the support of corporate professionals, including technical writers, learning technology specialists, graphic designers, information technology specialists, and consultants. The team consisted of five full-time employees and four external training consultants. Given a short timeframe for completion (management allowed a few months to design and implement the program), work began immediately to develop focused training based on the desired business impact (the business objectives), job performance competencies, and field sales encounters. Several members of the design team were concerned that traditional face-to-face learning methods could not be replaced by an interactive electronic program. The learning technology specialists addressed these concerns, and field testing established the electronic technology design as a success in achieving learning goals. The electronic training process that was developed for the sales engineers became known affectionately as the TLC Program, the Technology Learning

Competency Program. After design completion, it was implemented in June and July, shortly after the new incentive plan was
implemented.

The Technology Learning Competency Program (TLC)

The TLC Program was an interactive, self-paced learning process
designed to assess current skill level and needs of the sales engineer.
Each module was designed to build on a specific set of UPI sales
skills (that is, client partnerships, product pricing and contracting,
selling more profitable products, uncovering objections, handling
objections, defining product features as unique benefits for the customer, expanding existing contracts, handling dissatisfied customers, building community awareness of UPI, and UPI product
awareness/knowledge).

The TLC Program was designed to allow the participant to
respond to various sales-relationship scenarios and to determine the
appropriate decision to move closer to a sale. Each decision made by
the engineer activated another scenario, which allowed additional
choices or decisions to be made. The program continued on a predetermined path initiated by the engineer until a string of choices
confirmed the responses as appropriate or until the decision was
redirected. Video of a subject matter expert provided analysis of
decision choices and helpful suggestions. This took maximum
advantage of learning opportunities presented when a participant
worked through the program. The engineer experienced real-world
issues and situations, had the help of an expert, and was able to learn
from mistakes in a non-threatening manner.

A pre-test at the beginning of each module was used to determine the skill areas that needed improvement and to load the appropriate learning modules. All the 117 sales engineers were pre-tested
to establish a baseline. The program then linked participants to recommended modules that addressed their skill gaps. Each engineer
was allowed a two-month window to complete the required electronic training, either during or after hours as his or her schedule
allowed. So that they could be more effective coaches, the eight managers completed all modules plus a coaching module.

The TLC Program contained a programmed mechanism that captured the results from the various decision paths chosen by the participant. After each learning module, an individual report was
generated, which highlighted the learning achievement and the

decisions made by the engineer. This report was provided to each participant and his or her manager for discussion in the follow-up coaching session. This provided additional learning opportunities and a means for recognition and feedback. Sales engineers were asked to schedule the follow-up planning and coaching meeting with their managers to occur within two weeks of their TLC Program implementation.

Measurement Methods and Data Analysis

Measures to evaluate the effectiveness of a program can be designed and tracked through five distinct levels, as shown in Table 1.

In addition to the five levels of data illustrated in this table, intangible benefits are reported for important outcomes that cannot be converted to monetary values.

The executive vice president of international sales requested that the return on investment (Level 5) be calculated for this program because of the high cost and potential business impact of the TLC Program. Therefore, it became necessary to gather and analyze data at the five levels, plus any intangible benefits.

Table 1. Five Levels of Data.

Level and Type of Measure	Measurement Focus
Level 1. Reaction/Planned Action	Measures participant satisfaction and captures planned actions
Level 2. Learning	Measures changes in knowledge, skills, and attitudes
Level 3. Application	Measures changes in on-the-job behavior
Level 4. Business Impact	Measures changes in business impact variables
Level 5. Return on Investment	Compares program benefits with the costs

ROI Model and Process

Executive management expressed concern that the process used to evaluate TLC be a credible process. Figure 1 illustrates the ROI Process Model used to address this concern. This process has been applied in virtually every industry and in numerous international settings to evaluate training programs, HR programs, technology initiatives, and performance improvement programs. The process flows sequentially from step to step until the ROI is developed. The impact study captures both Level 3 (application) and Level 4 (business impact) data. The ROI (Level 5) is developed from Level 4 data. Improvements that cannot be converted to monetary values are reported as intangible benefits. A conservative approach is used to ensure that only benefits that can be legitimately attributed to the program are captured.

Figure 1. The ROI Process Model.

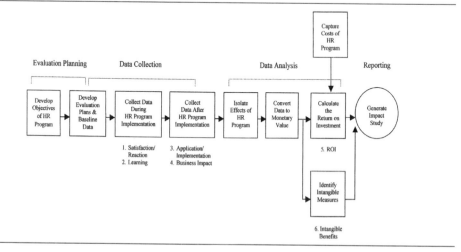

The Data Collection Plan and ROI Analysis Plan

After the business measures were determined and the framework for the TLC Training Program was known, the data collection plan focusing on Level 3 (Application) and Level 4 (Business Impact) measures was developed. The Level 3 measures were behavior changes and frequency of application linked to the TLC Program objectives. After exploring performance data availability in the ISO unit, the quality of the specific data, and the perceived linkage to the TLC Program, the Level 4 measures were targeted and included in the data collection plan: The data collection plan is presented in Figure 2.

The Level 4 data items were then transferred to the ROI analysis plan so that the planning process could be completed. The methods for isolation, data conversion, cost categories, and other items were determined and documented on the ROI analysis plan. The ROI analysis plan is presented in Figure 3.

Figure 2. Data Collection Plan – United Petroleum International.

Program: Technology Learning Competency Program (TLC)   **Responsibility:** _____   **Date:** 1999 _____

Level	Objective(s)	Measures/Data	Data Collection Method	Data Sources	Timing	Responsibilities
Level I **Reaction and Satisfaction**	Employee positive reaction to: • Appropriateness of the technology delivery program • Usefulness of the TLC • TLC application to the job	• Participants perception and attitude	• Online questionnaire	• Participant	• End of each segment (3-5 modules) • End of program	• Program coordinator
Level II **Learning**	• Module learning assignments based on knowledge/skill gaps: • Client partnerships • Product pricing & contracting • Identification & handling objections	A. Skill gaps identified B. Learning occurs as gaps closed through each module implemented	A. Online pre-test questionnaire on all modules B. Online post-test by module	• Participant	A. Prior to training to establish baseline A. Prior to each module as required B. At end of each module	• Program coordinator
Level III **Application & Implementation**	1. Review post-course report and participate in follow-up planning meeting with manager 2. Application of skills to achieve business posts	1. Goals set and achieved 2. Skills applied in sales planning and sales situations	1. And 2. followup questionnaire	1. And 2. Participants 1. And 2. Managers	1. Coaching and planning session within two weeks of TLC 1. And 2. Follow-up questionnaire four months after TLC	• Program coordinator intiates follow-up • Manager and participant initiate planning and coaching
Level IV **Business Impact**	1. Improved closing ration 2. Increased revenue 3. Customer satisfaction	1. Increase in monthly closes 2. Increase in profit margin 3. Customer satisfaction index	1. Performance monitoring 2. Performance monitoring 3. Customer survey (existing)	1. Sales recored–marketing 2. Sales record–marketing 3. Customer quarterly survey	1. Monthly 2. Monthly 3. Monthly	• Program coordinator
Level V **ROI**	Because of the strict requirement for development costs (see comments) an ROI at 20% will be acceptable.	**Comments:** *Because training will be completed for all current engineers within first year of roll-out, management desires to achieve a return on investment during the first year. Therefore, development costs will not be prorated over the life of the program as is customary.*				

Measuring ROI in an eLearning Sales Program **105**

Figure 3. ROI Analysis Plan - United Petroleum International.

Program: Technology Learning Competency Program (TLC) **Responsibility:** _____ **Date:** 1999

Data Items (Usually Level 4)	Methods for Isolating the Effects of the TLC Progam	Methods of converting Date to Monetary Values	Cost Categories	Intangible Benefits	Communication Targets for Final Report	Other Influences/ Issues During Application	Comments
Closes per month	• Participant estimates • Manager estimates	N/A; captured in monthly revenue below	• Development costs • Materials and software • Equipment • Time of subject matter experts • Salaries and venefits during traing (while on company time) • Analysis and evaluation costs	• Recruiting tool • Increase in employee satisfaction • Improved partnership and communication between manager and sales engineer	• Sales engineers • Leadership of sales organization • UPI executive management	• Customers may not be able to identify if or how "engineer skills" impact their satisfaction • Influence of other factors on the three measures • Quality of coaching/ expectations session • Short time frame inhibited ability to field test the TLC modules	• Must capture % of time that training occurs on company time
Monthly revenue	• Participant estimates • Customer estimates	Profit margin of revenue					
Customer satisfaction index		Executive management estimate					

Levels 1 and 2 Data

Level 1 data were captured through an online feedback questionnaire that assessed course content, usefulness of the TLC Program, and job applicability. Participants rated questions on a Likert-type scale from 1 to 7. Participant average for the overall course content was 6.6, and overall usefulness of the system was 6.5. Applicability of the course to the job was rated 6.8. Level 1 data are consolidated in the first three columns of Table 2.

Level 2 data were assessed using pre- and post-testing. The pre- and post-testing for TLC was designed based on job performance expectations. Subject matter experts (SMEs) determined the testing components, which were then validated by sales managers. The SMEs, working with the program designers, validated program content based on competency requirements and skill gaps of the sales organization. They also provided input to design pre-and post-tests. Pre-tests were administered electronically at the beginning of each learning module to determine individual knowledge and skill gaps. The results showed that participants averaged a 50 percent knowledge level on the pre-test and averaged a 91 percent knowledge level on the post-test. These Level 2 data are consolidated in the last two columns of Table 2.

Levels 3 and 4 Data

Level 3 (Application) included three components to evaluate results: (1) follow-up planning and coaching sessions between sales engineers and sales managers, (2) self-assessment of skill application using a follow-up questionnaire, and (3) managers' assessment of skill application using a follow-up questionnaire.

Engineers completed follow-up planning and discussion meetings with their respective managers within two weeks of completing the TLC Program. A plan including goals and expectations was created as a result of each discussion. To allow appropriate time for evaluation and application of skills, it was imperative for managers to have these planning and coaching sessions as close to the end of the training as possible. The sessions occurred during July and August and averaged two hours in length. Because of the dispersed locations of the engineers and managers, some of these meetings were conducted face-to-face and some by telephone or video conferencing.

Table 2. Reaction and Learning Results—1 to 7 Scale.

Reaction: Overall Course	Reaction: Overall Usefulness of TLC	Reaction: Job Applicability	Learning: Pre-test Overall Score	Learning: Post-test Overall Score
6.6	6.5	6.8	50%	91%

The follow-up questionnaire was developed during the program design phase and field-tested with a random sample of sales engineers and sales managers. By advice of the sales managers, the questionnaire was administered four months after the completion of the TLC Program. Four months was deemed an appropriate timeframe to determine the successful application of skills. A series of questions on the follow-up questionnaire also focused on engineers' progress with the improvement goals established in the follow-up discussions between managers and sales engineers. In addition, sales managers each received a follow-up questionnaire focusing on the performance of sales engineers and isolating the effects of the TLC Program. These performance data were consolidated and documented in the final evaluation report. Figure 4 presents a summary of the follow-up questions from the sales engineers' questionnaire.

Business impact data (Level 4) were monitored by reviewing the quarterly customer satisfaction index scores, the monthly sales closing averages, and the profit margin of monthly sales revenue. These data were readily available within the organization, and all but customer satisfaction were used in the determination of business impact and return on investment of the TLC Program. Customer satisfaction data were reviewed for progress, but a standard monetary value did not exist for improvements; therefore there was no conversion to a monetary value.

Figure 4. Summary of follow-up questions.

1. Did you have a follow-up coaching session with your sales manager?
2. Did you complete a follow-up plan and set related goals?
3. How do you rate the quality of the planning and discussion session with your manager?
4. Based on the discussion and planning session you had with your manager, what specific improvement goals have you completed? What improvement goals still need to be completed?
5. How have you and your job changed as a result of participating in TLC?
6. How are you specifically applying what you learned as a result of participating in TLC?
7. What is the impact of these changes for the customer and the ISO organization?
8. Rank (estimate the percentage) the effect each of the following had on any improvement in your sales performance. Allocate from 0 to 100% to the appropriate factors (the total percentage of all items selected must equal 100%):

TLC Training Program   ____%   Executive Management ____%
Influence

Market Influences   ____%   New Monetary Sessions ____%

Manager Coaching   ____%   Other   ____%
Incentives   (specify)

9. What barriers (if any) were a deterrent as you applied what you learned?
10. List any skills you did not have an opportunity to apply during the evaluation timeframe?
11. Estimate the total hours you were involved in accessing/completing TLC training during regular company work hours: _____ hours

Isolating the Effects

To assess the Levels 4 and 5 data accurately, it was imperative that the various influences on any improvement in sales performance be isolated. To isolate the effects of how each factor influenced sales (that is, TLC training, the new incentive plan, market changes, management influence, etc.), each had to be assessed by a credible source. The influence of each factor was determined by using participant and manager estimates regarding each factor. The data were gathered from the participants in the Levels 3 and 4 follow-up questionnaire and from the managers in a separate follow-up questionnaire. Table 3 reports the consolidated data.

Design and Implementation Costs

The development costs of $354,500 for this project included the salaries for development time of one project manager, five full-time employees, and four contract consultants. The costs associated with time spent in meetings and interviews with executive management, senior sales staff, and subject matter experts were also included. This included the time of the interviewer, as well as the people being interviewed. The cost of travel, meals, and lodging during development was also included.

Table 3. Consolidated Estimates—Isolating the Effects.

Influencing Factor	Sales Engineers Average from 104 Respondents	Sales Managers Average from 8 Respondents	Combined Average
New Incentive Plan	35%	37%	36%
TLC Training Program	38%	36%	37%
Executive Management Influence	8%	6%	7%
Coaching by Sales Manager	16%	18%	17%
Other (market changes, new products, product improvements, etc.)	3%	3%	3%

The material costs of $68,500 included a comprehensive workbook for participants, distribution of tutorial CDs, and some additional dial-up networking software.

The equipment cost of $91,000 included upgrades (systems, processors, and video/graphics capability) to the specified hardware setup. This cost category also included the purchase of several new laptops for the sales engineers, digital editing equipment for editing the video and graphics in each module, and two platform servers capable of handling the multi-operational usage.

Eight subject matter experts were assigned to the project. These eight lead sales engineers were paid their sales average ($150 per day) for the 18 days each spent on the module designs, video shoots, and other project duties.

The analysis and evaluation costs of $71,000 included all costs associated with the initial performance analysis and evaluation process (for example, employee time during interviews and questionnaires). This cost category also included the use of an outside consulting firm (The ROI Institute) to plan and implement the performance analysis and evaluation methodology for this project.

All the 117 sales engineers reported completing all modules during their personal time. Because they were compensated mostly by commissions, they usually spent their work hours conducting sales planning and call activities. Table 4 summarizes the fully-loaded costs for the TLC Program.

Table 4. Fully-Loaded Costs.

Development Costs	$354,500
Materials/Software	$68,500
Equipment	$91,000
SME Time (commission paid to expert sales engineers for lost opportunity) eight people @ $150/day X 18 days	$21,600
Analysis and Evaluation Costs	$71,000
TOTAL	**$606,600**

Because no sales were occurring for SMEs during the 18 project days, the commission payments may represent a cost to the sales bottom line. The management team felt the lead sales engineers would be able to maintain their average sales throughout the year even with their involvement in this project. Therefore, they did not feel that lost sales should be included as an opportunity cost. Salaries and benefits and opportunity costs for the "actual training time" are not included in the calculations because none of the 104 sales engineers reported implementing the TLC training during normal company work hours.

Levels 3 and 4 Results

The results of the initiative were encouraging. Prior year sales records revealed that sales engineers' overall performance showed an average of 14 closes per month at $980 profit margin per close. Six months after the implementation of TLC, the engineers averaged 16.65 closes per month at $1,350 profit margin per close. From the previous year, this was an average increase of 2.65 closes per month and an additional $370 profit margin on revenue.

The design team decided to use The ROI Institute's conservative process when calculating the ROI based on revenue generated from new or increased closes. This decision helped to enhance the credibility of the data because participant and manager estimates were the only methods used to isolate the impact of training. The profit margin portion of the revenue increase attributable to the training (TLC) was used as a basis for the ROI calculation.

The Level 5 data were calculated by comparing the cost with the net benefits attributable to the TLC implementation. The benefit attributed to the use of TLC for improvement was considered to be 37 percent, based on the combined participant and manager estimates from Table 3.

The benefits, except for improved customer satisfaction, were then converted to a monetary value, and a return on investment was calculated. Customer satisfaction improvements and other data that could not be converted to monetary values were captured as intangible benefits. Level 3 and Level 4 performance data and intangible benefits were documented in the final evaluation report.

The ROI was calculated as follows:

$$\text{ROI} (\%) = \frac{\text{Benefit} - \text{Costs}}{\text{Costs}} \times 100 = \underline{\hspace{1cm}} \%$$

ROI Results

Monitoring the performance records revealed the total increase in sales attributable to all influencing factors was $5,022,810. There was an average of 2.65 additional closes per month (16.65 − 14.0). However, based on the participant and manager estimates, only 37 percent of this increase in sales was influenced by the TLC Program.

The conservative adjustment of benefits resulting from the TLC program was a factor of 0.98 additional closes per month (2.65 x 0.37). This resulted in an average of $1,323 profit margin per close ($1,350 x 0.98). Multiplied by 12 months and 117 engineers to annualize, this produced $1,857,492 in monetary benefits attributable to TLC.

- 2.65 closes x 0.37 = 0.98 factor for additional closes attributable to TLC Program
- 0.98 x $1,350 per close = $1,323
- $1,323 x 12 months = $15,876 x 117 sales engineers = $1,857,492

The total cost of the TLC Training Program was $606,600. After rounding the benefits from the program, the ROI for the TLC Program was calculated as follows:

$$\text{ROI } (\%) = \frac{\$1,867,000 - \$606,000}{\$606,600} \text{ x } 100 = 206\%$$

In addition to the impact of the TLC training, participants and managers reported the new incentive plan implemented in June had influenced an increase in sales by 36 percent, or $1,808,000.

Intangible Benefits

The results from quarterly customer satisfaction surveys were used to compare the previous year with the current year. Positive improvements and trends were identified. These data were not converted to a monetary value because management had no standard monetary value for an increase in customer satisfaction. It was also difficult to determine how much the skills/behavior from the training actually influenced the improvement in customer satisfaction. Data to isolate and substantiate this would need to come directly from customers because many factors could influence their satisfaction level. When using estimates, only customers are likely to know the extent of such influences. However, executive management felt the customer satisfaction scores were a good indicator of how the organization was responding to the market.

The customer satisfaction scores showed an average improvement of 23 percent since the previous year. Sales engineers and sales managers reported additional intangible benefits, such as increased job satisfaction, better understanding of expectations, reduced turnover, and increased recruiting effectiveness of future sales engineers.

Learning Issues From the Study

This program demonstrated favorable results. The results can be attributed to several things: a comprehensive front-end analysis process that accurately identified the appropriate gaps and solutions, the support of corporate HR, the support of executive management, and the sales organization providing the resources and clarification of expected outcomes prior to designing this initiative.

A major learning issue involved meeting management's requirement for a short lead time to design and implement the program. Executive management expected the program to be implemented within a few months because the competitive environment and need for improved skills were having a negative impact on sales. This created little time to conduct a pilot program. Also, there was not enough time to create all the modules needed for the full range of competency and skill needs of the sales organization. The most salient competencies were targeted and given development priority.

The need to more accurately isolate the effects of this initiative was another learning issue. Several factors influenced the results. Although participant estimates can be effective (participants know what influences their performance), additional methods, like a control group arrangement or trend-line analysis, can often isolate the impact more convincingly.

Reporting to Stakeholder Groups

The target population for this initiative included four groups: the sales engineers, the leaders of the sales organization, the subject matter experts, and the executive management team of UPI. All played a critical role in the success of the TLC Program. All were provided a final report showing the results from the impact study.

The primary group was the 117 sales engineers who actually participated in the TLC Program. They were the most instrumental of the groups in creating the success enjoyed by TLC. They dedicated the time to the system and took full advantage of the opportunity to improve performance based on what they learned from the technology-supported training. They also provided tremendous constructive feedback to enhance the system for future engineers.

The second group consisted of the leaders of the sales organization, who were responsible and accountable for the success of sales at UPI. Ten people—including one executive vice president, one director, and eight sales managers—were key factors in the success. They supported the up-front analysis and the validation of the job skills and gaps that were to be measured. By conducting planning and coaching sessions with sales engineers and by discussing expectations, the leaders of the sales organization were essential factors in the transfer and application of skills on the job.

The third group was the SMEs, who provided timely and accurate feedback about each module being developed, and the corporate professionals and consultants, who demonstrated diligence and expertise. On frequent occasions, they worked beyond normal work hours to keep the project on track.

The fourth group was the members of the executive management team of UPI, who funded the project and showed interest in the entire training process. The executive management team supported the project by allocating the necessary resources and setting the expectations for outcomes.

Questions for Discussion

1. Identify the influencing factors that contributed to the success of the TLC Program.
2. How would you convince management that a control group arrangement would be beneficial to the study?
3. What recommendations would you make to management to convert customer satisfaction improvements to a monetary value?
4. How credible are the estimates in this evaluation?
5. How credible is this study?

Measuring ROI in Performance Management Training

Cracker Box, Inc.

This case study describes how one organization—a restaurant chain—built evaluation into the learning process and positioned it as an application tool. This approach is a powerful one that uses action plans, which participants develop during the training program to drive application, impact, and return-on-investment (ROI) data. This training program adds significant value to the restaurant store chain in this case study and shows how the evaluation process can be accomplished with minimum resources. The keys to success are planning for the evaluation, building it into the learning process, and using the data to help future participants.

Background
Situation

Cracker Box is a large, fast-growing restaurant chain located along major interstates and thoroughfares. In the past 10 years, Cracker Box has grown steadily and now has over 400 stores with plans for continued growth. Each store has a restaurant and a gift shop. A store manager is responsible for both profit units. The turnover of store managers is approximately 25 percent, lower than the industry average of 35 percent, but still excessive. Because of the store's growth and the turnover, the organization needs to develop almost 150 new store managers per year.

Store managers operate autonomously and are held accountable for store performance. Working with the members of the store team,

This case was prepared to serve as a basis for discussion rather than to illustrate either effective or ineffective administrative and management practices. All names, dates, places, and organizations have been disguised at the request of the author or organization.

managers control expenses, monitor operating results, and take actions as needed to improve store performance. Each store records dozens of performance measures in a monthly operating report and other measures weekly.

Stores recruit managers both internally and externally and require that they have restaurant experience. Many of them have college degrees. The training program for new managers usually lasts nine months. When selected, a store manager trainee reports directly to a store manager who serves as a mentor. Trainees are usually assigned to a specific store location for the duration of manager training. During the training period, the entire store team reports to the store manager trainee as the store manager coaches the trainee. As part of formal training and development, each store manager trainee attends at least three one-week programs at the company's Corporate University, including the Performance Management Program.

Performance Management Program

The Performance Management Program teaches new store managers how to improve store performance. Program participants learn how to establish measurable goals for employees, provide performance feedback, measure progress toward goals, and take action to ensure that goals are met. The program focuses on using the store team to solve problems and improve performance and also covers problem analysis and counseling skills. The one-week program is residential and often includes evening assignments. Corporate University staff and operation managers teach the program, and they integrate skill practice sessions throughout the instruction. Program sessions take place at the location of the Corporate University near the company's headquarters.

Needs Assessment

The overall needs assessment for this process was in two parts. First, there was a macrolevel needs assessment for the store manager position. The Corporate University's performance consultants identified specific training needs for new managers, particularly with issues involving policy, practice, performance, and leadership. This needs assessment was the basis for developing the three programs for each new manager trainee. The second part of the assessment was built into this program as the individual manager trainees provided input for a microlevel or store-level needs assessment.

The program facilitator asked participants to provide limited needs assessment data prior to the program. Each participant was asked to meet with the store manager (that is, his or her mentor) and identify at least three operating measures that, if improved, should enhance store performance. Each measure was to focus on changes that both the store manager and manager trainee thought should be made. These business impact measures could be productivity, absenteeism, turnover, customer complaints, revenues, inventory control, accidents, or any other measure that could improve performance. It would be possible for each participant in a specific manager trainee group to have different measures.

To ensure that the job performance needs are met, each participant was asked to review the detailed objectives of the program and select only measures that could be improved by the efforts of the team and skills taught in the program. The important point in this step is to avoid selecting measures that cannot be enhanced through the use of the input of the team and the skills covered in the program.

As participants register for the program, they are reminded of the requirement to complete an action plan as part of the application of the process. This requirement is presented as an integral part of the program and not as an add-on data collection tool. Action planning is necessary for participants to see the improvements generated from the entire group of program participants. Credit is not granted until the action planning process is completed.

Measurement Requirements
Why Evaluate This Program?

The decision to conduct an ROI analysis for this program was reached through a methodical and planned approach. A Corporate University team decided at the outset that data would be collected from this program. Therefore, the team built the evaluation into the program. This decision was based on the following reasons:

- This program is designed to add value at the store level and the outcome is expressed in store-level measures that are well-known and respected by the management team. The evaluation should show the actual value of improvement.
- This evaluation positions the data collection process from an evaluation perspective to an application process. The manager trainees did not necessarily perceive that the information they provided was for the purpose of evaluation, but saw it as more of an application tool to show the impact of their training.
- The application data enables the team to make improvements and

adjustments. The data also helps the team gain respect for the program from the operating executives as well as the store managers.

The ROI Process

The Corporate University staff used a comprehensive evaluation process in many of its programs. This approach, called the ROI process, generates the following six types of data.

- Reaction and satisfaction
- Learning
- Application and implementation
- Business impact
- ROI
- Intangible measures

To determine the contribution the training program makes to the changes in business impact measures, a technique to isolate the effects of the program is included in the process.

Figure 1 shows the ROI process model. It begins with detailed objectives for learning, application, and impact. It shows development of data collection plans and ROI analysis plans before data collection actually begins. Four different levels of data are collected, namely, the first four types of data listed above. The process includes a method to isolate the effects of a program and techniques to convert data to monetary value. The ROI is calculated when comparing the monetary benefits to the cost of the program. The intangible measures, the sixth type of data, are those measures not converted to monetary value. This comprehensive model allows the organization to follow a consistent standardized approach each time it is applied to evaluate training and development programs.

Planning for Evaluation

Planning for the evaluation is critical to saving costs and improving the quality and quantity of data collection. It also provides an opportunity to clarify expectations and responsibilities and shows the client group—in this case, the senior operating team—exactly how this program is evaluated. Two documents are created: The data collection plan and the ROI analysis plan.

Data Collection Plan

Figure 2 shows the data collection plan for this program. Broad objectives are detailed along the five levels of evaluation, which

Figure 1. The ROI process model.

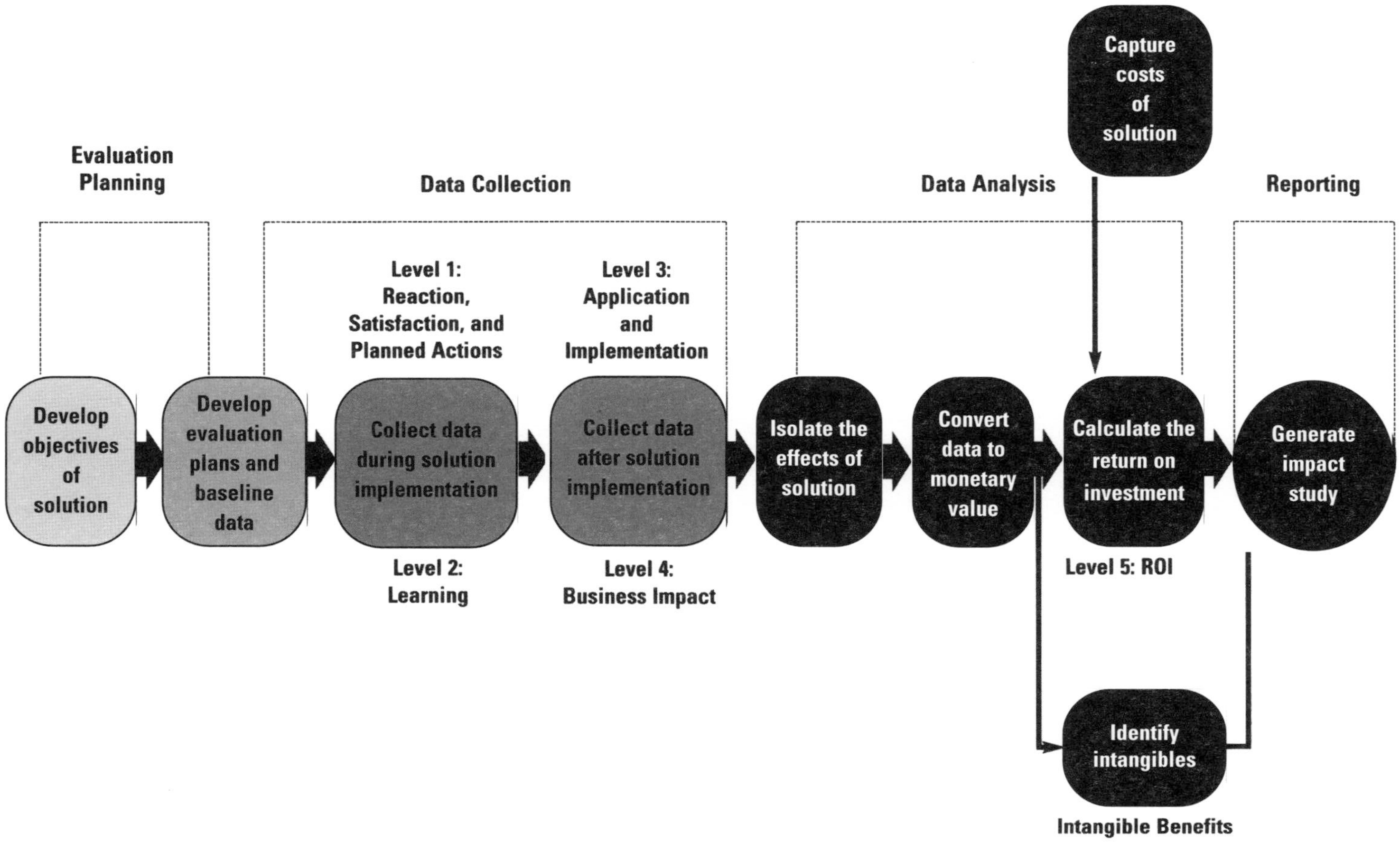

Figure 2. Data collection plan.

Program: Performance Management Program   **Responsibility:** _____   **Date:** _____

Level	Objective(s)	Measures and Data	Data Collection Method	Data Sources	Timing	Responsibilities
1	**Reaction and Satisfaction** • Obtain positive reaction to program and materials • Identify planned actions	• Average rating of 4.0 out of 5.0 on quality, quantity, and usefulness of material • 100% submit planned actions	• Standard feedback questionnaire	• Participant	• End of program	• Facilitator
2	**Learning** • Establishing employee goals • Providing feedback and motivating employees • Measuring employee performance • Solving problems • Counseling employees	• Be able to identify 100% of steps necessary to establish, monitor, and achieve goals • Demonstrate ability to provide employee feedback, solve problems	• Skill practice • Facilitator assessment • Participant assessment	• Participant	• During program	• Facilitator

3	**Application and Implementation** • Apply skills in appropriate situations • Complete all steps of action plan	• Ratings on questions • The number of steps completed on action plan	• Follow-up questionnaire • Action plan	• Participant • Participant	• Three months after program • Six months after program	• Corporate University staff
4	**Business Impact** • Identify three measures that need improvement	• Varies	• Action plan	• Participant	• Six months after program	• Corporate University staff
5	**ROI** • 25%					

Comments:

_____

_____

_____

_____

represent the first five types of data collected for programs. As the figure illustrates, the typical reaction and satisfaction data is collected at the end of the program by the facilitator. Learning objectives focus on the five major areas of the program: establishing employee goals, providing feedback and motivating employees, measuring employee performance, solving problems, and counseling employees. Learning measures are obtained through observations from the facilitator as participants practice the various skills.

Through application and implementation, participants focused on two primary broad areas. The first was to apply the skills in appropriate situations, and the second was to complete all steps in their action plan. In terms of skill application, the evaluation team developed a follow-up questionnaire to measure the use of the skills along with certain other related issues. This was planned for three months after the program. Six months after the program, the action plan data is provided to show the actual improvement in the measures planned.

Business impact objectives vary with the individual because each store manager trainee identifies at least three measures needing improvement. These measures appear on the action plan and serve as the basic documents for the Corporate University staff to tabulate the overall improvement.

The overall ROI objective is 25 percent, which was the standard established for internal programs of Cracker Box. This was slightly above the internal rate of return expected from other investments such as the construction of a new restaurant and gift shop.

ROI Analysis

The ROI analysis plan, which appears in figure 3, shows how the organization processes and reports data. Business impact data is listed and forms the basis for the rest of the analysis. The method for isolating the effects of the program at Cracker Box was participant estimation. The method to convert data to monetary values relied on three techniques: standard values (when they were available), expert input, or participant's estimate. Cost categories represent a fully loaded profile of costs, anticipated intangibles are detailed, and the communication targets are outlined. The ROI analysis plan basically represents the approach to process business impact data to develop the ROI analysis and to capture the intangible data. Collectively, these two planning documents outline the approach for evaluating this program.

Figure 3. ROI analysis plan.

Program: _Performance Management Program_   Responsibility: _____   Date: _____

Data Items (Usually Level 4)	Methods for Isolating the Effects of the Program and Process	Methods of Converting Data to Monetary Values	Cost Categories	Intangible Benefits	Communication Targets for Final Report	Other Influences and Issues During Application	Comments
• Three measures identified by manager trainee and manager	• Participant estimation	• Standard values • Expert input • Participant estimation	• Needs assessment • Program development • Program material • Travel and lodging • Facilitation and coordination • Participant salaries plus benefits • Training overhead • Evaluation	• Achievement • Confidence • Job satisfaction • Permanent store assignment	• Store managers • Participants • Corporate University staff • Regional operating executives • VP store operations • Senior VP human resources		

Client Signature: _____   Date: _____

Action Planning: A Key to ROI Analysis

Figure 4 shows the sequence of activities from introduction of the action planning process through reinforcement during the program. The requirements for the action plan was communicated prior to the program along with the request for needs assessment information. On the first day of training, Monday, the program facilitator described the action planning process in a 15-minute discussion. At Cracker Box, participants received specially prepared notepads on which to capture specific action items throughout the program. They were instructed to make notes when they learned a technique or skill that could be useful in improving one of the measures on their list of three. In essence, this notepad became a rough draft of the action plan.

The action planning process was discussed in greater detail in a one-hour session on Thursday afternoon. This discussion included three parts:

- Actual forms
- Guidelines for developing action plans and SMART (*s*pecific, *m*easurable, *a*chievable, *r*ealistic, and *t*ime based) requirements
- Examples to illustrate what a complete action plan should look like

Figure 4. Sequence of activities for action planning.

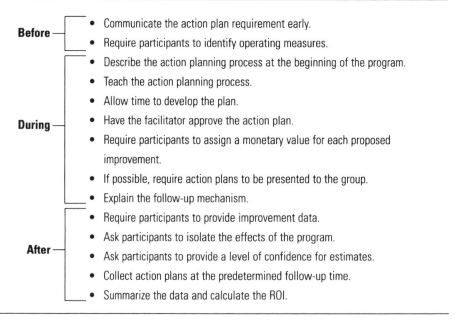

Before
- Communicate the action plan requirement early.
- Require participants to identify operating measures.

During
- Describe the action planning process at the beginning of the program.
- Teach the action planning process.
- Allow time to develop the plan.
- Have the facilitator approve the action plan.
- Require participants to assign a monetary value for each proposed improvement.
- If possible, require action plans to be presented to the group.
- Explain the follow-up mechanism.

After
- Require participants to provide improvement data.
- Ask participants to isolate the effects of the program.
- Ask participants to provide a level of confidence for estimates.
- Collect action plans at the predetermined follow-up time.
- Summarize the data and calculate the ROI.

Figure 5. Action plan form.

Name: _____ Instructor Signature: _____ Follow-Up Date: _____

Objective: _____ Evaluation Period: _____ to _____

Improvement Measure: _____ Current Performance: _____ Target Performance: _____

Action Steps	Analysis
1. _____	A. What is the unit of measure? _____
2. _____	B. What is the value (cost) of one unit? $ _____
3. _____	C. How did you arrive at this value? _____
4. _____	_____
5. _____	_____
6. _____	D. How much did the measure change during the evaluation period? _____ (monthly value)
7. _____	E. What percent of this change was actually caused by this program? _____ %
Intangible Benefits: _____	F. What level of confidence do you place on the above information? (100% = certainty and 0% = no confidence) _____ %

Comments: _____

Measuring ROI in Performance Management Training **127**

The program facilitator distributed the action planning forms in a booklet containing instructions, five blank action plans (only three are required, one for each measure), and the examples of completed action plans. On Thursday evening, participants completed the booklets in a facilitated session that lasted approximately one and a half hours. Participants worked in teams to complete all three action plans. Each plan took about 20 to 30 minutes to complete. Figure 5 sows a blank action plan. During the session, participants completed the top portion, the left column on which they list the action steps, and parts A, B, and C in the right column. They completed the remainder of the form—parts D, E, and F as well as intangible benefits and comments—in a six-month follow-up. The senior facilitator monitored most of these sessions and sometimes an operations executive was also present. The involvement of the operations executive provided an additional benefit of keeping the participants focused on the task. Also, this involvement usually impressed operating executives with the focus of the program and the quality of the action planning documents.

The action plan cold focus on any specific steps as long as they were consistent with the skills required in the program and were related to the business improvement measures. The most difficult part of developing the plan was to convert the measure to a monetary value. three approaches were offered to the participants. First, standard values are available for most of the operating measures. Operations managers had previously assigned a cost (or value) to a particular measure for use in controlling costs and to develop an appreciation for the impact of different measures. Second, when a standard value was not available, the participants were encouraged to use expert input. This option involved contacting someone in the organization who might know the value of a particular item. The program facilitator encouraged participants to call the expert on Friday morning and include the value in the action plan. Third, when a standard value or expert input was not available, participants were asked to estimate the cost or value using all of the knowledge and resources available to them. Fortunately, the measure was a concern to the trainee and the store manager so there was some appreciation for the actual value. An estimation was possible in every case when standard values and expert input were not available. It was important to require that this value be developed during the program or at least soon after completion of the program.

The next day, Friday, the participants briefly reviewed the action planning process with the group. Each action plan took about five minutes. To save time, each group chose one action plan to present to the entire group to underscore the quality of the action planning process. The program facilitator explained the follow-up steps to the group. Staff of the Corporate University and operation managers recommended that the manager trainee and the store manager discuss the document before they send a copy to the university staff. They should include contact information in case a staff member has a question about the data.

Results

Staff of the Corporate University and operation managers reported the results in all six categories developed by the ROI process, beginning with reaction and moving through ROI and the intangibles. Following are the results in each category together with additional explanation about how some of the data was processed.

Reaction and Learning

Reaction data is collected at the end of the program using a standard questionnaire, which focuses on issues such as relevance of the material, the amount of new information, and intention to use the skills. The content, delivery, and facilitation are also evaluated. Table 1 shows a summary of the reaction data on a rating scale in which one is unsatisfactory and five is exceptional.

Learning improvement is measured at the end of the program using a self-assessment and a facilitator assessment. Although these measures are subjective, they provide an indication of improvements in learning. Typical programs usually report significant improvements in both the self-assessments and facilitator-assessments. In this study, the facilitator-assessment data reported that all participants had acquired the skills at a satisfactory level.

Table 1. Reaction of program participants.

Topic	Rating
Relevance of material	4.3
Amount of new information	3.8
Intention to use skills	4.6
Content of the program	3.7
Delivery of the program	4.1
Facilitation of the program	4.2

Application and Implementation

To determine the extent to which the skills are being used and to check progress of the action plan, participants received a questionnaire three months after the program. This two-page, user-friendly questionnaire covered the following areas:

- Skill usage
- Skill frequencies
- Linkage to store measures
- Barriers to implementation
- Enablers for implementation
- Progress with the action plan
- Quality of the support from the manager
- Additional intangible benefits
- Recommendations for program improvements

Participants reported progress in each of the areas and indicated that they had significant use of the skills even beyond the projects involving action plans. Also, the store manager trainees indicated linkage of this program with many store measures beyond the three measures selected for action planning. Typical barriers of implementation that they reported included lack of time, understaffing, changing culture, and lack of input from the staff. Typical enablers were the support from the store manager and early success with the application of the action plan. This follow-up questionnaire allowed manager trainees an opportunity to summarize the progress with the action plan. In essence, this served as a reminder to continue with the plan as well as a process check to see if there were issues that should be explored. The manager trainees also gave the store managers high marks in terms of support provided to the program. Participants suggested several improvements, all minor, and store managers implemented those that added value. Explanations of some intangible benefits that participants identified appear later.

Business Impact

Participants collected business impact data that were specific to the manager trainees. Although the action plan contains some Level 3 application data (the left side of the form), the primary value of the action plan was business impact data obtained from the planning documents.

In the six-month follow-up the participants were required to furnish the following five items:

1. The actual change in the measure on a monthly basis is included in part D of the action plan. This value is used to develop an annual (first year) improvement.
2. The only feasible way to isolate the effects of the program is to obtain an estimate directly from the participants. As they monitor the business measures and observe their improvement, the participants probably know the actual influences driving a particular measure, at least the portion of the improvement related to their actions, which are detailed on the action plan. Realizing that other factors could have influenced the improvement, the manager trainees were asked to estimate the percent of improvement resulting from the application of the skills required in the training program (the action steps on the action plan). Each manager trainee was asked to be conservative with the estimate and express it as a percentage (part E on the action plan).
3. Recognizing that the above value is an estimate, the manager trainees were asked to indicate the level of confidence in their allocation of the contribution to this program. This is included in part F on the action plan, using 100 percent for certainty and 0 percent for no confidence. This number reflects the degree of uncertainty in the value and actually frames an error range for the estimate.
4. The participants were asked to provide input on intangible measures observed or monitored during the six months that were directly linked to this program.
5. Participants were asked to provide additional comments including explanations.

Figure 6 shows the completed action plan. The example focuses directly on absenteeism from participant number three. This participant has a weekly absenteeism rate of 8 percent and a goal to reduce it to 5 percent. Specific action steps appear on the left side of the form. The actual value is $41 per absence, an amount that represents a standard value. The actual change on a monthly basis is 2.5 percent, slightly below the target. The participant estimated that 65 percent of the change is directly attributable to this program and that he is 80 percent confident in this estimate. The confidence estimate frames a range of error for the 65 percent allocation, allowing for a possible 20 percent plus or minus adjustment in the estimate. The estimate is conservative, adjusted to the low side, bringing the contribution rate of this program to absenteeism reduction to 52 percent:

Figure 6. Action plan.

Name:	_John Mathews_	Instructor Signature: _____		Follow-Up Date: _1 September_
Objective:	_Reduce weekly absenteeism rate for team_		Evaluation Period: _March_ to _September_	
Improvement Measure:	_Absenteeism rate_	Current Performance: _8%_	Target Performance: _5%_	

Action Steps

1. _Meet with team to discuss reasons for absenteeism—using_   _10 March_
   problem-solving skills
2. _Review absenteeism records for each employee—look for_   _20 March_
   trends and patterns
3. _Counsel with "problem employees" to correct habits and_
   explore opportunities for improvement
4. _Conduct a brief "performance discussion" with an employee_
   returning to work after an unplanned absence
5. _Provide recognition to employees who have perfect_
   attendance
6. _Follow up with each discussion and discuss improvement or_   _31 March_
   lack of improvement and plan other action
7. _Monitor improvement and provide recognition when_
   appropriate

Intangible Benefits:
Less stress, greater job satisfaction

Analysis

A. What is the unit of measure?   _One absence_

B. What is the value (cost) of one unit? $ _41.00_

C. How did you arrive at this value?
   Standard value

D. How much did the measure change during the evaluation period?
   (monthly value)   _2.5%_

E. What percent of this change was actually caused by this program?
   _65_   %

F. What level of confidence do you place on the above information?
   (100% = certainty and 0% = no confidence)
   _80_   %

Comments: _Great program—it kept me on track with this problem._

$$65\% \times 80\% = 52\%$$

This particular location, which is known because of the identity of the store manager trainee, has 40 employees. Also, employees work an average 220 days. The actual improvement value for this example can be calculated as follows:

$$40 \text{ employees} \times 220 \text{ days} \times 2.5\% \times \$41 = \$9,020$$

This is a total first-year improvement before the adjustments. Table 2 shows the annual improvement values on the first measure only for the 14 participants in this group. (Note that participant number five did not return the action plan so that person's data was omitted from the analysis.) A similar table is generated for the second and third measures. The values are adjusted by the contribution estimate and the confidence estimate. In the absenteeism example, the $9,020 is adjusted by 65 percent and 80 percent to yield $4,690. This same adjustment is made for each of the values, with a total first-year adjusted value for the first measure of $68,240. The same process is followed for the second and third measures for the group, yielding totals of $61,525 and $58,713, respectively. The total first-year monetary benefit for this group is the sum of these three values.

Program Cost

Table 3 details the program costs for a fully loaded cost profile. The cost of the needs assessment is prorated over the life of the program, which is estimated to be three years with 10 sessions per year. The program development cost is prorated over the life of the program as well. The program materials and lodging costs are direct costs. Facilitation and coordination costs were estimated. Time away from work represents lost opportunity and is calculated by multiplying five days times daily salary costs adjusted for 30 percent employee benefits factor (that is, the costs for employee benefits). Training and education overhead costs were estimated. Actual direct costs for the evaluation are included. These total costs of $47,242 represent a conservative approach to cost accumulation.

ROI Analysis

The total monetary benefits are calculated by adding the values of the three measures, totaling $188,478. This leaves a benefits-to-cost ratio (BCR) ad ROI as follows:

Table 2. Business impact data.

Participant	Improvement ($ Values)	Measure	Contribution Estimate From Manager Trainees	Confidence Estimate	Adjusted $ Value
1	5,500	Labor savings	60%	80%	2,640
2	15,000	Turnover	50%	80%	6,000
3	9,020	Absenteeism	65%	80%	4,690
4	2,100	Shortages	90%	90%	1,701
5	0	—	—	—	—
6	29,000	Turnover	40%	75%	8,700
7	2,241	Inventory	70%	95%	1,490
8	3,621	Procedures	100%	80%	2,897
9	21,000	Turnover	75%	80%	12,600
10	1,500	Food spoilage	100%	100%	1,500
11	15,000	Labor savings	80%	85%	10,200
12	6,310	Accidents	70%	100%	4,417
13	14,500	Absenteeism	80%	70%	8,120
14	3,650	Productivity	100%	90%	3,285

Total annual benefit for first measure is $68,240.
Total annual benefit for second measure is $61,525.
Total annual benefit for third measure is $58,713.

Table 3. Program cost summary.

Items	Cost ($)
Needs Assessment (prorated over 30 sessions)	$ 1,500
Program Development (prorated over 30 sessions)	1,700
Program Materials, 14 @ $40	560
Travel and Lodging, 14 @ $900	12,600
Facilitation and Coordination	8,000
Facilities and Refreshments, 5 days @ $350	1,750
Participants' Salaries Plus Benefits, 14 @ 521 × 1.3	9,482
Training and Education Overhead (Allocated)	900
ROI Evaluation	10,750
	$ 47,242

$$\text{BCR} = \frac{\$188,478}{\$47,242} = 3.98$$

$$\text{ROI} = \frac{\$188,478 - \$47,242}{\$47,242} = 298\%$$

This ROI value of almost 300 percent greatly exceeds the 25 percent target value. The target audience considered the ROI value credible, although it is extremely high. Its credibility rests on the following principles on which the study was based:

1. The data comes directly from the participants in concert with their store manager.
2. Most of the data could be audited to see if the changes were actually taking place.
3. To be conservative, the data includes only the first year of improvements. With the changes reported in the action plans, there should be some second- and third-year value that has been omitted from the calculation.
4. The monetary improvement has been discounted for the effect of other influences. In essence, the participants take credit only for the part of the improvement related to the program.
5. This estimate of contribution to the program is adjusted for the error of the estimate, adding to the conservative approach.
6. The costs are fully loaded to include both direct and indirect costs.

7. The data is for only those individuals who completed and returned the action plans. No data appeared for participant five in table 2 because that person did not return an action plan.
8. The business impact does not include value obtained from using the skills to address other problems or to influence other measures. Only the values from three measures taken from the action planning projects were used in the analysis.

The ROI process develops convincing data connected directly to store operations. From the viewpoint of the chief financial officer, the data can be audited and monitored. It should be reflected as actual improvement in the stores. Overall, the senior management team considered the results credible and fully supported them.

Intangible Data

As a final part of the complete profile of data, the intangible benefits were itemized. The participants provided input on intangible measures at two time frames. The follow-up questionnaire provided an opportunity for trainees to indicate intangible measures they perceived to represent a benefit directly linked to this program. Also, the action plan had an opportunity for trainees to add additional intangible benefits. Collectively, each of the following benefits were listed by at least two individuals:

• A sense of achievement
• Increased confidence
• Improved job satisfaction
• Promotion to store manager
• Stress reduction
• Improved teamwork

To some executives these intangible measures are just as important as the monetary payoff.

The Payoff: Balanced Data

This program drives six types of data items: satisfaction, learning, application, business impact, ROI, and intangible benefits. Collectively these six types of data provide a balanced, credible viewpoint of the success of the program.

Table 4. Communication strategy.

Timing	Communication Medium	Target Audience
Within one month of follow-up	Detailed impact study (125 pages)	Program participants; Corporate University staff • Responsible for this program in some way • Involved in evaluation
Within one month of follow-up	Executive summary • Including business impact data	Corporate and regional operation executives
Within one month of follow-up	Report of results (1 page) • In-store manager magazine	Store managers
After registration	Report of results (1 page) • In prework material	Future participants

Communication Strategy

Table 4 shows the communication strategy for communicating results from the sty. All key stakeholders received the information. The communications were routine and convincing. The information to store managers and regional managers helped to build confidence in the program. The data provided to future participants was motivating and helped them to select measures for action plans.

Lessons Learned

It was critical to build evaluation into the program, positioning the action plan as an application tool instead of a data collection tool. This approach helped secure commitment and ownership for the process. It also shifted much of the responsibility for evaluation to the participants as they collected data, isolated the effects of the program, and converted the data to monetary values, the three most critical steps in the ROI process. The costs were easy to capture, and the report was easily generated and sent to the various target audiences.

This approach has the additional advantage of evaluating programs where a variety of measures are influenced. This situation is typical of leadership, team building, and communication programs. The application can vary considerably, and the actual business measure driven can very with each participant. The improvements are integrated after they are converted to monetary value. Thus, the common value among measures is the monetary value representing the value of the improvement.

Discussion Questions

1. Is this approach credible? Explain.
2. Is the ROI value realistic?
3. How should the results be presented to the senior team?
4. What can be done to east the challenge of converting data to monetary values?
5. How can the action planning process be positioned as an application tool?
6. What types of programs would be appropriate for this approach?

CHAPTER 8

Measuring ROI in Interactive Selling Skills

Retail Merchandise Company

The case study represents a classic application of the return-on-investment (ROI) process. An interactive selling skills program drives sales increases at a pilot group of retail stores. A control group arrangement isolates the effects of the program. The organization uses the results to make critical decisions.

Background Information

Retail Merchandise Company (RMC) is a large national chain of 420 stores, located in most major U.S. markets. RMC sells small household items, gifts of all types, electronics, and jewelry as well as personal accessories. It does not sell clothes or major appliances. The executives at RMC were concerned about the slow sales growth and were experimenting with several programs to boost sales. One of their concerns focused on the interaction with customers. Sales associates were not actively involved in the sales process, usually waiting for a customer to make a purchasing decision and then proceeding with processing the sale. Several store managers had analyzed the situation to determine if more communication with the customer would boost sales. The analysis revealed that very simple techniques to probe and guide the customer to a purchase should boost sales in each store.

The senior executives asked the training and development staff to experiment with a simple customer interactive skills program for a small group of sales associates. The training staff would prefer a

This case was prepared to serve as a basis for discussion rather than to illustrate either effective or ineffective administrative and management practices. All names, dates, places, and organizations have been disguised at the request of the author or organization.

program produced by an external supplier to avoid the cost of development, particularly if the program is not effective. The specific charge from the management team was to implement the program in three stores, monitor the results, and make recommendations.

The sales associates are typical of the retail store employee profile. They are usually not college graduates, and most have a few months, or even years, of retail store experience. Turnover was usually quite high, and formal training has not been a major part of previous sales development efforts.

The Solution

The training and development staff conducted a brief initial needs assessment and identified five simple skills that the program should cover. From the staff's analysis, it appeared that the sales associates did not have these skills or were very uncomfortable with the use of these skills. The training and development staff selected the Interactive Selling Skills program, which makes significant use of skill practices. The program, an existing product from an external training supplier, includes two days of training in which participants have an opportunity to practice each of the skills with a classmate followed by three weeks of on-the-job application. Then, in a final day of training, there is discussion of problems, issues, barriers, and concerns about using the skills. Additional practice and fine-tuning of skills take place in that final one-day session. At RMC, this program was tried in the electronics area of three stores, with 16 people trained in each store. The staff of the training supplier facilitated the program for a predetermined facilitation fee.

The Measurement Challenge

The direction from senior management was very clear: These executives wanted to boost sales and at the same time determine if this program represented a financial payoff, realizing that many of the strategies could be implemented to boost sales. Business impact and ROI were the measurement mandates from the senior team.

In seeking a process to show ROI, the training and development staff turned to a process that Jack Phillips developed. The ROI process generates six types of measures:

- Reaction and Planned Action
- Learning
- Application and Implementation
- Business Impact

- ROI
- Intangible measures

It also includes a technique to isolate the effects of the program or solution.

This process involves extensive data collection and analysis. As figure 1 shows, the process includes steps to develop the ROI, beginning with evaluation planning. Four types of data are collected, representing the four levels of evaluation. The analysis develops a fifth level of data as well as the intangible benefits. The process includes a method to isolate the effects of the program and a method to convert data to monetary value. The fully loaded costs are used to develop the actual ROI. This process was already in place at RMC, and training and development selected it as the method to measure the success of this program.

Planning for the ROI

An important part of the success of the ROI evaluation is to properly plan for the impact study early in the training and development cycle. Appropriate up-front attention saves time later when data are actually collected and analyzed, thus improving the accuracy and reducing the cost of the evaluation. This approach also avoids any confusion surrounding what will be accomplished, by whom, and at what time. Two planning documents are key to the up-front planning, and the training staff completed them before the program was implemented.

Following are descriptions of each document.

Data Collection Plan

Figure 2 shows the completed data collection plan for this program. The document provides a space for major elements and issues regarding collecting data for the different levels of evaluation. Broad program objectives are appropriate for planning, as the figure shows.

The objective at Level 1 for this program was a positive reaction to the potential use of the skills on the job. The gauge for this level was a reaction questionnaire that participants completed at the end of the program and facilitators collected. The goal was to achieve four out of five on a composite rating. Also, the questionnaire asked participants to indicate how often and in which situations they would actually use the skills.

The measurement of learning focused on learning how to use five simple skills. The measure of success was a pass or fail on the skill practice that the facilitator observed and for which the observer collected data on the second day of the program.

Figure 1. The ROI process model.

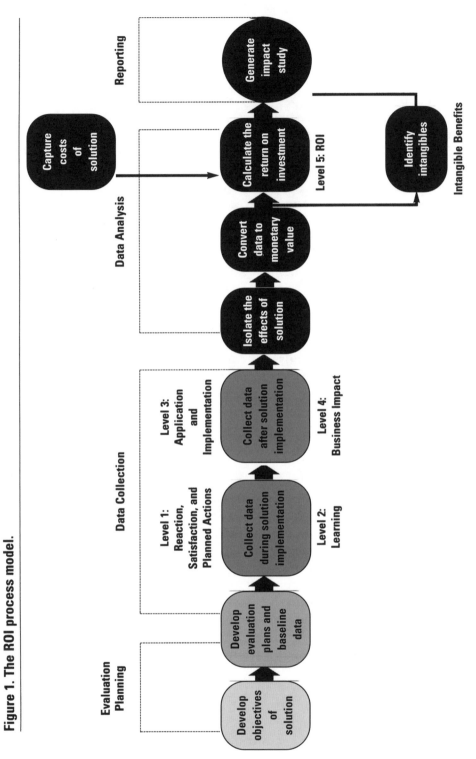

Figure 2. Data collection plan.

Program: _____ Responsibility: _____ Date: _____

Level	Broad Program Objectives	Measures	Data Collection Method and Instruments	Data Sources	Timing	Responsibilities
1	**Reaction and Satisfaction and Planned Actions** • Positive reaction—four out of five • Action items	• Rating on a composite of five measures • Yes or No	• Questionnaire	• Participant	• End of program (Third day)	• Facilitator
2	**Learning** • Learn to use five simple skills	• Pass or Fail on skill practice	• Observation of skill practice by facilitator	• Facilitator	• Second day of program	• Facilitator
3	**Application and Implementation** • Initial use of five simple skills • At least 50% of participants use all skills with every customer	• Verbal feedback • 5th item checked on a 1 to 5 scale	• Follow-up session • Follow-up questionnaire	• Participant • Participant	• Three weeks after second day • Three months after program	• Facilitator • Store training coordinator
4	**Business Impact** • Increase in sales	• Weekly average sales per sales associate	• Business performance monitoring	• Company records	• Three months after program	• Store training coordinator
5	**ROI** • 50%					

Comments: _____

Measuring ROI in Interactive Selling Skills **143**

For application and implementation evaluation, the objectives focused on two major areas. The first was the initial use of the five simple skills. Success was determined from verbal feedback that the facilitator obtained directly from participants in a follow-up session on the third day of training. The second major objective was for at least 50 percent of the participants to be using all of the skills with every customer. This information was obtained on the follow-up questionnaire, scheduled three months after completion of the program, at which the participants rated the frequency of utilization of the skills.

Business impact focused just on increase in sales. The average weekly sales per sales associate was monitored from company records in a three-month follow-up. Finally, a 50 percent ROI target was set, which was much higher than the standard for many other ROI evaluations. Senior executives wanted a significant improvement over the cost of the program to make a decision to move forward with a wide-scale implementation.

The data collection plan was an important part of the evaluation strategy. It provided clear direction on the type of data that would be collected, how it would be collected, when it would be collected, and who would collect it.

Isolating the Effects of the Program

One of the most important parts of this evaluation is isolating the effects of the training program. This is a critical issue in the planning stage. The key question is, "When sales data is collected three months after the program is implemented, how much of the increase in sales, if any, is directly related to the program?" While the improvement in sales may be linked to the training program, other nontraining factors contribute to improvement. The cause-and-effect relationship between training and performance improvement can be very confusing and difficult to prove, but it can be accomplished with an acceptable degree of accuracy. In the planning process the challenge is to develop one or more specific strategies to isolate the effects of training and include it on the ROI analysis plan.

In this case study, the issue was relatively easy to address. Senior executives gave the training and development staff the freedom to select any stores for implementation of the pilot program. The performance of the three stores selected for the program was compared with the performance of three other stores that are identical in every way possible. This approach, control group analysis, represents the most accurate way to isolate the effects of a program. Fortunately, other strategies from the list of 10 approaches in the ROI process, such as trend-line analysis and estimation, would also be feasible. Control group analysis, the best method, was selected given that the situation was appropriate.

The challenge in the control group arrangement is to appropriately select both sets of stores. The control group of three stores does not have the training, whereas the pilot group does. It was important for those stores to be as identical as possible, so the training and development staff developed several criteria that could influence sales. This list became quite extensive and included market data, store level data, management and leadership data, and individual differences. In a conference call with regional managers, this list was pared down to the four most likely influences. The executives selected those influences that would count for at least 80 percent of the differences in weekly store sales per associate. These criteria were as follows:

- *Store size*, with the larger stores commanding a higher performance level
- *Store location*, using a market variable of median household income in the are where customers live
- *Customer traffic levels*, which measures the flow of traffic through the store; this measure, originally developed for security purposes, provides an excellent indication of customer flow through the store
- *Previous store performance*, a good predictor of future performance; the training and development staff collected six months of data for weekly sles per associate to identify the two groups.

These four measures were used to select three stores for the pilot program and match them with three other stores. As a fallback position, in case the control group arrangement did not work, participant estimates were planned. In this approach, the individuals would be provided with their performance data and would be asked to indicate the extent to which the training program influenced their contribution. This data, which is an estimate, would be adjusted for the error of the estimate and used in the analysis.

ROI Analysis Plan

Table 1 shows the completed ROI analysis plan, which captures information on several key items necessary to develop the actual ROI calculation. The first column lists the business impact measure. This is in connection with the previous planning document, the data collection plan. The ROI analysis builds from the business impact data by addressing several issues involved in processing the data. The first issue is the method of isolating the effects of the program on that particular business impact measure. The third column focuses on the methods to convert data to monetary value. In this case, sales data would have to be converted to value-added data by adjusting it to the actual profit margin at the store level.

The next column focuses on the key cost categories that would be included in the fully loaded cost profile. Next are the potential intangible benefits, followed by the communication targets. It is important for several groups to receive the information from the impact study. Finally, the last column lists any particular influences or issues that might have an effect on the implementation. The training staff identified three issues, with two being very critical to the evaluation. No communication was planned with the control group so there would not be potential for contamination from the pilot group. Also, because the seasonal fluctuation could affect the control group arrangement, this evaluation was positioned between Father's Day and the winter holiday season, thus taking away huge surges in volume.

The data collection plan together with the ROI analysis plan provided detailed information on calculating the ROI and illustrating how the process will develop and be analyzed. When completed, these two planning documents provide the direction necessary for the ROI evaluation.

Results
Reaction and Learning

The first two levels of evaluation, reaction and learning, were simple and straightforward. The training staff collected five measures of reaction to determine if the objectives had been met. The overall objective was to obtain at least four out of five on a composite of these five measures. As table 2 illustrates, the overall objective was met. Of the specific measures, the relevance of the material and the usefulness of the program were considered to be the two most important measures. In addition, 90 percent of the participants had action items indicating when and how often they would use these skills. Collectively, this Level 1 data gave assurance that sales associates had a very favorable reaction to the program.

The measurement of learning was accomplished with simple skill practice sessions observed by the facilitator. Each associate practiced each of the five skills, and the facilitator inserted a check mark on the questionnaire when the associate successfully practiced. While subjective, it was felt that this approach provided enough evidence that the participants had actually learned these basic skills.

Table 1. ROI analysis plan.

Data Items	Methods of Isolating the Effects of the Program	Methods of Converting Data	Cost Categories	Intangible Benefits	Communication Targets	Other Influences and Issues
• Weekly sales per associate	• Control group analysis • Participant estimate	• Direct conversion using profit contribution	• Facilitation fees • Program materials • Meals and refreshments • Facilities • Participant salaries and benefits • Cost of coordination and evaluation	• Customer satisfaction • Employee satisfaction	• Program participants • Electronics Department managers at targeted stores • Store managers at targeted stores • Senior store executives district, region, headquarters • Training staff: instructors, coordinators, designers, and managers	• Must have job coverage during training • No communication with control group • Seasonal fluctuations should be avoided

Table 2. Level 1 reaction data on selected data.

Success with objectives	4.3
Relevance of material	4.4
Usefulness of program	4.5
Exercises and skill practices	3.9
Overall instructor rating	4.1
Composite	4.2

Application and Implementation

To measure application and implementation, the training and development staff administered a follow-up questionnaire three months after the end of the program. The questionnaire was comprehensive, spanning 20 questions on three pages, and was collected anonymously to reduce the potential for bias from participants. The questionnaire covered the following topics:

• Action plan implementation
• Relevance of the program
• Use of skills
• Changes in work routine
• Linkage with department measures
• Other benefits
• Barriers
• Enablers
• Management support
• Suggestions for improvement
• Other comment

While all of the information was helpful, the information on the use of skills was most critical. Table 3 shows the results from two of the 20 questions on the questionnaire. The first one provides some assurance that the participants are using the skills, as 78 percent strongly agree that they utilize the skills of the program. More important, the next question focused directly on one of the goals of the program. Fifty-two percent indicated that they use the skills with each customer, slightly exceeding the goal of 50 percent.

Because these are simple skills, with the opportunity to use them every day, this three-month follow-up provides some assurance that the associates have internalized the skills. The follow-up session three weeks after the first two days of training provided the first, early indication

Table 3. Level 3 selected application data on two of 20 questions.

	Strongly Agree	Agree	Neither Agree nor Disagree	Disagree	Strongly Disagree
I utilize the skills taught in the program.	78%	22%	0%	0%	0%

	With Each Customer	Every Third Customer	Several Times Each Day	At Least Once Daily	At Least Once Weekly
Frequency of use of skills.	52%	26%	19%	4%	0%

of skill transfer to the job. If the skills are still being used three months after training, it is safe to conclude that the majority of the participants have internalized them.

While many other data collection methods could have been used, it is important to understand the rationale for using the questionnaire. The most accurate, and expensive, method would be observation of the participants on the job by a third party. In that scenario, the "mystery shoppers" must learn the skills and be allowed to rate each of the 48 participants. This approach would provide concrete evidence that the participants had transferred the skills. This approach would be expensive, and it is not necessary under the circumstances. Because the management team is more interested in business impact and ROI, it has less interest in the lower levels of evaluation. Although some data should be collected to have assurance that the skills have transferred, the process does not have to be so comprehensive. This is a resource-saving issue and is consistent with the following guiding principles for the ROI process:

1. When a higher level evaluation is conducted, data must be collected at lower levels.
2. When an evaluation is planned for a higher level, the previous level of evaluation does not hae to be comprehensive.
3. When collecting and analyzing data, use only the most credible sources.
4. When analyzing data, choose the most conservative among alternatives.

5. At least one method must be used to isolate the effects of the project or initiative.
6. If no improvement data are available for a population or from a specific source, it is assumed that little or no improvement has occurred.
7. Estimates of improvement should be adjusted for the potential error of the estimate.
8. Extreme data items and unsupported claims should not be used in ROI calculations.
9. Only the first year of benefits (annual) should be used in the ROI analysis of short-term projects or initiatives.
10. Project or program costs should be fully loaded for ROI analysis.

These are macrolevel principles with a conservative approach for collecting and processing data. Guiding principle number two comes into play with this issue. When an evaluation is under way at a higher level than the previous level of evaluation, the earlier evaluation did not have to be comprehensive. This does not mean that Level 3 data cannot be collected or that it should not be collected. With limited resources, shortcuts must be developed and this principle allows us to use a less expensive approach. If the management team had asked for more evidence of customer interaction or wanted to know the quality and thoroughness of the actual exchange of information, then a more comprehensive Level 3 evaluation would be required and perhaps the evaluation would have even stopped at Level 3.

Business Impact

Weekly sales data were collected for three months after the program for both groups. Table 4 shows the data for the first three weeks after training, along with the last three weeks during the evaluation period. An average for the last three weeks is more appropriate than data for a single week because that could have a spike effect that could affect the results. As the data shows, there is a significant difference between the two groups, indicating that the training program is improving sales. The percent increase, directly attributable to the sales training, is approximately 15 percent. If only a business impact evaluation is needed, this data would provide the information needed to show that the program has improved sales. However, if the ROI is needed, two more steps are necessary.

Table 4. Level 4 data on average weekly sales.

Weeks After Training	Trained Groups ($)	Control Groups ($)
1	$ 9,723	$ 9,698
2	9,978	9,720
3	10,424	9,812
13	13,690	11,572
14	11,491	9,683
15	11,044	10,092
Average for Weeks 13, 14, 15	$12,075	$10,449

Converting Data to a Monetary Value

To convert the business data to a monetary value, the training and development staff had to address several issues. First, it is necessary to convert the actual sales differences to a value-added data—in this case, profits. The store level profit margin of 2 percent is multiplied by the difference or increase in sales. Table 5 shows the calculation, as the weekly sales per associate of $1,626 become a value-added amount of $32.50. Because 46 participants were still on the job in three months, the value-added amount gets multiplied by 46, for a weekly total of $1,495.

Mention of 46 participants brings another guiding principle—number six—into focus. That principle says, "If no improvement data are available for a population or from a specific source, it is assumed that little or no improvement has occurred." This is a conservative approach because the missing data is assumed to have no value. Two

Table 5. Annualized program benefits for 46 participants.

Average weekly sales per employee trained groups	$12,075
Average weekly sales per employee untrained groups	10,449
Increase	1,626
Profit contribution (2% of store sales)	32.50
Total weekly improvement ($\times$ 46)	1,495
Total annual benefits ($\times$ 48 weeks)	**$71,760**

of the participants are no longer on the job and instead of tracking what happened to them, this rule is used to exclude any contribution from that group of two. However, the cost to train them would be included, although their values are not included for contribution.

Finally, annual benefits are used to develop a total benefit for the program. The ROI concept is an annual value, and only the first-year benefits are used for short-term training programs. This is guiding principle number nine. Although this approach may slightly overstate the benefits for the first year, it is considered conservative because it does not capture any improvements or benefits in the second, third, or future years. This operating standard is also conservative and thus is a guiding principle. In summary, the total annualized program benefit of $71,760 is developed in a very conservative way using the guiding principles.

Program Cost

The program costs, shown in table 6, are fully loaded and represent all the major categories outlined earlier. This is a conservative approach, as described in guiding principle number 10. In this case, the costs for the development are included in the facilitation fee since the external supplier produced the program. The cost of the participants' time away from the job is the largest of the cost items and can be included, or the lost opportunity can be included, but not both. To be consistent, this is usually developed as the total time away from work (three days) is multiplied by the daily compensation rate including a 35 percent benefits factor. Finally, the estimated cost for the evaluation and the coordination of data collection is included. Since the company had an internal evaluation staff certified in the ROI process, the overall cost for this project was quite low and represents direct time involved in developing the impact study. The total fully loaded cost for the program was $32,984.

ROI Calculation

Two ROI calculations are possible with use of the total monetary benefits and total cost of the program. The first is the benefit-cost ratio (BCR), which is the ratio of the monetary benefits divided by the costs:

$$BCR = \frac{\$71,760}{\$32,984} = 2.18$$

Table 6. Cost summary for 48 participants in three courses.

Item	Cost ($)
Facilitation fees, three courses @ $3,750	11,250
Program materials, 48 @ $35 per participant	1,680
Meals and refreshments, three days @ $28 per participant	4,032
Facilities, nine days @ $120	1,080
Participants' salaries plus benefits (35% factor)	12,442
Coordination and evaluation	2,500
Total Costs	**32,984**

In essence, this suggest that for every dollar invested, 2.18 dollars are returned. When using the actual ROI formula, this value becomes:

$$\text{ROI (\%)} = \frac{\$71,760 - \$32,984}{\$32,984} \times 100 = 118\%$$

This ROI calculation is interpreted as follows: For every dollar invested, a dollar is returned and another $1.18 is generated. The ROI formula is consistent with ROI for other types of investment. It is essentially earnings divided by investment. In this case, the ROI exceeds the 50 percent target.

Intangibles

This program generated significant intangible benefits:

• Increased job satisfaction
• Improved teamwork
• Increased confidence
• Improved customer service
• Improved image with customers
• Greater involvement

Conclusions and Actions
Communication of Results

It was important to communicate the results of this evaluation to the senior executives who requested a program, to the sales associates who were part of it, and to other personnel who were affected by it. First, the senior executives need the information to make a decision. In a face-to-face meeting, lasting approximately one hour, the training and development staff presented all six types of data with the recommendation that the program be implemented throughout the store chain. An executive summary and PowerPoint slides were distributed.

The participants received a two-page summary of the data, showing the results of the questionnaire and the business impact and ROI achieved from the process. There was some debate about whether to include the ROI in the summary, but eventually it was included in an attempt to share more information with the participants.

The electronics department managers, the participants' managers, received the executive summary of the information and participated in a conference call with the training and development staff. This group needed to see the benefits of training since they had no alter and rearrange schedules to cover the jobs while the participants were in training.

Finally, the training staff received a detailed impact study (approximately 100 pages), which was used as a learning document to help them understand more about this type of evaluation. This document became the historical record about the data collection instruments and ROI analysis.

Action

As a result of the communication of the impact study, senior executives decided to implement the program throughout the store chain. For all six types of data, the results were very positive with a very high ROI, significantly exceeding the target. The implementation proceeded with the senior executives' request that the sales data for the three target stores be captured for the remainder of the year to see the actual one-year impact of the program. While the issue of taking one year of data, based on a three-month snapshot, appears to be conservative since the second- and third-year data are not used, this provided some assurance that the data does indeed hold up for the year. At the end of the year, the data actually exceeded the snapshot of performance in three months.

Lessons Learned

This evaluation provides some important insights into the ROI process. In the past, the store chain evaluated pilot programs primarily on Level 1 data (reactions from both the participants and their managers), coupled with the sales presentation from the vendor.

The ROI approach provides much more data to indicate the success of training. In essence, companies can use Level 4 and 5 data for making a funding decision instead of making a funding decision on the basis of reaction data, Level 1.

From a statistical significance viewpoint, the small sample size does not allow for making an inference about the other stores at a 95 percent confidence. In essence, due to the small sample size it is impossible to say that the other stores would have the same results as the three in question. A sample size of 200 stores would be needed for statistical soundness. However, the economics of the evaluation and the practicality of the pilot implementation drove the sample size in this case, and in most other cases. No group of senior executives would suggest a sample size of 200 stores to see if the program should be implemented in the other 220 stores. It is important to note in the results that statistical inference cannot be made, but it is also important to remember two points:

• The six types of data represent much more data than previously used to evaluate these types of programs.
• Second, most managers do not take other funding decisions based on data that has been collected, analyzed, and reported at a 95 percent confidence level.

Finally, another lesson was learned about this application of the ROI process. This is a very simple case allowing for a control group arrangement. Many other situations are not this simple, and other methods of isolation have to be undertaken. Other studies, while feasible, are more complex and will require more resources.

Questions for Discussion
1. Are the data and results credible? Explain.
2. How should the results be communicated?
3. With such a small sample, how can the issue of statistical significance be addressed?
4. The use of a control group arrangement is not possible in many situations. How can other potential approaches be utilized? Explain.
5. Would you implement this program in the other 417 stores? Explain.

CHAPTER 9

Measuring ROI for Retention Improvement

Southeast Corridor Bank

This study demonstrates how a retention improvement program generated an extremely high impact, including an impressive return-on-investment, using a strategic accountability approach to managing retention. By analyzing a turnover problem in branch bank operations, this case focuses on how the specific causes of turnover were determined, how the solutions were matched to the special causes, and how the calculation of the actual impact of the turnover reduction was developed. The strength of the case lies in the techniques used to ensure that the solutions were appropriate and that the turnover reduction represented a high-payoff solution.

Background

Southeast Corridor Bank (SCB), a regional bank operating in four states with 60 branches, had grown from a one-state operation to a multistate network through a progressive strategic campaign of acquisitions. As did many organizations, SCB faced merger and integration problems, including excessive employee turnover: SCB's annual turnover was 57 percent, compared with an industry average of 26 percent. The new senior vice president for human resources faced several important challenges when he joined SCB, among them the need to reduce turnover. Although management was not aware of the full impact of turnover, it knew turnover was causing operational problems, taking up much staff and supervisor time, and creating disruptive situations with customers.

A Strategic Accountability Approach

The strategic accountability approach outlined in figure 1 focuses on employee retention as an important part of strategy and is the basic model for this case study. As it had for many firms, retention had become a strategic issue because it can make the difference between mediocre and excellent profits. Accountability was built in throughout the process so management could fully understand the cost of the problem, the cost of the solutions, the potential impact of the solutions, and the actual impact of the solutions, all in monetary terms.

This approach moves logically from one step to another through a series of eight steps necessary to manage the process. It's easy to stay on track because, for the most part, each of the different steps has to be completed before moving to another. This approach brings structure, organization, and accountability to managing retention, and helps organizations avoid implementing solutions without analysis.

Figure 1. The strategic accountability approach to managing retention.

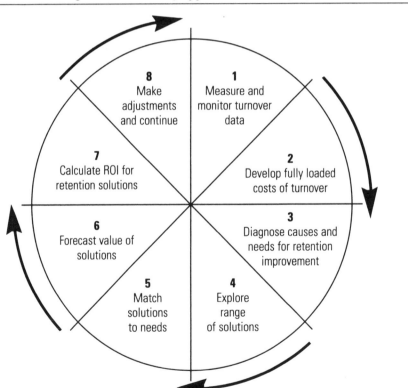

Step 1. Measure and Monitor Turnover

To properly monitor and measure turnover, several steps are important:
- Defining turnover consistently
- Reprting turnover rates by various demographics
- Reporting rates by critical job groups
- Including costs of turnover
- Comparing turnover data with benchmarking targets
- Developing trigger points that stimulate action

Step 2: Develop a Fully Loaded Cost of Turnover

The cost of turnover is one of the most underestimated and undervalued costs in most organizations. It is often misunderstood because it is not fully loaded and does not reflect the actual costs of a turnover statistic. Also, the impact of turnover is not regularly reported to the management team, so its members don't know the actual cost. When fully loaded costs are calculated for the organization for an entire year, the actual numbers can be extremely surprising.

When exploring turnover, usually only the costs for recruiting, selecting, and training are considered. These easily calculated costs are sometimes inappropriately reported as the cost of turnover but, in reality, other costs should be included. A more comprehensive list includes 12 categories. The first seven recommended categories are investments that are lost to some degree when an employee leaves; the last five are related to the effect of turnover on conducting business:
- Exit expense
- Recruiting expense
- Employment expense
- Orientatin expense
- Training expense
- Wage and salary expense while training
- Temporary replacement expense
- Lost productivity
- Quality problems
- Customer dissatisfaction
- Loss of expertise and knowledge
- Loss of management time because of turnover

Step 3. Diagnose Causes and Needs for Retention Improvement

Some causes of turnover may be obvious, but others can be extremely elusive. Collecting appropriate data often is a challenge because of the potential for bias and the inaccuracies that can surface

during data collection. A number of diagnostic processes are available, including the following:
- Demographic analysis
- Diagnostic instruments
- Focus groups
- Probing interviews
- Job satisfaction surveys
- Organizational commitment surveys
- Exit interviews
- Exit surveys
- Nominal group technique
- Brainstorming
- Cause-and-effect diagrams
- Force field analysis
- Mind mapping
- Affinity diagrams

Step 4. Explore a Range of Solutions

Many organizations are very creative in their approaches to retention problems, resulting in hundreds of excellent solutions. The critical point is to ensure that the solution is feasible for the organization. Most solutions fall into one of these categories:
- Offering a competitive total compensation package, which includes salary, benefits, bonuses, incentives, awards, and recognition
- Building a great place to work, wich includes teamwork, work environment, supportive culture, and enabling systems
- Providing growth opportunities, which includes work design, empowerment, career path development, training, and succession planning
- Creating a compelling future, which includes creating a profitable organization with a competitive advatage and developing mission, vision, and values.

Step 5. Match Solutions to Needs

This step is related to the need to forecast the value of solutions, which is discussed next. These two steps should be taken together because the solutions selected are assumed to meet specific needs, making the forecast of their anticipated value imperative. When attempting to match solutions to needs, five key concerns are considered:
- Avoiding mismatches
- Implementing only a minimum number of solutions
- Selecting a solution for a maximum return

- Verifying the match early
- Checking the progress of each solution

Step 6. Forecast the Value of Solutions

Developing a forecast for a solution's value allows the team to establish priorities, work with a minimum number of solutions, and focus on solutions with the greatest return-on-investment (ROI). Difficult, challenging, and sometimes risky, forecasting is an expert estimation of what a solution should contribute. It is imperative to accumulate as much data as possible to back up the estimate and build credibility for the process. The payoff value can be developed if the percentage of expected turnover reduction can be related to it. For example, if the number-one cause of turnover is removed with a particular solution, what percentage of the turnover would actually be eliminated? Sometimes employees can provide input on this as data is collected on the causes of turnover. This step may require several "what if" decisions that may result in various assumptions about the data. Also, this step may involve building on previous experiences to the extent possible. In some cases, the experiences of other organizations can be helpful.

Step 7. Measure ROI for Retention Solutions

Another often-neglected step is the calculation of the actual financial impact of a turnover reduction strategy. This step is often omitted because it appears to be unnecessary. If accumulating a number of solutions is the only measure of success of turnover reduction or prevention, the impact of those solutions may be unimportant. But from a senior executive's point of view, accountability is not complete until impact and ROI data have been collected, at least for major solutions. The ROI methodology generates six types of data about the success of a turnover reduction strategy:
1. Reaction to and satisfaction with the solution
2. Skill and knowledge acquisition
3. Application and implementation progress
4. Business impact improvement
5. Return-on-investment, expressed as an ROI formula
6. Intangible measures not converted to monetary values

This methodology also includes a technique for isolating the effects of a turnover solution. The ROI process has achieved widespread application for evaluating all types of programs and solutions (Phillips, 2002).

Step 8. Make Adjustments

The extensive set of data collected from the ROI process will provide information for making adjustments and changes in turnover reduction strategies. The information reveals the success of the turnover reduction solution at all levels, from reaction to ROI. It also examines barriers to success, identifying specifically what kept the solution from being effective, or prevented it from becoming more effective. It also identifies the processes in place that enable or support a turnover reduction solution. All of the information allows for adjusting or repositioning the solution so it can be revised, discontinued, or amplified. The next step in the process goes back to the beginning, monitoring the data to ensure that turnover levels continue to meet expectations . . . and the cycle continues.

Measuring and Monitoring Turnover

SCB monitored turnover by two categories, defining employee departures as either voluntary separations or terminations for performance. Departures due to retirement or disability were not included in the definition. A termination for performance involved an important problem that might have been rectified if the performance deficiency had been recognized or prevented early.

The turnover rate was monitored by job group, region, and branch bank. Branches had the highest turnover, averaging 71 percent in the previous year, far exceeding any expectations and industry averages of turnover acquired from other financial institutions and the American Bankers Association. Turnover was also considered excessive in a few entry-level clerical job classifications in regional and corporate offices.

Impact of Turnover

The impact of turnover was developed at the beginning of the study. External turnover studies in the banking industry had revealed that the cost of turnover for bank employees ranged from 110 percent to 125 percent of annual pay (Creery and Creery, 1988). This fully loaded cost had been published in several trade publications, using the 12 cost categories listed earlier in Step 2. When reviewing the proposed program and the proposed method for calculating the payoff, the senior executive team suggested a lower value. In essence, the senior team thought that turnover wasn't quite that expensive and suggested only 90 percent (0.9 times an employee's annual pay).

Determining the Cause of Turnover

Three basic techniques were used to pinpoint the actual cause of turnover. First, as described earlier, the analysis of individual job groups and tenure within job groups gave insight into where the turnover was occurring, the magnitude of the problem, and some indication of the cause. Much of the turnover occurred in the first six to 18 months of employment. Second, exit interviews with departing employees were examined to see if specific reasons for departure could be pinpointed. As with most exit data, accuracy was a concern: The departing employees may have been biased when reporting their reasons for leaving. The desire to avoid burning bridges could have left the data incomplete and inaccurate. Third, recognizing this problem, the HR team used the nominal group technique to determine more precisely the actual causes of turnover. This process is described next.

Nominal Group Technique

The nominal group technique was selected because it allowed unbiased input to be collected efficiently and accurately across the organization. A focus group was planned with 12 employees in each region, for a total of six groups representing all the regions. In addition, two focus groups were planned for the clerical staff in corporate headquarters. This approach provided approximately a 10 percent sample, which was considered a sufficient number to pinpoint the problem.

Participants in the focus groups, who represented areas in which turnover was highest, described why their colleagues were leaving, not why they themselves would leave. Data was taken from individuals in a carefully structured format during two-hour meetings at each location, using third-party facilitators, and was integrated and weighted so the most important reasons were clearly identified. This process had the advantages of low cost and high reliability, as well as a low degree of bias. Only two days of external facilitator time was needed to collect and summarize data for review.

The nominal group technique unfolded quickly in 10 steps:

1. The process steps were briefly described along with a statement of confidentiality. The importance of the participants' input was underscored so they understood what they must do and the consequences for the bank.
2. Participants were asked to make a list of specific reasons why they felt their colleagues had left the bank or why others might leave. It was stressed that the question dealt with the actions or potential actions of employees other than themselves, although the bank

realized that the participants' comments would probably reflect their own views (and that was what was actually needed).

3. In a round-robin format, each person revealed one reason for turnover, which was recorded on flipchart paper. At this point, no attempt was made to integrate the issues, just to record the data on paper. The lists were placed on the walls so that when this step was complete as many as 50 or 60 items were listed and visible.

4. The next step was to consolidate and integrate the list. Some of the integration was easy because the items contained the same words and meanings. In other cases, it was important to ensure that the meanings for the cause of the turnover were the same before items were consolidated. (When this process was complete the list might have contained 30 or 40 different reasons for turnover).

5. Participants were asked to review all the items, carefully select those they considered to be the top 10 causes, and list them individually on index cards. Participants were instructed not to concern themselves about which cause was number one. (In this process, participants may become convinced that their original list was not complete or accurate or may identify other reasons for turnover).

6. Participants ranked their to 10 items by importance, with the first item as the most important.

7. In a round-robin format, each individual revealed his or her number-one item, and 10 points were recorded on the flipchart paper next to the item. The next individual revealed his or her number-one issue and so on until the entire group had offered the top reason. Next, the number-two reason was identified, and nine points were recorded on the flip chart paper next to the item. This process continued until all reasons had been revealed and points recorded.

8. The numbers next to each item were totaled. The item with the most points was the leading cause of turnover, and the one with the second-highest number of points was the second most important cause of turnover. This continued until the top 15 causes had been captured as the weighted average causes of turnover from that group.

9. This process was completed for all six regional groups and the clerical staff groups. Trends began to emerge quickly from one group to the other.

10. The actual raw scores were then combined to integrate the results of the six regional focus groups and the clerical group.

The top 15 scores were the top 15 reasons for turnover across all the branches and clerical groups.

Specific Needs

The following list shows the 10 most important reasons for turnover in the bank branches:

1. Lack of opportunity for advancement
2. Lack of opportunity to learn new skills and new product knowledge
3. Pay level not adequate
4. Not enough responsibility and empowerment
5. Lack of recognition and appreciation of work
6. Lack of teamwork in the branch
7. Lack of preparation for customer service problems
8. Unfair and unsupportive supervisor
9. Too much stress at peak times
10. Not enough flexibility in work schedules

A similar list was developed for the clerical staff, but the remainder of this case study will focus directly on the efforts to reduce turnover in the branch network. Branch turnover was the most critical issue, involving the highest turnover rates and the largest number of employees, and the focus group results provided a clear pattern of specific needs. Recognizing that not all the causes of turnover could be addressed immediately, the bank's management set out to work on the top five reasons while it considered a variety of options. Eventually, a skill-based pay system was created.

Solution: Skill-Based Pay

A skill-based pay system addressed the top five reasons for turnover. The program was designed to expand the scope of the jobs, with increases in pay for acquiring skills, and to provide a clear path for advancement and improvement. Jobs were redesigned from narrowly focused teller duties to an expanded job with a new title: The tellers all become banking representative I, II, or III. Table 1 shows the basic job duties with new initial wage rates. A branch employee would be considered a banking representative I if he or she could perform one or two simple tasks, such as processing deposits and cashing checks.

As an employee at the banking representative I level took on additional responsibilities and performed different functions, he or she wold be eligible for a promotion to banking representative II. If the

Table 1. Proposed job levels.

Banking Representative Level	Job Duties	Hourly Wage Rate
I	Basic teller transactions (deposits, check cashing, etc.)	$6.00
II	Same as above, plus opening and closing accounts and processing CDs, savings bonds, special transactions, etc.	$7.50
III	Same as above, plus processing limited liability consumer loans, applications for all consumer loans, home equity loans, referrals for mortgage loans, etc.	$9.00

representative could perform all the basic functions of the branch bank, including processing consumer loan applications, a promotion to banking representative III was appropriate. Training opportunities were available to help employees develop the needed job-related skills and structured on-the-job training was provided through the branch managers, assistant managers, and supervisors. Self-study information was also available. The concept of performing multiple tasks was intended to broaden responsibilities and empower employees to perform a variety of tasks that would provide excellent customer service. Pay increases recognized skill acquisition, demonstrated accomplishment, and increased responsibility.

Although the skill-based system had some definite benefits from the employee's perspective, there were also benefits fot the bank. Not only was turnover expected to lessen, but actual staffing levels were expected to be reduced in larger branches. In theory, if all employees in a branch could perform all the duties, fewer employees would be needed. Prior to this time, minimum staffing levels were required in certain critical jobs, and those employees were not always available for other duties.

In addition, the bank anticipated improved customer service. The new approach would prevent customers from having to wait in long lines for specialized services. For example, in the typical branch bank, it had not been unusual to see long lines for such special functions as opening a checking account, closing out a CD, or taking a consumer loan application, while such activities as paying bills and receiving deposits often required little or no waiting. With each employee performing all the tasks, shorter waiting lines would not only be feasible, but expected.

To support this new arrangement, the marketing department referred to the concept in its publicity about products and services. Included with the checking account statements was a promotional piece labeled "In our branches there are no tellers." This document described the new process and stated that all the branch employees could perform all branch functions and consequently provide faster service.

Measuring Success

Measuring the success of the new solution required collecting data at four levels. At the first level, reaction and satisfaction were measured during meetings with the employees and during regularly scheduled training sessions. This measurement provided input on employee acceptance of the new arrangement and the difference elements of the program. Using brief surveys, data was collected on a five-point scale. As expected, the results were positive, averaging a 4.2 composite rating.

At the second level, learning was measured in two different ways. For each training and learning opportunity, skill acquisition and knowledge increase was measured. Informal self-assessments were take for many of the programs. A few critical skills required actual demonstration to show that employees could perform the skill (for example, documentation, compliance, and customer services). When learning measurements revealed unacceptable performance, participants were given an opportunity to repeat training sessions or take more time to practice. In a limited number of cases, a third opportunity was provided. After one year of operation, only two employees were denied promotions based on their poor performance in training programs.

At the third level, application and implementation were measured by collecting four types of data, as shown in table 2. Actual participation in the program reflected the willingness of individuals to pursue skill acquisition through a variety of efforts. The results were impressive.

In all, 95 percent of the branch employees wanted to participate in the program. The remaining 5 percent were content with the banking representative I classification and were not interested in learning new skills. Actual requests for training and learning opportunities were a critical part of the formal process. Employees had to map out their own developmental efforts, which were approved by the branch manager. In all, some 86 requests per month were logged, almost over-taxing the system in providing training and learning opportunities. Reviews

Table 2. Selected application and implementation data.

	1 Year Before	1 Year After
Participation in program	N/A	95%
Requests for training	45 per month	86 per month
Review situations	N/A	138
Actual promotions	139	257

N/A = not applicable

of the status and progress—to be considered for the promotion for the next level—were significant, as this review was the formal way of demonstrating the skills required for promotion. The number of actual promotions increased quickly: As the table shows, actual promotions during the year before the program had been 139, increasing to 257 during the year after the program was initiated.

The categories of business-impact measures that were monitored are shown in table 3, along with their definitions. In all, nine categories of data were expected to be influenced to some degree by this project, although the first four were considered to be the primary measures.

The most important expected benefit was a reduction in turnover, the major thrust of the project. The second measure was staffing levels: With more highly skilled employees, fewer staff should be needed, at least for the larger branches. The third measure was customer service: With fewer customers waiting in line and less need to move from one line to another, customers should be more satisfied. The fourth measure was job satisfaction: Employees should be more satisfied with their work, their jobs, and career possibilities. Finally, an increase in loan volume was attributed to the project because there would be fewer customers waiting in line. Consequently, customers would visit more often or would not leave in frustration because of delays. This was expected to result in increases in the number of deposits, consumer loans, new accounts, and transactions, as well as increases in successful cross-selling. This was expected to result in some increases in the number of deposits. However, these las five categories were measures of each branch and were expected to move very little because of this project.

Isolating the Effects of the Project

In almost any situation, multiple influences affect specific business measures, so an important concern was to isolate the actual impact of the skill-based pay project from other influences. To add

Table 3. Business measures influenced by the project.

Business-Impact Measures	Definitions
1. Branch employee turnover (monthly)	Avoidable turnover (total number of employees leaving voluntarily and for performance reasons divided by the average number of employees in the branch for the month). This number was multiplied by 12 to develop the annual turnover rate.
2. Staffing level	The total number of employees in the branch, reported monthly.
3. Customer satisfaction	Customer reaction to the job changes (faster service, fewer lines) measured on a 1-to-5 scale.
4. Job satisfaction	Employee feedback on selected measures on the annual feedback survey process.
5. Deposits	Savings, checking, and securities deposits by type and product.
6. Loan volume	Consumer loan volume by loan type.
7. New accounts	New accounts opened for new customers.
8. Transaction volume	Number of face-to-face transactions, paying and receiving, by major category.
9. Cross-selling	New products sold to existing customers.

credibility and validity to the analysis, a specific method was used to isolate the effects of the project for each data item used in the ROI calculation. As shown in table 4, this method relied on estimates from branch managers and the branch staff. In brief group meetings, the branch staff members were provided the actual results of the turnover reduction and were asked to allocate the percentage of the reduction linked directly to the skill-based pay effort. Each branch provided this information.

As a first step in the process, branch team members discussed the other factors that could have contributed to turnover reduction (only two were identified). They were asked to discuss the linkage between each factor and the actual turnover reduction. This discussion, in a focus group format, improved the accuracy of the estimation. However, since these were estimates, an error adjustment was made: Individuals were asked to indicate the level of confidence in their estimate using a scale of 0 to 100 percent, with 0 percent meaning no confidence and 100 percent meaning absolute certainty. This percentage was used as a discount for that employee's allocation. For example, if an individual allocated 60 percent of the turnover reduction to this specific project and was 80 percent confident in that allocation, the adjusted value would be 48 percent (60 percent times 80 percent). This method of isolation provided a conservative estimate for the effect of skill-based pay on turnover reduction. In this data item, the branch manager input was combined with that of the staff employees on equal weighting. Essentially, the results were averaged.

For the staffing levels item, actual improvements were judged by the branch managers. In essence, using the process described above, branch managers indicated the degree to which the new project had resulted in actual staff reductions. Because staff reductions only occurred in 30 percent of the branches (the larger ones), this estimate only involved those branch managers. No other factors seemed to have contributed to the staff reduction, so these branch managers gave credit for the entire reduction to the skill-based project.

Table 4 shows the method for isolating each measure that was a part of the planning for the study. Increases in deposits, loan volume, new accounts, transactions, and cross-selling were minimal and were influenced by many variables other than the new program. Consequently, no attempt was made to isolate the effect on these items or to use

Table 4. Business measures and planned analysis.

Data Item	Method of Isolating the Effects	Method of Converting Data
Employee turnover	Branch manager estimation Staff estimation	External studies
Staffing levels	Branch manager estimation	Company payroll records
Customer service	Customer input	N/A
Job satisfaction	Staff input	N/A
Deposits, loan volume, new accounts	Branch manager estimation	Standard value (percent margin)
Transaction volume, cross-selling	Branch manager estimation Staff estimation	Standard value (average percent margin)

N/A = not applicable

the improvements in the ROI analysis. However, they were listed as intangibles, providing evidence that they have been affected by the turnover reduction program.

Survey cards completed at the end of a transaction and deposited at the entrance to the branch provided a sample of customer reactions. The customers appreciated the new approach, liked the service delivered, and indicated that they would continue to use the branch. The annual employee job satisfaction survey showed that employees were pleased with the improvements in advancement opportunities, the chance to use skills, performance-based pay, and other related changes. Because customer service and job satisfaction measures were not isolated or converted to monetary volume, they were not used in the ROI calculation. However, these measures were very important and influential in the final evaluation and were listed as intangible benefits.

Converting Data

Table 4 also shows the method used (or planned) to convert data to monetary value. Turnover was converted to monetary value starting with a value from external studies. The specific amount was calculated using 0.9 times the annual salary as the cost of one turnover, a value considered conservative: Several studies had values ranging from 1.1 to 1.25 times annual earnings. It was important that the cost of one turnover was developed and agreed to in a meeting with the senior management prior to the actual calculation of values. The fact that the average annual salary of the branch bank staff below manager level was $18,500 meant that, collectively, the staffing reductions translated into significant savings that far exceeded expectations. For each potential employee departure that was prevented, a $16,650 ($18,500 × 0.9) average savings was realized.

Table 5 shows a turnover reduction of 174. The estimated contribution factor (the percent of the reduction linked to the solution), after the confidence error adjustment, was multiplied by the 174 to yield 120 prevented turnovers. The contribution factor and confidence estimates had been obtained in branch meetings, as described earlier. The average cost of a turnover ($16,650) was multiplied by 120 to yield an annual value of almost $2 million. At that point in data collection, the second-year value was not known, so that amount was doubled for an estimate of two-year savings.

The method for converting staffing levels to a monetary value was to use the actual salaries for the jobs that had been eliminated. Only a few branches were affected. The actual number was multiplied by the average salary of the branch staff. The value was captured for one year and projected for another year assuming the same level. A two-year timeframe was used because it was considered to be a conservative way to evaluate (that is, one year of actual data and a forecast of one year). Although the program was expected to provide extended value, additional benefits beyond the two years were excluded. This was the conservative basis of the ROI Methodology.

Analysis

The turnover reduction at the branches was significant, dropping from 71 percent to 35 percent in one year. Although some of the smaller branches had no staffing changes, the larger branches had fewer staff members. In all, 30 percent of the branches were able to have at least one fewer part-time or full-time staff member. Ten percent of the branches were able to reduce the staff by two individuals.

Table 5 shows the calculations of the total annual and projected benefits for the two-year period. Different scenarios could have been considered, such as capturing the first-year benefit only, but benefits had to be captured or projected for a two-year period, as the costs had been. The total two-year benefit was $4,625,000.

Project Cost

Table 6 shows the fully loaded cost of the skill-based pay project. The initial analysis costs were included, along with time, direct costs, and travel expenses for the focus groups because developing the program required the time and materials for these. The next two categories were the branch staff time, which represented an estimate of all the time employees had to spend away from their normal work to understand the program and learn new skills. The next category was the actual salary increases—the additional salaries in the branches as a result of earlier promotions. The total amount of first-year promotions ($977,600) was reduced by the rate of promotions in the year before the program was implemented.

The ongoing administration and operation involved the time required for the HR staff to administer the program. Finally, the evaluation costs represented the costs related to developing the study of the project's affect on the business. The total cost presented in this table includes several items that were involved only in the one-year actual cost and one-year forecast; these costs are the totals for the project in those categories. Across all categories for two years, the total cost was $1,290,396.

Table 5. Calculation of actual business results.

	Preceding Year	One Year After	Actual Difference	Contribution Factor	Confidence Estimate	Adjusted Amount	Unit Amount	First-Year Benefits	Two-Year Benefits
Turnover	336 (71%)	162 (35%)	174	84%	82%	120	$16,650	$1,998,000	$3,996,000
Staffing Levels	480 (average)	463 (end of year)	17	100%	100%	17	$18,500	$314,500	$629,000

Table 6. Fully loaded project costs.

Project Costs	Year 1	Year 2
Initial analysis	$14,000	—
Program development	2,500	—
Participant time	345,600	$195,000
Branch manager time	40,800	30,200
Salary increases	446,696	203,900
Administration/operation	4,600	4,100
Evaluation	3,000	—
	$ 857,196	$ 433,200

ROI and Its Meaning

The two-year monetary benefits were combined with costs to develop the benefit cost ratio (BCR) and the ROI using the following formulae:

$$BCR = \frac{\text{Solution Benefits}}{\text{Solution Cost}} = \frac{\$4,625,000}{1,290,396} = 3.58$$

$$ROI = \frac{\text{Net Solution Benefits}}{\text{Solution Cost}} = \frac{\$4,625,000 - \$1,290,396}{1,290,396} \times 100 = 258\%$$

This BCR value indicates that for every $1 invested in the project, $3.58 is returned. In terms of ROI, for every $1 invested, $2.58 is returned after the costs are captured. These results are excellent, since most ROI studies have target (expected) values in the 25-percent range. The ROI was only one measure and should be considered in conjunction with the other measures. However, because it was an estimate that was developed using a conservative approach, it probably underestimated the actual return from this project.

Communicating Results

The results were communicated to the senior management team in an executive staff meeting in which approximately 30 minutes were allocated to the project report. The communications were very important and covered three points:

1. The project was quickly reviewed, including the description of the solution.
2. The methodology used for evaluating the project was described.

3. The results were revealed one level at a time, presenting the following types of data:

- Reaction of employees to, and satisfaction with, the skill-based pay system
- Learning the system and how to us it
- Application of the system
- Business impact of skill-based pay
- ROI in skill-based pay
- Intangible measures linked to skill-based pay

This presentation provided a balanced profile of the project and was convincing to the senior management team. This was the first time an HR solution to a problem had been evaluated using a balanced measurement approach that included ROI. The intangible measures also were important, particularly the customer service improvement. Overall, the senior team was very pleased with the success of the project and impressed with the analysis.

Lessons Learned

Although this project arrived at the right solution, a few lessons were learned. First, because forecasting is such an important step in the strategic accountability approach to managing retention, perhaps it would have been safer to forecast the ROI at the time the solution was developed. In particular, increasing the branch salaries to the extent planned for this solution was risky: It would have been difficult to retract this program if it did not show enough value to make it worthwhile. Also, the branch managers and regional managers were not entirely convinced that skill-based pay would add value, and additional effort was needed to capture their buy-in and help them understand the full cost of turnover. They needed to see how this system could alleviate many of their problems and add monetary value to the branches. A forecasted ROI could have provided more confidence before the program was put it place, but although this was considered, it was not pursued.

Finally, the time that would have to be spent by branch managers should have been estimated at a higher level, as they had to deal with numerous requests for training and juggle schedules to ensure the staff maintained the training they needed. Also, managers had to provide additional training and spend the time necessary to confirm that the bank representatives had obtained the skills necessary for promotion.

Questions for Discussion

1. This case study illustrtaes how the actual causes of turnover were determined. What is your reaction to this process?
2. Why do many organizations spend so little time determining the causes of turnover?
3. Calculating the ROI of a turnover reduction program is rarely done, yet it can have tremendous benefits. Why is this step often omitted?
4. How can the data from this project be used in the future?
5. Critique the overall approach to this retention project, highlighting weaknesses and strengths.

References

Creery, Presley T., and K.W. Creery. *Reducing Labor Turnover in Financial Insitutions.* Westpoint, CT: Greenwood Press, 1988.

Phillips, Patricia P. *The Bottomline on ROI.* Atlanta: Center for Effective Performance, 2002.

CHAPTER

Measuring ROI in a Masters Degree

Federal Information Agency

The Federal Information Agency (FIA) provides various types of information to other government agencies and businesses as well as state and local organizations, agencies, and interested groups. Operating through a network across the United States, the work is performed by several hundred communication specialists with backgrounds in systems, computer science, electrical engineering, and information science. Almost all the specialists have bachelor's degrees in one of these fields. The headquarters and operation center is in the Washington, D.C., area, where 1,500 of these specialists are employed.

Problem and Solution

FIA has recently experienced two problems that have senior agency officials concerned. The first problem is an unacceptable rate of employee turnover for this group of specialists—averaging 38 percent in the past year alone. That has placed a strain on the agency to recruit and train replacements. An analysis of exit interviews indicated that employees leave primarily for higher salaries. Because FIA is somewhat constrained in providing competitive salaries, it has become extremely difficult to compete with private sector for salaries and benefits. Although salary increases and adjustments in pay levels will be necessary to lower turnover, FIA is exploring other options in the interim.

The second problem concerns the need to continuously update the technical skills of the staff. While the vast majority of the 1,500

This case was prepared to serve as a basis for discussion rather than to illustrate either effective or ineffective administrative and management practices. All names, dates, places, and organizations have been disguised at the request of the author or organization.

specialists have degrees in various fields, only a few have master's degrees in their specialty. In this field, formal education is quickly outdated. The annual feedback survey with employees reflected a strong interest in an internal master's degree program in information science. Consequently, FIA explored implementing an in-house master's degree in information science conducted by the School of Engineering and Science at Regional State University (RSU). The master's degree program would be implemented at no cost to the participating employee and conducted on the agency's time during routine work hours. Designed to address both employee turnover and skill updates, the program would normally take three years for participants to complete.

Program Description

RSU was selected for the master's program because of its reputation and the match of its curriculum to FIA needs. The program allows participants to take one or two courses per semester. A two-course per semester schedule would take three years to complete with one course in the summer session. Both morning and afternoon classes were available, each representing three hours per week of class time. Participants were discouraged from taking more than two courses per term. Although a thesis option was normally available, FIA requested a graduate project be required for six hours of credit as a substitute for the thesis. A professor would supervise the project. Designed to add value to FIA, the project would be applied in the agency and would not be as rigorous as the thesis. Participants sign up for three hours for the project in both year two and three.

Classes were usually offered live with professors visiting the agency's center. Occasionally, classes were offered through videoconference or independent study. Participants were asked to prepare for classroom activities on their own time, but were allowed to attend classes on the agency's time. A typical three-year schedule is shown in Table 1.

Senior management approved the master's curriculum, which represented a mix of courses normally offered in the program and others specially selected for FIA staff. Two new courses were designed by university faculty to be included in the curriculum. These two represented a slight modification of existing courses and were tailored to the communication requirements of the agency. Elective courses were not allowed for two reasons. First, it would complicate the offering to a certain extent, requiring additional courses, facilities, and professors— essentially adding cost to the program. Second, FIA wanted a prescribed,

Table 1. Typical three-year schedule.

M.S.—Information Science

	Year 1	Year 2	Year 3
Fall	2 Courses—6 hours	2 Courses—6 hours	2 Courses—6 hours
Spring	2 Courses—6 hours	2 Courses—6 hours	2 Courses—6 hours
Summer	1 Course—3 hours	1 Course—3 hours	Graduate Project—3 hours
		Graduate Project—3 hours	

Graduate Project—6 hours (Year 2 and 3)
Total Semester Hours—48

customized curriculum that would add value to the agency while still meeting the requirements of the university.

Selection Criteria

An important issue involved the selection of employees to attend the program. Most employees who voluntarily left the agency resigned within the first four years and were often considered to have high potential. With this in mind, the following five criteria were established for identifying and selecting the employees to enroll in the program:

1. A candidate should have at least one year of service prior to beginning classes.
2. A candidate must meet the normal requirements to be accepted into the graduate school at the university.
3. A candidate must be willing to sign a commitment to stay with the agency for two years beyond program completion.
4. a candidate's immediate manager must nominate the employee for consideration.
5. A candidate must be considered "high potential" as rated by the immediate manager.

The management team was provided initial information on the program, kept informed of its development and progress prior to actual launch, and briefed as the program was described and selection criteria was finalized. It was emphasized that the selection should be based on objective criteria, following the guidelines offered. At the same time, managers were asked to provide feedback as to the level of interest and specific issues surrounding the nomination of candidates.

A limit of 100 participants entering the program each year was established. This limit was based on two key issues:

1. The capability of the university in terms of staffing for the program—RSU could not effectively teach more than 100 participants each semester.
2. This was an experiment that, if successful, could be modified or enhanced in the future.

Program Administration

Because of the magnitude of the anticipated enrollment, FIA appointed a full-time program administrator who was responsible for organizing and coordinating the program. The duties included registration of the participants, all correspondence and communication with the university and participants, facilities and logistics (including materials and books), and resolving problems as they occur. FIA absorbed the total cost of the coordinator. The university assigned an individual to serve as liaison with the agency. This individual was not additional staff; the university absorbed the cost as part of the tuition.

The Drivers for Evaluation

This program was selected for a comprehensive evaluation to show its impact on the agency using a four-year timeframe. Four influences created the need for this detailed level of accountability:

1. Senior administrators had requested detailed evaluations for certain programs considered to be strategic, highly visible, and designed to add value to the agency.
2. This program was perceived to be very expensive, demanding a higher level of accountability, including return on investment (ROI).
3. Because retention is such a critical issue for this agency, it was important to determine if this solution was the appropriate one. A detailed measurement and evaluation should reflect the success of the program.
4. The passage of federal legislation and other initiatives in the United States, aimed at bringing more accountability for taxpayers' funds, has created a shift in increased public sector accountability.

Consequently, the implementation team planned a detailed evaluation of this program beyond the traditional program evaluation processes. Along with tracking costs, the monetary payoff would be developed, including ROI in the program. Because this is a very complex and comprehensive solution, other important measures would be monitored to present an overall, balanced approach to the measurement.

Recognizing the shift toward public sector accountability, the human resources staff had developed the necessary skills to implement the ROI process. A small group of HR staff members had been certified to implement the ROI process within the agency. The ROI is a comprehensive measurement and evaluation process that develops six types of data and always includes a method to isolate the effects of the program (Phillips, Stone, and Phillips, 2001).

The evaluation of the master's program was conducted by several of these team members with the assistance of the original developer of the ROI process, Dr. Jack J. Phillips.

Program Costs

The cost of the program was tabulated and monitored and reflected a fully loaded cost profile, which included all direct and indirect costs. One of the major costs was the tuition for the participants. The university charged the customary tuition, plus $100 per semester course per participant to offset the additional travel, faculty expense, books, and handouts. The tuition per semester hour was $200 ($600 per three-hour course).

The full-time administrator was an FIA employee, receiving a base salary of $37,000 per year, with a 45 percent employee benefits upload factor. The administrator had expenses of approximately $15,000 per year. Salaries for the participants represented another significant cost category. The average salary of the job categories of the employees involved in the program was $47,800, with a 45 percent employee benefits factor. Salaries usually increase about 4 percent per year. Participants attended class a total of 18 hours for each semester hour of credit. Thus, a three-hour course represented 54 hours of off-the-job time in the classroom. The total hours needed to complete the program for one participant was 756 hours (14×54).

Classroom facilities was another significant cost category. For the 100 participants, four different courses were offered each semester and each course was repeated at a different time slot. With a class size of 25, eight separate semester courses were presented. Each semester, half the scheduled courses were offered in the summer. Although the classrooms used for this program were those normally used for other training and education programs offered at the agency, the cost for providing the facilities was included. (Because of the unusual demand, an additional conference room was built to provide ample meeting space). The estimate for the average cost of all meeting rooms was $40 per hour of use.

The cost for the initial assessment was also included in the cost profile. This charge, estimated to be about $5,000, included the turnover analysis and was prorated for the first three years. FIA's development costs for the program were estimated to be about $10,000 and were prorated for three years. Management time involved in the program was minimal, but estimated to be about $9,000 over the three-year period. This consisted primarily of meetings and memos regarding the program. Finally, the evaluation costs, representing the cost to actually track the success of the program and report the results to management, was estimated to be $10,000.

Table 2 represents the total costs of the initial group in the program for three years using a fully loaded cost profile. All of the cost categories described above are included. This value is necessary for the ROI calculation.

Data Collection Issues

To understand the success of the project from a balanced perspective, a variety of types of data had to be collected throughout program implementation. During the initial enrollment process, meetings

Table 2. Total fully loaded costs of master's program for 100 participants.

	Year 1	Year 2	Year 3	Total
Initial analysis (prorated)	$1,667	$1,667	$1,666	$5,000
Development (prorated)	3,333	3,333	3,334	10,000
Tuition—regular	300,000	342,000	273,000	915,000
Tuition—premium	50,000	57,000	45,500	152,500
Salaries/Benefits (participants)	899,697	888,900	708,426	2,497,023
Salaries/Benefits (program administrator)	53,650	55,796	58,028	167,474
Program coordination	15,000	15,000	15,000	45,000
Facilities	43,200	43,200	34,560	120,960
Management time	3,000	3,000	3,000	9,000
Evaluation	3,333	3,333	3,334	10,000
Total	$1,372,880	$1,413,229	$1,145,848	$3,931,957

were conducted with participants to obtain their commitment to provide data at different timeframes. The program administrator had regular access to participants who were willing to provide data about their reaction to the program, and detail the extent of knowledge and skill enhancement and the successes they achieved on the job. Measures were taken at four distinct levels:

1. Reaction to individual courses and the program, including the administrative and coordination issues
2. The knowledge and skills obtained from the individual courses and learning about the program
3. Application and implementation of the program as learning is applied on the job and the program is coordinated effectively
4. Changes in business measures in the agency directly related to the program

In addition to these data items, program costs were monitored so that the return on investment could be calculated.

Collecting different types of data required measures to be taken at different timeframes. It was agreed at the beginning of the program that some data categories would be collected at the end of each semester. Reaction would be measured, and learning would be monitored with individual grade point averages. At periodic intervals, follow-up data was collected to reflect the progress of the program and its application on the job. Finally, business impact data directly linked to the program was measured during the program as well as at the conclusion. While this program was perceived to have a long-term impact, data had to be collected throughout the process to reflect any early impact that developed.

Data Collection Plan

The program administrator was responsible for the initial data collection and semester feedback sections. Individual faculty members were asked to collect reaction and learning measures at the end of each course. While most of the data would come directly from the participants, the records from the agency were monitored for certain business measures, such as turnover. In addition, immediate managers of participants provided input concerning the actual use of the program on the job. Figure 1 shows the data collection plan for this program.

Reaction and Satisfaction

Reaction to the program was collected at specific time periods. A few issues involving reaction and satisfaction were collected from prospective participants at an information briefing when the program

Figure 1. Data collection plan.

Program: _____ Federal Information Agency Responsibility: _____

Level	Broad Program Objective(s)	Measures	Data Collection Method/Instruments	Data Sources	Timing	Responsibilities
1	**REACTION/SATISFACTION** • Positive reaction to program, content, quality, and administration	• 4.0 on a scale from 1-5	• Reaction questionnaire	• Participants	• At the intro of the program • End of course • End of semester	• Program administrator • Faculty • Program administrator
2	**LEARNING** • Maintain above-average grades • Understand the purpose and the participant's role in the program	• 3.0 grade point average out of a possible 4.0 • 4.0 on a scale from 1-5	• Formal and informal testing in each course • Questionnaire at the end of initial meeting	• Participants • Participants	• End of each course • At the intro of the program	• Faculty • Faculty
3	**APPLICATION/ IMPLEMENTATION** • Use of the knowledge and skills on the job • Develop and apply innovative projects to add operational value • Enjoy a very high completion rate	• Various measures on a scale of 1-5 • Completion of project • Completion rate of 80%	• Questionnaires • Action plans • Monitoring records	• Participants • Participants • Agency records	• End of each year • One-year follow-up • End of program	• Program administrator • Program administrator • Program administrator

	Broad Program Objective(s)	Measures	Data Collection Method	Data Sources	Timing	Responsibilities
4	**BUSINESS IMPACT** • Reduce avoidable turnover • Improve job satisfaction/commitment • Career enhancement • Upgrade technology and agency capability • Improve operational results • Recruiting success	• Number of avoidable exits each month divided by the average number each month • 4.0 on a scale of 1-5 • Monetary values • Number of candidates	• Monitoring records • Questionnaires • Action plans • Monitoring records	• Agency records • Participants • Managers • Participants • Agency records	• Monthly • End of each year • End of program • One-year follow-up	• HR staff • Program administrator • Program administrator • Program administrator
5	**ROI** • Achieve a 25% return on investment					

Comments: _____

was announced. Perceived value, anticipated difficulty of the courses, and usefulness of the program on the job were captured in initial meetings. Next, reaction measures were collected for each individual course as the participants rated the course material, instructor, delivery style, and learning environment. Also, at the end of each semester, a brief reaction questionnaire was collected to provide constant feedback of perceptions and satisfaction with the program. Upon completion of the program, an overall reaction questionnaire was distributed.

Learning

The initial meeting with the participants provided an opportunity to collect information about their understanding of how the program works and their role in making the program successful. Most of the learning took place in individual courses. The faculty member assigned grades based on formal and informal testing and assessment. These grades reflected individual learning, skills, and knowledge. Professors used a variety of testing methodology such as special projects, demonstrations, discussion questions, case studies, simulations, and objective tests. The overall grade point average provided an ongoing assessment of the degree to which the participants were learning the content of the courses.

Application and Implementation

Application and implementation measures were assessed at several different time intervals. At the end of each year, a questionnaire was distributed where the participants indicated the success of the program in three areas:
1. The opportunities to use the skills and knowledge learned in the program
2. The extent to which the skills have actually been used on the job
3. The effectiveness in the use of the skills

In addition, several questions focused on the progress with (and barriers to) the implementation of the program. At this level of analysis, it was important to determine if the program material was actually being used on the job. Program statistics were collected, including dropout and completion rates of the participants.

Business Measures

Because the program was implemented to focus on retention of specialists, the primary business measure was turnover. Turnover rates for the participants in the program were compared directly with individuals not involved in the program to determine if the rates were significantly reduced. In addition to avoidable turnover, tenure of employees was tracked, which reflected the average length of service of the target job group. It was anticipated that the program would have an impact on a variety of other business measures as well, including the following:

1. Productivity (from projects)
2. Quality (from projects)
3. Enhanced agency capability
4. Technology upgrade
5. Job satisfaction
6. Employee commitment
7. Recruiting success
8. Career enhancement

In the planning process, it was decided that these measures would be explored to the extent feasible to identify improvements. If not, the perceived changes in these business measures would be collected directly from the participants.

Graduate Projects

An important part of the program was a graduate work-study project required to complete the master's degree. The project involved at least two semesters of work and provided six hours of credit. It was supervised by a faculty member and approved by the participants' immediate manager. The project had to add value to the agency in some way as well as improve agency capability, operations, or technology upgrade. At the same time, it had to be rigorous enough to meet the requirements of the university. In a sense, it was a master's thesis, although the participants were enrolled in a nonthesis option. Through this project, the participants were able to apply what they had learned. The project was identified during the first year, approved and implemented during the second year, and completed in the third year.

This project provided an excellent opportunity for participants to support the agency and add value to agency operations. As part of the project, participants developed an action plan detailing how their project would be used on the job. The action plan, built into the graduate project, provided the timetable and detail for application of the project. A part of the action plan is a detail of the monetary contribution to the agency (or forecast of the contribution). That was required as part of the project and, ultimately, became evidence of contribution of the project. Follow-up on the action plan provided the monetary amount of contribution from the graduate project.

Data Collection Summary

Table 3 shows a summary of the various instruments used to collect data, along with the level of evaluation data. As this table reveals, data collection was comprehensive, continuous, and necessary for a program with this much exposure and expense. Data collected at Levels 1, 2, and 3 were used to make adjustments in the program. Adjustments were made throughout the program as feedback was obtained. This action is particularly important for administrative and faculty-related issues.

ROI Analysis Plan

Figure 2 presents a completed planning document for the ROI analysis. This plan, which was completed prior to the beginning of the program, addresses key issues of isolating the influence of the program, converting the data to monetary values, and costing the program. As figure 2 reveals, avoidable turnover, the key data item, is listed along with the technology and operations improvement expected from individual graduate projects. It was anticipated that the program would pay off on turnover and improvements from projects.

Recruiting success is also listed as a measure for potential isolation and conversion. An increase in the number of applicants interested in employment with FIA was anticipated as the communication and publicity surrounding the program became known in various recruiting channels. Other business impact measures were considered to be intangible and are listed in the intangible benefits column. Intangible benefits are defined as those measures purposely not converted to monetary values. During the planning stage, it was anticipated that measures such as improved job satisfaction, enhanced agency capability, and improved organizational commitment would not be converted to monetary value. Although very important, these measures would be listed as intangible benefits—only if they were linked to the program.

The cost categories discussed earlier were detailed in this planning document. Costs are fully loaded and include both direct and indirect categories. The communication targets were comprehensive. Seven groups were identified as needing specific information from this study.

The ROI analysis and data collection plans provide all the key decisions about the project prior to the actual data collection and analysis.

Table 3. Data summary by evaluation level.

Type of Instrument	Reaction/ Satisfaction	Learning	Application/ Implementation	Business Impact
1. Questionnaire after intro to program	X	X		
2. End-of-course instructor evaluation	X			
3. End-of-semester evaluation questionnaire	X			
4 Individual course tests		X		
5. Annual evaluation questionnaire			X	
6. Action plans with follow up			X	X
7 One-year follow-up questionnaire			X	X
8. Monitoring records				X

Isolating the Effects of the Program

Several methods were used to isolate the effects of the program, depending on the specific business impact measure. For avoidable turnover, three methods were initially planned. A comparison group was identified, which would serve as the control group in a traditional control group experiment. The individuals selected for the master's program would be matched with others not in the program, using the same tenure and job status characteristics. Recognizing the difficulty of success with a control group arrangement, both the participants and managers were asked to indicate the percent of the turnover reduction they believed to be directly related to this program. A questionnaire was provided to obtain this input.

For the technology and operations improvement data, participants' estimates were used as a method for isolating the effects of the program using data from action plans for the projects. The same approach was planned for isolating the effects of the program on recruiting success.

Figure 2. ROI analysis plan.

Program: _____ M.S. In Information Science   Responsibility: _____   Date: _____

Data Items (Usually Level 4)	Methods for Isolating the Effects of the Program/Process	Methods of Converting Data to Monetary Values	Cost Categories	Intangible Benefits	Communication Targets for Final Report	Other Influences/Issues During Application	Comments
• Avoidable turnover	• Comparison group • Participants' estimates • Manager estimates	• External studies	• Initial analysis • Program development • Tuition • Participant salaries/benefits • Program coordination costs • Facilities • Management time • Evaluation	• Improved job satisfaction • Improved operational commitment • Career enhancement • Enhanced agency capability • Technology upgrade	• Participants • Immediate managers of participants • Program sponsor • Senior agency administrators • Agency HR staff • RSU administrators • All agency employees	• Need to monitor external employment conditions • Need to identify other potential internal influences on turnover reductions	Payoff of program will probably rest on turnover reduction and improvements from projects
• Technology and operating improvements	• Participants' estimates	• Standard values • Historical costs • Expert input • Participants' estimates					
• Recruiting success	• Participants' estimates	• Internal expert estimates					

Converting Data to Monetary Values

The methods used to convert data to monetary values varied as well. For avoidable turnover, external studies were used to pinpoint the approximate value. From various databases, studies in similar job categories had revealed that the cost of turnover for these specialized job groups was somewhere between two and three times the average annual salary. This was considerably higher than the HR staff at FIA anticipated. As a compromise, a value of 1.75 times the annual salary was used. While this value is probably lower than the actual fully loaded cost of turnover, it is conservative to assign this value. It is much better to use a conservative estimate for this value than to calculate the fully loaded cost for turnover. Most retention specialists would agree that 175 percent of annual pay is a conservative, fully loaded cost of turnover for information specialists.

To obtain the monetary values of project improvements, participants were asked to use one of four specific methods to identify the value:

1. Standard values were available for many items throughout the agency, and their use was encouraged when placing monetary values on a specific improvement.
2. Historical costs could be used, capturing the various costs of a specific data item as it is improved, by the project. These cost savings values are taken directly from general ledger accounts and provide a very credible cost value.
3. If neither of the above methods is feasible, expert inut, using internal sources, was suggested.
4. Finally, if the other methods failed to produce a value, participants were instructed to place their own estimates for the value. In those cases, the confidence of the estimate would be obtained.

For recruiting success, internal expert estimates would be used, directly from the recruiting staff. Collectively, these techniques provided an appropriate array of strategies to convert data to monetary values.

Reaction and Satisfaction Measurements

Reaction measurements, taken during the initial program introductions, were informal and confirmed that the participants recognized the value of the program and its usefulness to them as well as the agency. Also, any concerns about the difficulty of the program were addressed during that meeting.

Two opportunities to collect reaction and satisfaction data occurred at the end of each semester. For each course, the instructor obtained direct feedback using standard instrumentation. Table 4 shows the faculty evaluation selected for this program. It was a slightly modified version of what RSU normally collects for its instructors. In addition to providing feedback to various RSU department heads, this information was provided to the program administrator as well as the major sponsor for this project. This constant data flow was an attempt to make adjustments if the faculty was perceived to be unresponsive and ineffective in delivering the desired courses. As table 4 shows, on a scale from one to five, the responses were extremely effective. The only concerns expressed were with the presentation and ability to relate to agency needs. At several different times, adjustments were made in an attempt to improve these two areas. The ratings presented in table 4 were the cumulative ratings over the three-year project for the 100 participants who initially began the program.

At the end of each semester, a brief scannable questionnaire was collected to measure satisfaction with and reaction to the program. Table 5 shows the various items rated on this questionnaire. The goal was to have a composite of at least four out of five for this program, and it was achieved. The only areas of concern were the quality of the faculty, the amount of new information, and the appropriateness of the course material. Adjustments were made to improve these areas.

Learning Measurements

Learning was primarily measured through formal testing processes used by individual faculty members. As stated earlier, a variety of methods were used ranging from objective testing to simulations. The tests yielded an individual grade that translated into a grade point average. The grade objective for the overall program was to maintain a 3.0 grade

Table 4. Reaction and satisfaction with faculty.

Issue	Average Rating*
Knowledge of topic	4.35
Preparation for classes	4.25
Delivery/Presentation	3.64
Level of involvement	4.09
Learning environment	4.21
Responsiveness to participants	4.31
Ability to relate to agency needs	3.77

*On a 1-5 scale, with 5 = exceptional

Table 5. Measures of reaction to and satisfaction with the program.

Issue	Average Rating*
Value of program	4.7
Difficulty of program	4.1
Usefulness of program	4.5
Quality of faculty	3.p
Quality of program administration	4.4
Appropriateness of course material	3.9
Intent to use course material	4.2
Amount of new information	3.7
Recommendation to others	4.6

*On a 1-5 scale, with 5 = exceptional

point average out of a possible 4.0. Table 6 shows the cumulative grade point average through the three-year period ending with an average of 3.18, exceeding the target for the overall program.

Application and Implementation Measures

Application and implementation were measured with three instruments: the annual questionnaire at the end of each program year, the follow-up on the action plans, and a one-year follow-up questionnaire. The two questionnaires (annual and follow-up) provided information about overall application and use of the program and course material. Table 7 shows the categories of data for the annual questionnaire, which, for the most part, was duplicated in the follow-up

Table 6. Cumulative grade point averages.

Year	Cumulative Grade Point Average *
Year 1	3.31
Year 2	3.25
Year 3	3.18

*Out of a possible 4.0

questionnaire. As this table reveals, nine topical areas were explored with the focus on the extent to which the participants were using the program and the skills and knowledge learned. It also explored improvements and accomplishments over and above the individual project improvement. Barriers and enablers to implementation were detailed, in addition to input on the management support for the program, along with recommendations for improvement.

Several questions were devoted to each of these categories. For example, table 8 presents application data for knowledge and skills, showing four specific areas and the ratings obtained for each. While these ratings reveal success, there was some concern about the frequency of use and opportunity to use skills. The input scale for these items was adjusted to job context. For example, in the frequency of skills, the range of potential responses was adjusted to reflect anticipated responses and, consequently, in some cases it may have missed the mark. Some skills should be infrequently used because of the skills and the opportunity to use them. Thus, low marks on these two categories were not particularly disturbing considering the varied nature of program application.

Business Impact

Although business data was monitored in several ways, the annual and follow-up questionnaire obtained input on the perceived linkage with impact measures. As shown in table 7, one category of data provided the opportunity for participants to determine the extent to which this program influenced several impact measures. As

Table 7. Categories of data for annual questionnaire.

- Course sequencing/availability
- Use of skills/knowledge
- Linkage with impact measures
- Improvements/accomplishments
- Project selection and application
- Barriers to implementation
- Enablers to implementation
- Management support for program
- Recommendations for improvement

Table 8. Application data: Use of knowledge and skills.

Issue	Average Rating*
Opportunity to use skills/knowledge	3.9
Appropriateness of skills/knowledge	4.1
Frequency of use of skills/knowledge	3.2
Effectiveness of use of skills/knowledge	4.3

*On a 1-5 scale, with 5 = exceptional

far as actual business improvement value, two data items were converted to monetary values: turnover and project application.

Turnover Reduction

The primary value of the program would stem from annual turnover reduction of the target group. Table 9 shows the annualized, avoidable turnover rates for three different groups. The first is the total group of 1,500 specialists in this job category. The next group is the program participants, indicating that of the 100 initial participants, 12 left during the program (5 percent, 4 percent, 3 percent), and three left in the first year following completion, for a total of 15 in the four-year time span. For the similar comparison group, 100 individuals were identified and the numbers were replenished as turnover occurred. As the numbers revealed, essentially the entire comparison group had left the agency by the end of the third year. This comparison underscores the cumulative effect of an excessive turnover rate. Using the comparison group as the expected turnover rate yields a total expected turnover of 138 in the four-year period (34 percent, 35 percent, 33 percent, 36 percent). The actual, however, was 15 for the same period. Thus, the difference in the two groups (138 − 15) equals 123 turnover statistics prevented with this program, using the control group arrangement to isolate the results of the program.

The participants and managers provided insight into the percent of the turnover reduction attributed to the program. For their estimate, the process starts with the difference measured in the total group compared to the actual. Using a base of 100, the total group was expected to have 144 turnover statistics (39 percent, 36 percent, 35 percent, 34 percent). The difference between the total group and the actual turnover statistic is 129 (144 − 15 = 129). Because there were other contributing factors, participants were asked to indicate what percentage

Table 9. Turnover data.

Annualized Avoidable Turnover	1 Year Prior to Program	1st Year September to August	2nd Year September to August	3rd Year September to August	1 Year Post-program
Total Group 1,500	38%	39%	36%	35%	34%
Program Participants Group	N/A	5% (5 participants)	4% (4 participants)	3% (3 participants)	3% (3 participants)
Similar Group	N/A	34%	35%	33%	36%

Four-Year Expected Turnover Statistics = 138
Four-Year Actual Turnover Statistics = 15
Four-Year Total Group Turnover Statistics = 144

of this reduction they attributed to the program. The participants' and managers' estimates were combined (using a simple average to reflect equal weight) to yield a 93 percent allocation to this program. The confidence estimate for this value is 83 percent (the average of the two). Obviously, both groups realized that this program was accomplishing its major goal of reducing turnover. Thus, if 129 are adjusted by 93 percent and 83 percent, the yield is 100 turnover statistics. Given the choice of using 123 or 100, the lower number is used, although it might not be as credible as the actual control group comparisons. It is conservative to indicate that at least 100 turnover statistics were prevented in the four-year time frame for this analysis.

The value for the turnover reduction is rather straightforward, with 1.75 times the annual earnings used as a compromised value. The total value of the turnover improvement is $100 \times \$47,800 \times 1.75 = \$8,365,000$. This is a significant, yet conservative, value for the turnover reduction.

Project Values

The participants developed projects that were designed to add value to the agency by improving capability and operations. Table 10 shows the summary of the data from the projects. Eighty-eight individuals graduated from the program, and all had approved and implemented projects. Of that number, 74 actually provided data on their project completion in the one-year follow-up on their action plan. Of that number, 53 were able to convert the project to a monetary value. The participants were asked to estimate the amount of improvement that was

Table 10. Monetary values from project.

Number of Projects Approved and Implemented	88
Number of Projects Reporting Completion	74
Number of Projects Reporting Monetary Values	53
Number of Projects with Usable Monetary Values	46
Average Value of Project (Adjusted)	$ 55,480
Highest Value of Project (Adjusted)	$ 1,429,000*
Lowest Value of Project (Adjusted)	$ 1,235
Average Confidence Estimate	62%
Total Value (Adjusted Twice)	$ 1,580,000

*Discarded in the analysis

directly related to the project (percent), recognizing that other factors could have influenced the results. The values are reported as adjusted values in table 10. Only 46 of those were useable values, as unsupported claims and unrealistic values were omitted from the analysis. For example, the highest value ($1,429,000) was eliminated because of the shock value of this number and the possibility of error or exaggeration. The average confidence estimate was 62 percent. When each project value is multiplied by the individual confidence estimate, the total adjusted usable value is $1,580,000.

Intangibles

The intangible benefits were impressive with this program. Recruiting success was not converted to monetary value, but included instead as a subjective intangible value. All of the intangible measures listed in the initial data collection plan were linked to the program, according to participants or managers. A measure was listed as an intangible if at least 25 percent of either group perceived it as linked to the program. Thus, the intangibles were not included in the monetary analysis but were considered to be important and included in the final report.

BCR and ROI Calculations for Turnover Reduction

The benefits-cost ratio (BCR) is the total monetary benefits divided by the total program costs. For turnover reduction, the BCR calculation becomes:

$$BCR = \frac{\text{Monetary Benefits}}{\text{Total Program Costs}} = \frac{\$8,365,000}{\$3,931,957} = 2.13$$

The ROI calculation for the turnover reduction is the net program benefit divided by the cost. In formula form it becomes:

$$ROI = \frac{\text{Monetary Benefits} - \text{Total Program Costs}}{\text{Total Program Costs}} = \frac{\$4,433,043}{\$3,931,957} \times 100 = 113\%$$

BCR and ROI Calculations for Total Improvement

The BCR for the value obtained on turnover reduction and project completion yields the following:

$$BCR = \frac{\$8,365,000 + \$1,580,000}{\$3,931,957} = \frac{\$9,945,000}{\$3,931,957} = 2.53$$

The ROI—usable program benefits for the two improvements—is as follows:

$$ROI = \frac{\$9,945,000 - \$3,931,957}{\$3,931,957} \times 100 = 153\%$$

Communicating Results

Because these are large values, it was a challenge to communicate them convincingly to the senior team. The conservative nature of this approach helps defend the analysis and make the results more credible and believable. The step-by-step results were presented to the senior team using the following sequence:

1. A brief review of the project and its objectives
2. Overview of the methodology
3. Assumptions used in the analysis
4. Reaction and satisfaction measures
5. Learning measures
6. Application and implementation measures
7. Business impact measures
8. ROI
9. Intangibles
10. Barriers and enablers
11. Interpretation and conclusions
12. Recommendations

This information was presented to the senior team in a one-hour meeting and provided an opportunity to present the methodology and results. This meeting had a three-fold purpose:

1. Present the methodology and assumptions for capturing the ROI, building credibility with the process and analysis
2. Using a balanced approach, show the impact of a major initiative and how it provides a payoff for the agency and taxpayers
3. Show how the same type of solution can be implemented and evaluated in the future

The project was considered a success.

Questions for Discussion

1. Can the value of this program be forecasted? If so, how?
2. Most of these costs are estimated or rounded off. Is this appropriate? Explain.
3. What issues surface when developing cost data? How can they be addressed?
4. are the ROI values realistic? Explain.
5. Is this study credible? Explain.
6. How can this type of process be used to build support for programs in the future? Explain.

CHAPTER

Measuring ROI in an
Absenteeism Reduction Program

Metro Transit Authority

This case illustrates how changes in human resource policies and selection processes can reduce absenteeism and prevent major problems in business operations. Because of unscheduled absences, the unavailability of bus drivers caused route schedule delays and bottlenecks, which resulted in dissatisfied customers, a loss of revenue, and increased operating costs. New guidelines and disciplinary policies for unscheduled absences, as well as a change in hiring practices, were initiated to correct the situation. The ability to demonstrate the costs associated with the absenteeism problem led to the two solutions being implemented. The evaluation team was able to isolate the effects of each of the two HR initiatives and calculate the operational savings to demonstrate an impressive return on investment.

Background

The Metro Transit Authority (MTA) operates a comprehensive transportation system in a large metropolitan area. More than 1,000 buses function regularly, providing essential transportation to citizens in the metro area. Many passengers depend on the bus system for their commute to and from work, as well as other essential travel. MTA employs more than 2,900 drivers to operate the bus system around the clock.

This case was prepared to serve as a basis for discussion rather than to illustrate either effective or ineffective administrative and management practices. All names, dates, places, and organizations have been disguised at the request of the author or organization.

As with many transit systems, MTA was experiencing excessive absenteeism with bus drivers, and the problem was growing. Just three years ago, absenteeism was 7 percent, compared with the most recent three-month period of 8.7 percent—too excessive to keep the transit system operating in a consistent manner.

To ensure that buses ran on time, a pool of substitute drivers was employed to fill in during unexpected absences. The number of drivers in the pool was a function of the absenteeism rate. At the time of this study, the pool consisted of 231 substitute drivers. When the drivers in the pool were not needed as substitutes, they performed almost no essential work for the Transit Authority although they were required to report to work. When a substitute driver was used, this usually delayed the bus schedule, making the bus late for subsequent stops.

Causes of Problems and Solutions

To determine the cause of absenteeism, an analysis was conducted using focus groups, interviews, and an analysis of human resources records. Focus groups included bus drivers and their supervisors. Interviews were conducted with supervisors and managers. HR records were examined for trends and patterns in absenteeism. The conclusions from the analysis were as follows:

- Individuals who were frequently absent had a pattern of absenteeism that dated back to the beginning of their employment and, in most cases, was present in other employment situations.
- Many of the absences could be avoided. The problem was primarily a motivation and discipline issue.
- The prevailing attitude among employees was to take advantage of the system whenever possible, up to the threshold of being terminated.

As a result of these findings, MTA initiated two solutions:

1. **A no-fault disciplinary system was implemented.** With this policy, an employee who experiences more than six unexpected (unplanned) incidences in a six-month period was terminated— no questions asked. A sickness that extends more than one day was considdered on incidence. Thus, the policy would not unfairly penalize those who are absent for legitimate sickness or for scheduled surgery and other medical attention. The no-fault system was implemented after extensive negotiations with the union. Whe unio officials realized the impact of excessive absenteeism, they agreed with the new policy.
2. **The selection process for new drivers was modified.** During the initial screening, a list of questions was developed and used to screen out applicants who had a history of absenteeism dating

back to their high school days. The questions, with scoring and interpretation, were added to the current selection process and required approximately 30 minutes of additional time during the initial employment interview.

To bring appropriate attention to the absenteeism issue and to generate results as soon as possible, both solutions were implemented at the same time.

Objectives of the Solutions

The expected outcomes were established early, in the form of implementation and impact objectives. The objectives of the two solutions were to:

- Communicate the no-fault policy, including how the policy would be applied and the rationale for it
- Experience little or no adverse rection from current employees as the no-fault absenteeism policy was implemented
- Maintain present level of job satisfaction as the absenteeism solutions were implemented and applied
- Use the new screening process for each selection decision so that a systematic and consistent selection process would be in place
- Implement and enforce the no-fault policy consistently throughout all operating units
- Reduce driver absenteeism at least 2 percent during the first year of implementation of the two solutions
- Improve customer service and satisfaction with a reduction in schedule delays caused by absenteeism

Supervisors were required to conduct meetings with their employees to explain the need for the policy and how it would be applied. Supervisors completed a meeting report form after the meeting and returned it to the HR department.

The no-fault policy has the potential of influencing employment termination by essentially increasing employee turnover, which could have created problems for some supervisors. Because of this, it was important to demonstrate to the management team that these programs were effective when administered properly. Also, senior management were interested in knowing the payoff for these types of initiatives; they needed to be convinced that the company was receiving an adequate return on investment.

Data Collection

Figure 1 shows the data collection plan for the absenteeism reduction solutions at Metro Transit Authority. The objectives are de-

Figure 1. Data collection plan.

Program: Absenteeism Reduction **Responsibility:** _____ **Date** January 15

Level	Broad Program Objective(s)	Measures	Data Collection Method/Instruments	Data Sources	Timing	Responsibilities
1	**REACTION/SATISFACTION** • Positive employee reaction to the no-fault policy	• Positive reaction from employees	• Feedback questionnaire	• Employees	• At the end of the employee meetings	• Supervisors
2	**LEARNING** • Employee understanding of the policy	• Score on posttest, at least 70	• True/false test	• Employees	• At the end of the employee meetings	• Supervisors
3	**APPLICATION/ IMPLEMENTATION** 1. Effective and consistent implementation and enforcement of the programs 2. Little or no adverse reaction from current employees regarding no-fault policy 3. Use the new screening process	1. Supervisors' response on program's influence 2. Employee complaints and union cooperation	1. and 2. Follow-up questionnaire to supervisors (two sample groups) 3. Sample review of interview and selection records	1. Supervisors 2. Company records	1. Following employee meetings, sample one group at three months and another group at six months 2. Three months and six months after implementation	• HR program coordinator

4 | **BUSINESS IMPACT**

1. Reduce driver absenteeism a least 2% during first year	1. Absenteeism	1. Monitor absenteeism	1. Company records	1. Monitor monthly and analyze one year pre- and one-year post-implementation	• HR program coordinator
2. Maintain present level of job satisfaction as new policy is implemented	2. Employee satisfaction	2. Follow-up questionnaire to supervisors	2. Supervisors	2. Three months and six months after employee meetings	
3. Improve customer service and satisfaction with reduction in schedule delays	3. Delays impact on customer service	3. Monitor bus schedule delays	3. Dispatch records	3. Monthly	

5 | **ROI**

Target ROI ≥ 25%

Comments: _____

_____

_____

_____

_____

Source: Phillips, Jack J., Stone, Ron D., and Phillips, Patricia P. (2001). *The Human Resources Scorecard: Measuring the Return on Investment.* Boston: Butterworth-Heinemann.

fined, and the data collection methods selected are typical for those types of programs. Absenteeism, the primary business data, is monitored on a postprogram basis and compared with preprogram data. Table 1 shows the absenteeism rate for the years prior to, and after, implementing both the no-fault policy and the new selection process. A complete year of data was collected to show the full impact of both solutions to capture the delayed effect in influencing the absenteeism measure. In addition, bus schedule delays of more than five minutes caused by unexpected absenteeism were monitored and are reported in Table 1.

Also, for implementation and business measures, a questionnaire was developed and administered to a sample of supervisors to determine the extent to which the programs were implemented and were perceived to be operating effectively. Input was sought regarding problems and issues, as well as success stories and changes in job satisfaction.

Learning measures were taken with a simple 10-item true/false test. To ensure that employees understood the policy, the test was administered by supervisors in meetings with employees. Scores were attached with the record of the meeting, along with the time, place, agenda, and a list of the attendees. A sample of test scores revealed an average value above the minimum acceptable level of 70.

Table 1. Absenteeism and bus delays before and after implementation.

	Unscheduled Absenteeism Percent of Scheduled Days Worked		Absenteeism Related Bus Delays Percent of All Delays	
	PRE	POST	PRE	POST
July	7.2	6.3	23.3	18.3
August	7.4	5.6	24.7	18.0
September	7.1	5.0	24.9	17.5
October	7.8	5.9	26.1	18.2
November	8.1	5.3	25.4	16.7
December	8.4	5.2	26.3	15.9
January	8.7	5.4	27.1	15.4
February	8.5	4.8	26.9	14.9
March	8.6	4.9	26.8	14.7
April	8.5	4.9	27.8	14.4
May	8.8	4.0	27.0	13.6
June	8.8	4.9	26.4	13.7
Three-month average	8.7%	4.8%	27.1%	13.9%

Reaction measures were taken with a simple questionnaire using an objective format. The questionnaire was distributed at the meetings to obtain reaction to the no-fault policy.

Figure 2 shows the return-on-investment (ROI) analysis plan for evaluating the absenteeism reduction initiatives. Major elements of the plan are discussed below.

Isolating the Effects of the Solutions

Several approaches were considered for the purpose of isolating the effects of the two solutions. Initially, a control group arrangement was considered, but was quickly discarded for three important reasons:

1. To purposely withhold the policy change for a group of employees could create contractual and morale problems for the individuals in the control group.
2. Because the new policy would be known to all employees, contamination would occur in the control group, at least temporarily, as employees learned about the "crackdown" on absenteeism. The policy would have the short-term effect of reducing absenteeism in those areas where it was not implemented.
3. Because of the operational problems and customer service issues associated with absenteeism, it was not desirable to withhold a needed solution just for experimental purposes.

Trendline analysis was initially feasible because only a small amount of variance was noticeable in the preprogram trend data. Because of the possibility of this option, in the planning stage, trendline analysis was considered as a method to estimate the impact of both absenteeism initiatives. However, because multiple influences on absenteeism later developed, such as a change in economic conditions, the trendline analysis was aborted.

Finally, as a backup strategy, estimations were taken directly from supervisors as they completed the follow-up questionnaire. Supervisors were asked to identify various factors that had influenced the absenteeism rate and to allocate percentages to each of the factors, including the new screening process and no-fault policy.

Converting Data to Monetary Values

Because the primary business measure was absenteeism, a monetary value had to be developed for the cost of an unexpected absence. The value could subsequently be used to calculate the total

Figure 2. ROI analysis plan.

Program: Absenteeism Reduction   **Responsibility:** _____   **Date:** _____ January 15

Data Items (Usually Level 4)	Methods for Isolating the Effects of the Program/ Process	Methods of Converting Data to Monetary Values	Cost Categories	Intangible Benefits	Communication Targets for Final Report	Other Influences/ Issues During Application	Comments
1. Absenteeism	1. Trendline analysis and supervisor estimates	1. Wages and benefits and standard values	**Screening Process** • Development • Interviewer preparation • Administration • Materials	• Sustain employee satisfaction • Improve employee morale	• Senior management • Managers and supervisors • Union representatives • HR staff	• Concern about supervisors' consistent administration • Partner with union reps on how to communicate results of study to employees	
2. Employee Job Satisfaction	2. Supervisor estimates	N/A		• Improve customer satisfaction			
3. Bus Schedule Delays (Influence on Customer Satisfaction)	3. Management estimates	N/A	No-Fault Policy • Development • Implementation • Materials	• Fewer disruptive bottlenecks in transportation grid • Ease of implementation by supervisors			

Source: Phillips, Jack J., Stone, Ron D., and Phillips, Patricia P. (2001). *The Human Resources Scorecard: Measuring the Return on Investment.* Boston: Butterworth-Heinemann.

cost of the absenteeism improvement. Although several approaches to determine the cost of absenteeism were possible, the analysis at MTA was based on the cost of replacement driver staffing.

Substitute drivers, as well as the regular drivers, were expected to work an average of 240 days per year, leaving 20 days for vacation, holidays, and sick days. The average wages for the substitute drivers is $33,500 per year and the employee benefits factor is 38 percent of payroll. When a regular driver is unexpectedly absent, he or she could charge the absence either to sick leave or vacation, thus substituting a planned paid day (vacation) for the unexpected absence.

The number of substitute drivers planned was a function of expected absenteeism. Consequently, the substitute driver staffing level did not always meet the exact level needed for a specific day's unscheduled absences. Because of the service problems that could develop as a result of understaffing, the company planned for an excessive number of substitute drivers for most days.

To minimize potential delays, all substitute drivers were required to report to work each day. Substitute drivers not used in driver seats essentially performed no productive work that could be counted as added value. During the previous year, overstaffing had occurred about 75 percent of the time for weekdays and nonholidays. That overstaffing represented 4,230 days of wasted time. During the weekends and holidays, which represent 114 days, overstaffing had occurred almost half of the time, representing a total of 570 wasted days.

On some days, there was actually a shortage of substitute drivers, which caused the buses to run late, and overtime had to be used to make the adjustment. During the previous year, there had been 65 instances in which a driver was unavailable, and it was estimated that in 45 of those situations, a regular driver was paid double time to fill in the schedule. In the other 15 situations, the bus route was cancelled.

A final, and very significant, cost of absenteeism was the cost of recruiting, training, maintaining, and supervising the substitute driver pool, beyond the actual salaries paid and benefits provided. These items include recruiting and employment, training and preparation, office space, administration and coordination, and supervision. This item was estimated at 25 percent of the actual annual pay. Here is how the total direct cost of absenteeism was developed from the above information.

Average daily cost of wages and benefits for a substitute driver:

$$\$33,500 \times 1.38 \div 240 = \$192.63$$

Approximate cost of overstaffing, weekdays:

$$192.63 \times 4{,}230 = \$814{,}800$$

Approximate cost of overstaffing, weekends and holidays:

$$192.63 \times 570 = \$109{,}800$$

Approximate cost of understaffing, overtime (only one salary is used for double-time pay):

$$192.63 \times 45 = \$8{,}670$$

Approximate cost of recruiting, training, maintaining, and supervising pool of drivers:

$$33{,}500 \times 231 \times 0.25 = \$1{,}934{,}600$$

Costs for Solutions

The cost for the new screening process contains four components: development, interviewer preparation, administrative time, and materials.

The total development cost, including pilot testing, was $20,000. An additional $5,000 was charged for preparing the interviewers to administer the test. The materials and time were variable costs, depending on the number of drivers employed. About 400 drivers were hired each year. For each new driver hired, an average of three candidates are interviewed. Thus, 1,200 interviews are conducted each year, with an average time of 30 minutes each. The average hourly wage for the interviewers is $14.50 per hour. The materials are $2 per test. Table 2 shows the cost of the screening process.

Table 2. Cost of screening process.

Development cost	$20,000
Interviewer preparation	$5,000
Administrative time (1,200 × 1/2 × $14.50)	$8,700
Materials (1,200 @ $2.00)	$2,400
TOTAL	$36,100

The cost for the no-fault policy included development and implementation. The development cost was incurred internally and was estimated to be $11,000, representing the time of internal specialists. The material distributed to employees accounted for another $3,800. The costs of meetings with all supervisors and with employees were estimated at $16,500. The cost for routine administration was not included because the alternative to continue to administer the no-fault policy is to administer a progressive discipline process, and the two should take about the same amount of time. Table 3 shows the cost of the no-fault policy.

Results: Reaction, Learning, and Application

Employees expressed some concern about the new policy, but the overall reaction to the change was favorable. They perceived the new policy to be fair and equitable. In addition, employees scored an average of 78 on the true/false test about the no-fault policy. A score of 70 on the end-of-meeting test was considered acceptable.

A follow-up questionnaire, administered anonymously to a sample of supervisors, indicated that the policy had been implemented in each area and had been applied consistently. Although supervisors reported some initial resistance from the habitual absenteeism violators, the majority of employees perceived the policy to be effective and fair. The supervisors also reported that the new policy took less time to administer than the previously used progressive discipline approach.

A review of HR records indicated that 95 percent of the supervisors conducted the meeting with employees and completed a meeting report form. In addition, a review of a sample of interviews and selection records indicated that the new screening process was used in every case.

Business Impact

Absenteeism dramatically declined after implementing both processes, yielding an average absenteeism rate of 4.6 percent for the

Table 3. Cost of no-fault policy.

Development cost		$11,000
Materials		$3,800
Meeting time		$16,500
	TOTAL	$31,300

last three months of the evaluation period, compared with the pre-program rate of 8.7 percent for the same period one year earlier. In the MTA situation, a reduction in absenteeism generates a cost savings only if the substitute driver pool was reduced. Because the pool staffing was directly linked to absenteeism, a significant reduction was realized. Table 4 shows the cost savings realized, using the approach shown earlier in this case.

In addition, on the questionnaires, supervisors estimated and allocated percentages for the contribution of each factor to absenteeism reduction. The results are presented in Table 5.

The bus schedule delays caused by absenteeism declined from an average of 27.1 percent for the three months prior to the initiatives to 13.9 percent for the last three months of the evaluation period.

In addition, several intangible measures were identified, including increased morale, improved customer service, and fewer bottlenecks in the entire system.

Table 4. Cost of absenteeism comparisons.

Cost Item	One Year Prior to Initiatives	One Year After Initiatives
Cost of overstaffing, weekdays	$814,000	$602,400
Cost of overstaffing, weekends and holidays	$109,800	$51,500
Cost of understaffing	$8,670	$4,340
Cost of recruiting, training, and maintaining driver pool	$1,934,600	$1,287,750
Total cost of absenteeism	$2,867,070	$1,945,990

Table 5. Supervisor estimates to isolate the effects of the solutions.

Factor	Contribution Percentage	Confidence Percentage
No-fault policy	67%	84%
Screening	22%	71%
Economic conditions	11%	65%
Other	1%	90%

Monetary Benefits

Because the total cost of absenteeism for drivers is known on a before-and-after basis (as shown in table 4), the total savings can be developed as follows:

Preprogram	$2,867,070
Postprogram	$1,945,990
Savings	$921,080

The contribution of the no-fault policy:

$$\$921,080 \times 67\% \times 84\% = \$518,383 = \$518,000$$

The contribution of the new screening process:

$$\$921,080 \times 22\% \times 71\% = \$143,873 = \$144,000$$

Total first year benefit = $518,000 + $144,000 = $662,000

Costs

The total costs for both solutions (as shown in tables 2 and 3) are as follows:

$$\text{Total costs} = \$36,100 + \$31,300 = \$67,400$$

ROI Calculation

The benefits-cost ratio (BCR) and ROI are calculated as follows:

$$BCR = \frac{\$662,000}{\$67,400} = 9.82$$

$$ROI(\%) = \frac{\$662,000 - \$67,400}{\$67,400} = 882\%$$

Questions for Discussion

1. What are feasible ways to isolate the effects of the solutions?
2. Can the cost of absenteeism be developed for MTA? Explain.
3. are the costs of the solutions adequate? Explain.
4. Critique the actual monetary benefits of the reduction in absenteeism.
5. Is this study methodology credible? Explain.
6. Is the ROI value realistic? Explain.
7. How should the results be communicated to various groups?

CHAPTER

Measuring ROI in Effective Meeting Skills

TechnoTel Corporation

Long, meaningless meetings can seriously impair workplace productivity. This case study presents the benefits that can be achieved by reducing the length of meetings, the number of meetings, and the number of meeting participants. The program evaluated is a two-day workshop intended to teach managers, supervisors, and project leaders skills in planning, managing, and facilitating the meeting process. A needs assessment, which included dialogue between the Chief Learning Officer and the President of Manufacturing led to the identification of application and business impact measures. Pre-program data were collected using a meeting profile worksheet, and post-program data were collected using a comprehensive questionnaire. Participant estimates were used to isolate the effects of the workshop on the time savings resulting from less time in meetings, fewer meetings, and fewer people attending meetings. Standard values of time (salary and benefits) were used to convert data to monetary values. Fully-loaded program costs were developed.

Program Need

TechnoTel Corporation is a maker of telecommunications equipment. Although the firm has twenty-two locations, this case study takes place in Frankfurt, Germany. A comprehensive needs

This case was prepared to serve as a basis for discussion rather than to illustrate either effective or ineffective administrative and management practices. All names, dates, places, and organizations have been disguised at the request of the authors or organization.

assessment targeting managerial and supervisory competencies revealed a lack of effective meeting skills, including the ability to prepare, conduct, facilitate, and follow up on meetings. This needs assessment was initiated by a conversation between the Chief Learning Officer (CLO) and the President of Manufacturing in Frankfurt.

The President of manufacturing explained to the CLO his concerns that the learning function placed too much emphasis on activity. An example of his observation was presented in a meeting with the CEO during which the CLO reminded executives how many programs the learning function was developing. He explained to her in manufacturing the focus is on efficiencies – building more with less while improving quality.

> **President:** In the manufacturing division we focus on efficiencies—building more with less as well as ensuring quality. We recognize that, while the organization is doing well economically, there has to be some way to manage our resources. We want to make sure that we are getting the most for the investments we make, even when we make them in our people.
>
> But, I look around and I see waste—time being one of the biggest waste factors. Meetings and training appear to be unproductive.
>
> For example, my managers and supervisors, as good as they are technically, cannot run an effective meeting. They invite everyone they can think of, with half of the participants sitting around looking at their watches, checking BlackBerries, or configuring process design models. When the meeting is underway, there is no structure and no agenda. The meetings invariably run over the time allotted. On top of this, there is a meeting on everything. My team spends more time meeting than any other group only to leave the meetings and do nothing as a result of them.

His concern was the time wasted in meetings. According to the president, there were:

- Too many meetings
- Too many people attending the meetings
- Meetings were too long

He explained his concern that time in meetings meant money wasted and productivity lacking. While no definitive dollar amount was known, it was estimated that the cost of lost productivity due to time wasted was in the hundreds of thousands in U.S. dollars per year.

The conversation set the stage for further investigation as to why so many meetings were being held, why too many people were attending the meetings, and why the meetings were too long. With clear instructions not to disrupt productivity anymore than necessary, the president agreed to allow the CLO to delve deeper into the cause of the meeting problem by asking some of his staff. Three focus groups, each including eight managers, supervisors, project leaders, and/or employees who participate in meetings on a routine basis, would be conducted to find the cause of the business problems identified by the president.

Focus Groups

Prior to the focus group selection, the president initiated a communiqué explaining that the learning function was in the process of helping him identify the cause of so many meetings in the division. It was also communicated that if a cause was identified, consideration would be given to a variety of solutions. The decision as to which solution would be made based on cost and convenience, as well as potential effectiveness.

Each focus group was scheduled at the plant for a maximum of two hours. Participants were randomly selected from 150 managers, supervisors, and project leaders, along with the employees at large, to participate in the focus group, then randomly assigned to the focus group in which they would participate. In some cases a person identified to participate in the focus group process would have a conflict and could not participate at the designated time. When this occurred, they would swap their time with someone scheduled for a more convenient time slot. In those few cases when a selected participant was unwilling, a new participate was selected.

The focus group was structured, focusing specifically on the cause of each of the business problems identified by the president. Each business problem was written on separate pages on a flip chart. Each focus group participant was given a stack of large Post-it® Notes.

The facilitator explained the purpose of the focus groups, then flipped the page on the flip chart to the first business problem:

- There are too many meetings

Each participant was given approximately two minutes to comment on this issue. Then the facilitator wrote a question on a second flip chart:

- What is happening or not happening on the job that is causing there to be too many meetings?

Focus group participants were asked to write down their observations on the Post-it Notes, one per note. Then the facilitator would asked to post their observation on the flip chart. The facilitator, along with participants, organized the responses into meaningful categories and discussed them to ensure clarity in the meaning of the observations.

The facilitator then wrote another question on the flip chart:

- What knowledge, skills, or information are needed in order to change what is happening or not happening on the job that is causing there to be too many meetings?

Again, the focus group participants wrote their answers on the Post-it Notes and placed them on the flip chart. The responses were again categorized.

A final question was written on the flip chart:

- How best can the knowledge, skills, and information identified be presented so that they will change what is happening or not happening on the job that is causing there to be too many meetings.

Once again, participants provided their responses, and the responses were posted and grouped into meaningful categories. This process of identifying job performance needs, learning needs, and preferences for acquiring knowledge was repeated for each of the other two business needs: 1) too many people attending meetings and 2) meetings are too long.

The facilitator, along with the help of the CLO, reviewed the findings and developed a summary table that was presented to the president along with the proposed solution. Table 1 presents the summary of the focus group results.

Table 1. Summary of Needs Assessment

Level of Need	Needs
Economic Need	**What is the economic opportunity or problem?** Specific dollar amount unknown. Estimate hundreds of thousands in U.S. dollars due to time wasted in meetings.
Business Need	**What are the specific business needs?** • Too many meetings • Too many people attending meetings • Meetings are too long
Job Performance Need	**What is happening or not happening on the job that is causing the business need?** • Meetings are not planned • Agendas for meetings are not developed prior to the meeting • Agendas for meetings are not being followed • Consideration of time and cost of unnecessary meetings is lacking • Poor facilitation of meetings • Follow-up on actions resulting from the meeting is not taking place • Conflict that occurs during meetings is not being appropriately managed • Proper selection of meeting participants is not occurring • Good meeting management practices are not implemented • Consideration of cost of meetings is not taking place
Learning Need	**What knowledge, skill, or information is needed in order to change what is happening or not happening on the job?** • Ability to identify the extent and cost of meetings • Ability to identify positives, negatives, and implications of basic meeting issues and dynamics • Effective meeting behaviors
Preferences	**How best can this knowledge, skill, or information be communicated so that change on the job occurs?** • Facilitator-led workshop • Job aids and tools provided • Relevant and useful information a requirement

Solution

The summary of needs and a proposed two-day workshop were presented to the president. Program objectives suggest that upon completion of the workshop, participants would have:

- The tools and techniques to prepare, conduct, and follow up on meetings
- An understanding of the human dynamics of meetings
- Strategies for participating in or leading meetings more effectively

In addition to these program outputs, participation in the program was expected to lead to shorter meetings, fewer meetings, and a fewer number of participants attending meetings.

Program Design

To meet the identified objectives, the two-day Effective Meeting Skills workshop included a variety of knowledge-based exercises as well as skill-based practices and tasks. Table 2 presents the complete outline for the program.

To assist the transfer of skills to the job, a brief action plan was required so that participants could identify specific new and enhanced behaviors and track their progress as they conduct future meetings. Although an important part of the program, the action plan was used primarily to assist participants in their tracking actual use of knowledge and skills.

Along with the action plan, a meeting profile was designed into the program to capture the current level and cost of meetings. It also provided baseline data for comparing improvements resulting from the program. Table 3 presents the meeting profile.

Target Audience

While the target audience would include all managers, supervisors, and project leaders throughout TechnoTel, the more immediate need was in the Manufacturing Division. The president was interested in conducting the program for 150 of his managers. However, due to the concern about productivity interruption and the president's skeptism toward another training program, he wanted to ensure that the investment was achieving some return. He

Table 2. Outline for the Effective Meetings Program

1. Meeting activity profile completed by participants
2. Definition for an effective meeting
3. Criteria for effective meetings
4. Causes behind ineffective meetings
5. Tips for conducting effective meetings
   a. Determine purpose
   b. Recognize the type of meeting
   c. Arrange seating appropriately
   d. Set the agenda
   e. Assemble a set of all appropriate attendees
   f. Establish ground rules
   g. Bring closure and plan follow-up
6. Skill practices
7. Key roles in meetings
8. Meeting tasks
9. The human function in meetings
10. Debriefing model
11. Brainstorming
12. Decision making
13. Encouraging participation
14. Handling group dynamics
15. Dealing with difficult participants
16. Providing feedback
17. Handling conflict
18. Meeting simulations/exercises
19. Action plan requirements

Table 3. Meeting Profile

Current Meeting Activity (Month Before Program)

• Number of meetings chaired each month	_____	A
• Average number of individuals attending each meeting each month	_____	B
• Average length of time for each meeting (in hours)	_____	C
Total Time Consumed in Meetings (A × B × C)	_____	D
• Average hourly compensation of attendees (salary plus benefits)	_____	E
Total Meeting Costs (D × E)	_____	F

committed to allow three groups of twenty-four participants to be targeted for athe comprehensive evaluation. Understanding that the benefits of the program would be reported for only the seventy-two participants and that the program costs would reflect only the costs of the seventy-two participants, the president saw value in the process and wanted confidence that training was more than an activity. He also made it clear that the value returned should exceed the investment being made in the program.

Evaluation Need

The nature of the business and the president's interest in accountability led the president to request a comprehensive evaluation of the program. Not only was he interested in whether or not the program resulted in reduced meetings and fewer participants, but expressed interested in whether the benefits of his putting his people through the program exceeded the costs.

The president's desire to ensure a positive return on his investment, as well as the corporate learning department's desire to gather data to improve the program overall, led the learning staffs plan of a comprehensive evaluation. Therefore, the learning staff implemented the ROI Methodology in its entirety.

Evaluation Methodology

The ROI Methodology had been integrated into TechnoTel's corporate learning function two years prior to the launch of the Effective Meeting Skills program. TechnoTel has successfully sustained the use of this process because it:

- Reports a balanced set of measures
- Follows a methodical step-by-step process
- Adheres to standards and philosophy of maintaining a conservative approach and credible outcomes

The ROI Methodology categorizes evaluation data into five levels as shown in Table 4. These five levels tell the complete story of program success. The five levels balance economic impact with measures that address individuals' perspectives of the program and success with the transfer of learning.

Table 4. The Evaluation Framework

Level	Measurement Focus
1. Reaction, and Planned Action	Measures participant satisfaction with the program and captures planned action
2. Learning	Measures changes in knowledge, skills, and attitudes
3. Application and Implementation	Measures changes in on-the-job behavior
4. Impact	Measures changes in critical business measures
5. Return-on-Investment (ROI)	Compares the monetary benefits to the costs

Level 1: Reaction and Planned Action

This initial level of evaluation is the most commonly used within the TechnoTel learning environment. Reaction and satisfaction data are collected using a standard end-of-course questionnaire. Planned actions are often collected using action plans, however, a question asking the participants' intent to use what they learned is included on the end-of-course questionnaire and suffices for the planned action measure when action plans are not used.

The TechnoTel learning environment is interested in a variety of measures at Level 1, some of which are relevant only to the learning staff and their efforts to improve the learning process. These measures address course design and delivery as well as participant perception of the learning environment. Because management is interested in potential use of all programs, TechnoTel's Level 1 evaluation also answers five important questions:

1. Is the program relevant to participants' jobs?
2. Is the program important to participants' jobs?
3. Do participants intend to use what they learned in the program?
4. Did the program provide participants with new information?
5. Would participants recommend the programs to others?

An acceptable rating, using a 1 to 5 rating scale (1 = Worst Case; 5 = Best Case), for all TechnoTel courses is 4.0 or above. Any measures that fall below these ratings are flagged and actions are taken to improve them in future courses.

Level 2: Learning

Participant understanding of the knowledge and skills taught in a program is imperative to their ability to change behavior. Learning measurement at TechnoTel takes place during the program through a variety of techniques such as tests, facilitator assessment, peer assessment, self-assessment, observation, and reflective thinking with documentation. The questions that TechnoTel strives to answer when measuring learning are:

1. Do participants understand what they are supposed to do and how to do it?
2. Are participants confident to apply their newly acquired knowledge and skills when they leave the classroom?

Level 3: Application and Implementation

For many programs, TechnoTel's supervisors and managers are interested in what participants do with what they learn. When this is the case, programs are evaluated at Level 3 using a variety of techniques including self-administered questionnaires, 360-degree feedback, observations, focus groups, and interviews. Because there is more to learning transfer than just attending the program or course, it is important to TechnoTel to gather data related to how the organizational system (management, technology, and so forth) supports the transfer of training. With these considerations, three basic questions are answered at Level 3 for some TechnoTel learning initiatives:

1. How much have participants changed their approach, behavior, or performance?
2. If they are applying their knowledge and skills, what is supporting their effort?
3. If they are not applying their knowledge and skills, why not?

Level 4: Impact

For many programs TechnoTel is interested in impact on output, quality, cost, and time-measures. For these programs, the organization may also want to know how programs influence customer satisfaction and employee satisfaction—measures that are critical to organizational success but not monetized but only tracked using corporate metrics. The ultimate question answered at Level 4 is, "So what?" By answering this basic question, stakeholders gain an understanding of the consequences of participant application of newly acquired knowledge and/or skill.

Level 5: ROI

This final measure of success answers the question: "Do the monetary benefits of the program exceed the costs?"

For some programs, the organization is not interested in calculating ROI. But for programs that are costly or high profile, that drive business impact, or that are of particular interest to management, ROI is important. A standard ROI target of 25 percent is set for programs being evaluated to this level. This represents a slightly higher ROI than the ROI being achieved by other investments made by TechnoTel.

The balanced set of measures that is yielded by answering the key questions posed at each level of evaluation provides TechnoTel's corporate learning department a complete story of program success. Through this story, the department not only improves the immediate learning process, but also enhances how the system as a whole works to ensure successful transfer of learning and the achievement of desired outcomes. TechnoTel uses all of this information in combination with the ROI metric to determine if a program is a wise investment—either alone or in comparison to alternative programs that may yield similar outcomes.

Step-By-Step Process

The ten steps in the ROI Methodology constitute a methodical process to evaluation. As shown in Figure 1, the evaluation process begins with identifying program objectives and evaluation planning. From there, execution requires that data be collected and analyzed before developing a final report.

Data Collection Procedures

A pragmatic approach to data collection was taken for the evaluation of the Effective Meeting Skills program. Because the cost of the program (as will be described in a later section) was not excessive, the corporate learning department staff determined that the prudent approach for this particular evaluation would be to keep

Figure 1. The ROI Methodology™

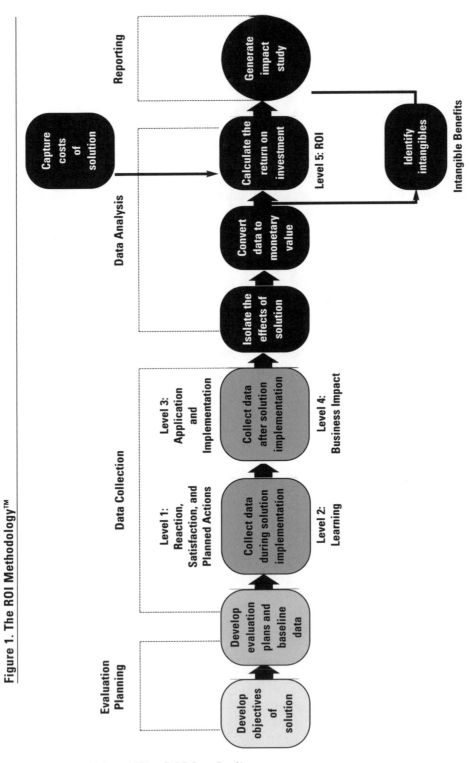

the cost low while ensuring credible results. The data collection process began with a review of the objectives and measures of success, identification of the appropriate data collection methods and the most credible sources of data, and a determination of the timing of data collection.

Program Objectives and Measures

The needs assessment identified the knowledge and skill deficiencies that kept managers from conducting effective meetings. Through the needs assessment process and the design of the Effective Meeting Skills program, specific outputs were defined, as well as specific impact measures that would result if participants applied their newly acquired knowledge and skills. Measures of success at Level 1 are standard (4.0 out of 5.0), as is the measure of success at Level 5 (25 percent); measures of success for the other levels of evaluation were dependent on the program or the client expectations. In this case, the president of the division implementing the workshop was interested in improvement in the impact measures; even though he did not specify what improvement he was looking for, he did indicate by his request that the benefits should exceed the cost of the program. Therefore, the improvement must be such that when converted to monetary value a positive ROI was achieved. Table 5 summarizes the program's objectives and the measures used to determine success.

Data Collection Methods

Data were collected for this evaluation using multiple methods: end-of-course questionnaire, action plans, meeting profile, written test, skills practice observation, and a follow-up questionnaire. The successful meeting profile was designed into the program (see Table 3). It was used at the beginning of the program to capture the current level and costs of meetings. When completed, this exercise showed participants how much time they spent in meetings and the overall cost of meetings. These data served as baseline for comparing improvements identified in the follow-up questionnaire. The written test measured the improvements in knowledge of basic issues and meeting dynamics, and skill practices measured success in using effective meeting skills.

The action plan was an important part of understanding how participants applied what they learned when they returned to the

Table 5. Objectives and Measures of Success for the Effective Meeting Skills Program

	Broad Objectives	Measures
Reaction Objectives	Positive reaction and planned action with the knowledge and skills presented in the course	Ranking of 4 our to 5 on: • Relevance • Importance • Intent to use • New information • Recommendation to others
	Planned action	Three different actions to be taken when returning to the job from each participant
Learning Objectives	Ability to identify the extent and cost of meetings	Given cost guidelines, determine the cost of last three meetings
	Ability to identify positives, negatives, and implications of basic meeting issues and dynamics	From a list of 30 positive and negative meeting behaviors, correctly identify the implications of each behavior
	Acquisition of effective meeting behaviors	Demonstrate appropriate responses to eight of ten active role play scenarios
Application Objectives	Use of effective meeting behaviors	Reported changes in behavior toward planning and conducting meetings
	Barriers to application	Number and variety of barriers identified
	Enablers to application	Number and variety of enablers identified
Impact Objectives	Shorter meetings	Reported time savings
	Fewer meetings	Reported time savings
	Fewer meeting participants	Reported time savings
	Other benefits related to improvement in productivity	Reported times savings, cost savings, output improvement, quality improvement, project turnaround, etc.
ROI	25%	

job; however, the follow-up questionnaire was the primary data collection method for Level 3 and Level 4 follow-up data. Table 6 presents the complete follow-up questionnaire.

Because of their desire to limit the cost of the evaluation, the corporate learning department staff decided on the most feasible methods for data collection. Cost data were developed using company records, and Table 7 summarizes the other data collection methods.

Table 6. Effective Meeting Skills Follow-up Impact Questionnaire

Are you currently in a people management role/capacity? Yes ☐ No ☐

1. Listed below are the objectives of the Effective Meetings program. After reflecting on this program, please indicate the degree of success in meeting the objectives:

As a result of this program, participants will have:	Failed	Limited Success	Generally Successful	Completely Successful
a. The tools and techniques to prepare for, conduct and follow-up on meetings	☐	☐	☐	☐
b. An understanding of the human dynamics of meetings	☐	☐	☐	☐
c. Strategies to participate in, and lead or chair meetings more effectively	☐	☐	☐	☐

2. Did you develop and implement an on-the-job action plan for Effective Meetings?
Yes ☐ No ☐

If yes, please describe the nature and outcome of the plan. If not, explain why.

_____

_____

_____

3. Please rate, on a scale of 1 to 5, the relevance of each of the program elements to your job, with (1) indicating no relevance and (5) indicating very relevant.

	1	2	3	4	5
a. Interactive Activities	☐	☐	☐	☐	☐
b. Groups Discussions	☐	☐	☐	☐	☐
c. Networking Opportunities	☐	☐	☐	☐	☐
d. Reading Materials/Video	☐	☐	☐	☐	☐
e. Program Content	☐	☐	☐	☐	☐

Table 6. *(continued)*

4. Have you used the written materials since you participated in the program?
   Yes ☐   No ☐

   Please explain. _____

   _____

5. Please indicate the degree to which you have changed the use of the following items/
   actions/behaviors enhanced as a result of your participation in **Effective Meetings**:

	No Change	Little Change	Some Change	Significant Change	Very Much Change	No Opportunity To Use Skill
a. Participating Effectively in Meetings	☐	☐	☐	☐	☐	☐
b. Avoiding Meetings Unless They are Necessary	☐	☐	☐	☐	☐	☐
c. Minimizing the Number of Participants Attending Meetings	☐	☐	☐	☐	☐	☐
d. Setting Objectives for Meetings	☐	☐	☐	☐	☐	☐
e. Developing an Agenda for Each Meeting	☐	☐	☐	☐	☐	☐
f. Controlling Time of Meetings	☐	☐	☐	☐	☐	☐
g. Enhancing Participant Satisfaction in Meetings	☐	☐	☐	☐	☐	☐
h. Arranging the Meeting Site for Maximum Effectiveness	☐	☐	☐	☐	☐	☐
i. Scheduling the Optimum Time for Meetings	☐	☐	☐	☐	☐	☐
j. Communicating the Ground Rules for Meetings	☐	☐	☐	☐	☐	☐
k. Assigning Appropriate Roles for Meeting Participants	☐	☐	☐	☐	☐	☐
l. Reaching Consensus in Meetings When Appropriate	☐	☐	☐	☐	☐	☐
m. Listening Actively to Meeting Participants	☐	☐	☐	☐	☐	☐
n. Encouraging Participation in Meetings	☐	☐	☐	☐	☐	☐
o. Using Brainstorming in Meetings When Appropriate	☐	☐	☐	☐	☐	☐
p. Dealing with Difficult Meeting Participants	☐	☐	☐	☐	☐	☐
q. Providing Feedback to Meeting Participants	☐	☐	☐	☐	☐	☐
r. Handling Conflict in Meeting	☐	☐	☐	☐	☐	☐
s. Keeping the Meeting on Focus	☐	☐	☐	☐	☐	☐
t. Accomplishing Meeting Objectives	☐	☐	☐	☐	☐	☐
u. Evaluating the Meeting Process	☐	☐	☐	☐	☐	☐
v. Implementing Action Plans	☐	☐	☐	☐	☐	☐
w. Planning a Follow-up Activity	☐	☐	☐	☐	☐	☐

Table 6. *(continued)*

6. List the five (5) **Effective Meeting** behaviors or skills you have used most frequently as a result of the program.

   _____

   _____

   _____

7. What has changed about your meeting activity profile as a result of this program? (Fewer meetings, fewer participants, shorter meetings, etc.)

   _____

   _____

   _____

8. Please estimate the following monthly time-saving measures. Use the most recent month compared to the month before attending this program. Provide only improvements directly related to this program and only when the time saved is used productively.

   ☐ Number of meetings avoided each month with improved
   planning and analysis   _____

   ☐ Average time saved per meeting per month (in hours)   _____

   ☐ Average number of participants reduced per meeting per month   _____

9. What level of confidence do you place on the above estimations?
   (0 percent = No Confidence, 100 percent = Certainty)

   _____ percent

10. Please identify any specific accomplishments/improvements that you can link to this program (on time schedules, project completion, response times, better decisions, more ideas from group, etc.)

    _____

    _____

    _____

11. What specific value in U.S. dollars can be attributed to the above accomplishments/improvements? Use first-year values only. While this is a difficult question, try to think of specific ways in which the above improvements can be converted to monetary units. Along with the monetary value, please indicate the basis of your calculation.

    $ _____

    Basis _____

    _____

12. What level of confidence do you place on the above estimations?
    (0 percent = No Confidence, 100 percent = Certainty)

    _____ percent

13. Other factors often influence improvements in performance. Please indicate the percent of
    the above improvement that is related directly to this program.

    _____ percent

    Please explain. _____

    _____

14. Do you think the **Effective Meetings** program represented a good investment for
    TechnoTel?

    Yes ☐ No ☐

    Please explain. _____

    _____

    Was it a good investment of your time?

    Yes ☐ No ☐

    Please explain. _____

    _____

15. Indicate the extent to which you think the **Effective Meetings** program has influenced
    each of these measures in your work unit, department, or business unit:

	No Influence	Some Influence	Moderate Influence	Significant Influence	Very Much Influence
a. Productivity	☐	☐	☐	☐	☐
b. Customer Response Time	☐	☐	☐	☐	☐
c. Cost Control	☐	☐	☐	☐	☐
d. Employee Satisfaction	☐	☐	☐	☐	☐
e. Customer Satisfaction	☐	☐	☐	☐	☐
f. Quality	☐	☐	☐	☐	☐
g. Other _____	☐	☐	☐	☐	☐

16. What barriers, if any, have you encountered that have prevented you from using skills or knowledge gained in this program. Please explain, if possible.

_____

_____

17. What enablers, if any, are present to help you use the skills or knowledge gained from this program? Please explain.

_____

_____

18. What additional benefits have been derived from this program?

_____

_____

19. What specific suggestions do you have for improving this program?

_____

_____

20. Other Comments:

_____

_____

Table 7. Data Collection Methods

	Level 1	Level 2	Level 3	Barriers/ Enablers	Level 4	Costs
End-of-Course Questionnaire	X					
Meeting Profile		X				
Written Test		X				
Skill Practice Observation		X				
Action Plan	X		X			
Questionnaire			X	X	X	
Company Records						X

Data Sources

Data source selection is a critical step in data collection in that the source drives the credibility and validity of the study. Who knows best about the measures being taken? The primary source of data for the effective meeting skills evaluation was the participants. The managers and project leaders participating in the workshop know the extent to which they apply their knowledge and skills; they are the people who plan and lead the meetings; they are the people who recognize the cost of too many unproductive meetings (they are the ones calling the meetings). Although it may have been valuable to administer surveys to the professional staff participating in the meetings, this step would have added additional cost to the data collection process. The information they would have provided would have been valuable, but the perceived value of their input did not appear to outweigh the time and cost involved in collecting and analyzing the additional data. It was decided that the participants would serve as the source of data for this evaluation.

While the program was implemented to all 150 managers and supervisors, the president agreed to allow 72 people (three groups) to participate initially in the evaluation. This limitation would save cost and time of evaluation and would provide the president the data he needed to make a fair assessment of the success of the program.

Data Collection Timing

When conducting a comprehensive evaluation such as that completed for the Effective Meeting Skills workshop, data is collected at two different timeframes: Levels 1 and 2 data are collected during the program, and Levels 3 and 4 data are collected after participants have had time to apply knowledge and skills on a routine basis. It was determined that, given the type of skills being developed in the Effective Meeting Skills program and the numerous opportunities managers have to apply the skills, three months would be ample time for the acquired skills to be internalized and produce results. Therefore, three months after completing the program, participants would receive the follow-up questionnaire.

Table 8 presents the complete data collection plan. The corporate learning staff presented the data collection plan and the ROI analysis plan (described in the next section) to the division president for concurrence prior to execution.

Table 8. Data Collection Plan.

Evaluation Purpose: _____

Program: Effective Meetings   **Responsibility:** _____   **Date:** _____

Level	Broad Program Objective(s)	Measures	Data Collection Method/Instruments	Data Sources	Timing	Responsibilities
1	REACTION/SATISFACTION & PLANNED ACTIONS • Positive Reaction • Planned Actions	• Average rating of at least 4.0 on 5.0 scale on quality, usefulness and achievement of program objectives. • 100% submit planned actions	• End of Course Questionnaire • Completed Action Plans	Participants	• End of Course	Facilitator
2	LEARNING • Identify the extent and cost of meetings • Identify positives, negatives and implications of basic meeting issues and dynamics • Acquisition of Effective Meeting Behaviors	• Given cost guidelines, identify the cost of last three meetings • From a list of 30 positive and negative meeting behaviors, correctly identify the implications of each behavior • Demonstrate appropriate response to 8 of 10 active role play scenarios	• Meeting Profile • Written Test • Skill Practice Observation	Participants	• At the Beginning of Program • At the Beginning of the Program (Pre) • At the End of the Program (Post) • During Program	Facilitator
3	APPLICATION/ IMPLEMENTATION • Use of Effective Meeting behaviors • Examine the need for a meeting and scrutinize the list of participants invited	• Reported actions to influence more effective meetings • Reported use of effective meeting planning and meeting conduct behaviors	• Action Plan • Questionnaire (For 3 Groups)	Participants	3 Months	Program Owner
4	BUSINESS IMPACT • Time savings from fewer meetings, shorter meetings, and fewer participants (Hours Savings Per Month) • Variety of Business Impact Measures from more successful meetings	• Time savings • Time savings, cost savings, output improvement, quality improvement, project turn-around, etc. as reported	• Questionnaire (For 3 Groups)	Participants	3 Months	Program Owner
5	ROI Target ROI at least 25 percent		Comments: _____			

Success with Data Collection

A data collection administration strategy is important for ensuring that the appropriate amount of data is provided. In the case of the Effective Meeting Skills workshop, the administrative strategy consisted of four primary actions:

1. The evaluation strategy was presented at the beginning of the program.
2. The facilitators reinforced the need for participants to respond to the follow-up questionnaire at the end of the program.
3. The division president signed a letter that was distributed three days prior to the questionnaires being mailed.
4. The questionnaire did not require that participants include their name or other demographic information; therefore, respondents remained anonymous.

All participants responded to the Level 1 and 2 evaluations; the follow-up for Levels 3 and 4 proved to be challenging, however. The overall response rate was 67 percent (48 respondents), which was satisfactory to the evaluation team and the division president. Unfortunately, only forty-three percent (31 respondents) of the participants provided useable data on Questions 8 and 9 (see Table 6). These two questions were directly related to follow-up on the impact measures. With the understanding that the results would reflect only that which occurred for those responding, the division president was satisfied with the response rate.

Data Analysis Procedures

Data analysis comprises five key steps, each of which was carefully considered during the evaluation of this workshop:

1. Isolating the effects of the program
2. Converting data to monetary value
3. Tabulating fully loaded costs
4. Identifying intangible benefits
5. Comparing the monetary benefits to the costs

Isolating the Effects of the Program

This step of the ROI Methodology answers the question, "How do you know it was your program that influenced the measures?"

Isolating the effects of the program considers all other variables that may have influenced improvement in specific measures of success for a program. Four of the ten potential techniques were considered for the Effective Meeting Skills workshop: control group, trend-line analysis, forecasting, and participant estimations.

Because only 72 of the 150 were being evaluated, it was first suggested that a control group arrangement could be used to isolate the effects of the program. The thought was that those managers and supervisors not participating in the evaluation process could serve as the control group. After much deliberation, however, it was agreed that it would be difficult to maintain the integrity of the experiment and it would be disruptive.

Participants completed a meeting profile during the program to determine the time, frequency, and participation of meetings, along with the costs. To collect similar data from the control group, its members would have to complete meeting profiles as well. This would not only contribute the contamination of the experiment, but would require additional work for the control group members. It was important to the division president to keep the evaluation low key by not requiring too much additional work and by not disrupting the organization. For these reasons, the control group arrangement was eliminated as an option.

Historical data were not available for the primary measure (time savings), so trend-line analysis and forecasting were inappropriate as well. The only remaining option was the use of participant estimations for isolating the effects of the workshop on the three impact measures: shorter meetings, reduced number of meetings, and fewer participants attending meetings.

Converting Data to Monetary Value

When moving from Level 4 to Level 5 evaluation, this step is the most critical because it determines the numerator (top number) in the ROI equation. Ten techniques to convert data to monetary value are possible. For this evaluation, however, the technique was apparent. As the outcome measures were all time related, the standard value of hourly compensation (salary plus benefits) for the participant chairing the meeting as well as those attending the meeting was used. If other business meausres improved due to the programs, they would be converted to money using particpant estimates unless standard values were available.

Tabulating Fully Loaded Costs

To calculate ROI, it is imperative to use the fully loaded costs of the program. Costs categories for the Effective Meeting Skills workshop were:

- Needs assessment (facilitator time, participant time, materials, refreshments)
- Program fee (facilitator costs, materials, program design, and development)
- Travel, lodging, meals
- Facilities
- Participants' salaries and benefits for their time in the classroom
- Evaluation costs

Identifying Intangible Benefits

Intangible benefits are any unplanned benefits derived from the program or any benefits not converted to monetary value. There were many intangible benefits of the Effective Meeting Skills workshop, which will be listed in the Eavluation Results section that follows.

Calculating ROI

The ROI equation compares net benefits (earnings) to the program costs (investment). It can be reported as a BCR by comparing the benefits to the program costs. ROI is well-used within the TechnoTel organization. Managers and professionals recognize the acronym for what it is; therefore, to ensure that the corporate learning department speaks the same language as the business, the following equation is used to report ROI:

$$BCR = \frac{Benefits}{Costs}$$

$$ROI = \frac{Net\ Program\ Benefits}{Costs} \times 100$$

A 25 percent ROI target is standard for most programs being evaluated at this level. Because of the nature of the program, the evaluation team and the division president believed this to be a conservative target.

Table 9 presents the completed ROI analysis plan. As in the case of the data collection plan, the ROI analysis plan was presented to the division president prior to implementing the evaluation. The division president concurred with the plan.

The ROI Methodology used for evaluating the Effective Meeting Skills program adhered to a set of operating standards or guiding principles, as presented in Table 10. These Twelve Guiding Principles keep the process consistent and conservative.

Table 10. Twelve Guiding Principles of ROI

1. When conducting a higher-level evaluation, collect data at lower levels.
2. When planning a higher level evaluation, the previous level of evaluation is not required to be comprehensive.
3. When collecting and analyzing data, use only the most credible sources.
4. When analyzing data, select the most conservative alternatives for calculations.
5. Use at least one method to isolate the effects of the program or project.
6. If no improvement data are available for a population or from a specific source, assume that little or no improvement has occurred.
7. Adjust estimates of improvements for the potential error of the estimates.
8. Avoid use of extreme data items and unsupported claims when calculating ROI calculations.
9. Use only the first year of annual benefits in the ROI analysis of short-term solutions.
10. Fully load all costs of the solution, project, or program when analyzing ROI.
I11. Intangible measures are defined as measures that are purposely not converted to monetary values.
12. Communicate the results of the ROI Methodology to all key stakeholders.

Evaluation Results

The results of the study indicated that the program was successful. Participants enjoyed the workshop, but, even more important, they saw it as relevant and useful. Participants quickly grasped the ability to define meeting costs and began implementing the new

Table 9. ROI Analysis Plan.

Program: ___Effective Meetings___   Responsibility: _____   Date: _____

Data Items (Usually Level 4)	Methods for Isolating the Effects of the Program/Process	Methods of Converting Data to Monetary Values	Cost Categories	Intangible Benefits	Communication Targets for Final Report	Other Influences/Issues During Application	Comments
• Time Savings	• Participant's Estimate	• Hourly Wage and Benefits	• Needs Assessment • Program Fee Per Participant	• Improvement in individual productivity not captured elsewhere	• Business Unit President	• Participants must see need for providing measurement	• Participants will identify specific improvements as a result of meetings being conducted more effectively
• Miscellaneous Business Measures	• Participant's Estimate	• Participant's Estimate - (using standard values when available)	• Travel / Lodging Meals • Facilities	• Stress reduction • Improved planning and scheduling	• Senior Managers • Managers of Participants	• Follow-up process will be explained to participants during program	
			• Participant Salaries Plus Benefits • Evaluation Costs	• Greater participation in meetings	• Participants • Training and Development Staff	• Three groups will be measured	

knowledge and skills. Although there were some barriers to application, they were minimal. From the perspective of the division president, however, the impact on time spent in meetings was significant; the investment returned positive results.

Level 1: Reaction and Planned Action

Level 1 objectives included reaction measures important to improving facilitation, content, and materials. The key measures of interest, however, addressed issues indicating intent to use, including three defined actions to be taken upon return to the job. The measure of success was a minimum score of 4.0 out of 5.0. Results were successful in regard to relevance, importance, intent to use, and willingness to recommend the workshop to others. Only one measure (new information) fell below the 4.0 target. This was anticipated, in that most of the concepts were familiar, but the packaging and tools provided a new perspective on the familiar topics.

The participants listed three defined actions they planned to take when returning to the job. The most noted action was implementing the meeting activity profile as a routine tool when reflecting on meetings each month. Also, participants indicated they would follow the seven steps to conducting an effective meeting as listed in the program outline (see Table 2).

Level 2: Learning

Level 2 objectives suggested that participants should be able to:

- Identify the extent and cost of meetings
- Identify positives, negatives, and implications of basic meeting issues and dynamics
- Acquire effective meeting behaviors.

The meeting profile identifying costs of meetings was successfully completed by participants. They felt comfortable with the tool and indicated the ability to complete similar items during the follow-up. A simple multiple-choice test was administered to ensure that participants understood the basic issue of meetings. The average score the test was a 92 out of a possible 100.

Exercises and skill practice indicated that participants were equipped with the knowledge and skills to successfully conduct meetings while reducing the cost of meetings by conducting shorter meetings, fewer meetings, and including fewer meeting participants.

Level 3: Application and Implementation

The follow-up evaluation (see Table 6) took place three months after the workshop. Questions 4, 5, 6, 16, and 17 related to application of knowledge and skills. The fundamental question with regard to application was Question 5, which assessed how much participants had changed their approach to planning and conducting meetings using the knowledge and skills they learned from the workshop. Table 11 summarizes the degree of change in behavior that occurred. For the most part, participants did change their meeting practices; some measures, however, indicated that little change occurred in some areas. Providing feedback to meeting participants (item Q), evaluating the meeting process (item U), and planning follow-up activity (item W), and planning follow-up activity appeared to be the least used skills.

Examining the barriers (Question 16) to the use of the knowledge and skills learned in the workshop shed some light on the reasons why there was less change in some areas than in others. The most often cited barrier was time. Some participants indicated they did no have the time to evaluate the success of the meeting or follow-up with meeting participants; however, others indicated that both of these actions were a valuable part of the meeting process.

Enabling factors (Question 17) supported the use of meeting skills learned in the workshop. The most often cited enabling factors were the job aids and materials participants took with them from the course. The workbook was cited as being the most valuable tool. Some participants indicated that senior management's interest in the tools and the workshop encouraged them to take the application of what they learned seriously.

Level 4: Impact

The intended outcomes of the Effective Meeting Skills workshop were shorter meetings, fewer meetings, and fewer meeting participants. Other measures of improvement were of interest, but the president was specifically interested in the payoff of the program with respect to these measures. By applying the knowledge and skills learned in the workshop, improvement in these three time-related

Table 11. Level 3 Evaluation Responses

	No Change	Little Change	Some Change	Significant Change	Very Much Change	No Opportunity To Use Skill
A. Participating Effectively in Meetings	0	0	25%	44%	31%	0
B. Avoiding Meetings Unless they are Necessary	0	0	19%	46%	35%	0
C. Minimizing the Number of Participants Attending Meetings	0	0	19%	50%	31%	0
D. Setting Objectives for Meetings	0	0	25%	42%	33%	0
E. Developing an Agenda for Each Meeting	0	4%	27%	44%	25%	0
F. Controlling Time of Meetings	0	0	6%	44%	50%	0
G. Enhancing Participant Satisfaction in Meetings	0	10%	31%	44%	15%	0
H. Arranging the Meeting Site for Maximum Effectiveness	0	0	4%	65%	31%	0
I. Scheduling the Optimum Time for Meetings	0	0	25%	42%	33%	0
J. Communicating the Ground Rules for Meetings	0	4%	27%	44%	25%	0
K. Assigning Appropriate Roles for Meeting Participants	0	0	6%	44%	50%	0
L. Reaching Consensus in Meetings When Appropriate	0	0	13%	52%	35%	0
M. Listening Actively to Meeting Participants	0	0	4%	65%	31%	0
N. Encouraging Participation in Meetings	0	0	25%	42%	33%	0
O. Using Brainstorming in Meetings When Appropriate	0	4%	27%	44%	25%	0
P. Dealing with Difficult Meeting Participants	0	0	6%	44%	50%	0
Q. Providing Feedback to Meeting Participants	0	19%	56%	25%	0	0
R. Handling Conflict in Meeting	0	4%	31%	50%	15%	0
S. Keeping the Meeting on Focus	0	0	25%	42%	33%	0
T. Accomplishing Meeting Objectives	0	4%	27%	44%	25%	0
U. Evaluating the Meeting Process	0	10%	38%	38%	15%	0
V. Implementing Action Plans	0	2%	33%	46%	19%	0
W. Planning a Follow-up Activity	0	6%	42%	35%	17%	0

measures occurred. Table 12 presents a comparison of the original meeting profile data obtained from participants during the program to the average post-program data. The average amounts taken from Question 8 are subtracted from the average pre-program data to get the average post-program data. Only 31 participants (43 percent) responded to Questions 8 and 9; the average confidence in the estimates for the group responding was 81 percent. The figure shows that the intended outcomes (reduction in the number of meetings, less time spent in meetings, and fewer participants attending meetings) were achieved as a result of the program.

Table 12. Improvement in Time Spent on Meetings

Current Meeting Activity (Month Before Program)		Average Pre-Program Data	Average Post-Program Data
Number of meetings chaired each month	A	6.5	5.2
Average number of individuals attending each meeting each month	B	7.2	5.1
Average length of time for each meeting (in hours)	C	2.6	1.7
Total Time Consumed in Meetings (A × B × C)	D	121.68	45.1

Averaged Responses to Question 8 (Follow-up Questionnaire)	
Meetings Avoided	
Estimate of number of meetings avoided each month	1.3
Shorter Meetings	
Estimate of average time saved per meeting (in hours)	0.9
Reduced Number of Participants in Meetings	
Estimate of number of participants reduced for each meeting	2.1

Number completing programs	72 (three groups)
Number of questionnaires returned	48 (67 percent)
Number of questionnaires with usable data for questions 8 and 9	31 (43 percent)
Average value of confidence level from Question 9	81 percent

Other measures improved as a result of the program as well. Respondents indicated improvement in overall productivity and quality of the meetings, and six managers placed monetary values on these measures. However, the monetary payoff of the program is based on the time savings from the above measures. The other measures were reported as "other benefits" because they were not as credible as the time savings.

Level 5: ROI

The ROI for the Effective Meeting Skills workshop was calculated based on time savings. To calculate the ROI, improvement in time savings due to shorter meetings, fewer meetings, and fewer meeting participants were converted to monetary value and then compared to the costs of the program.

Monetary Benefits

The data conversion technique used was a standard value of time, which equates to average hourly compensation of attendees plus the benefits factor of 32 percent. The average hourly cost of an attendee was calculated to be $31. As shown in Table 13, an average monthly savings in meeting costs based on the three measures was $2,373.98.

Table 13. Monetary Benefits of Time Savings

Current Meeting Activity (Month Before Program)		Average Pre-Program Data	Average Post-Program Data	
Number of meetings chaired each month	A	6.5	5.2	
Average number of individuals attending each meeting each month	B	7.2	5.1	
Average length of time for each meeting (in hours)	C	2.6	1.7	
Total Time Consumed in Meetings (A × B × C)	D	121.68	45.1	
Average hourly compensation of attendees (salary plus benefits)	E	$31.00	$31.00	
Total Meeting Costs (D × E)	F	$3,772.08	$1,398.10	
Meetings Avoided				
Estimate of number of meetings avoided each month			1.3	G
Shorter Meetings				
Estimate of average time saved per meeting (in hours)			0.9	H
Reduced Participants in Meetings				
Estimate of number of participants reduced for each meeting			2.1	I
Total Savings				
Monthly Meeting Savings (Pre – Post Costs)			$2,373.98	J
Annual Savings (J × 12)			$28,487.76	K

This amount represents the difference in pre-program costs ($3,772.08) and post-program costs ($1,398.10). The ROI is an annual value, and the division president wanted to see a payoff within one year. The savings were annualized using this monthly average, yielding a monetary benefit of $28,487.76 for one participant.

To calculate the full benefits of the program, the monthly value was multiplied by the number of participants who provided useable data (31); the error adjustment was also considered (81 percent). The full value of the Effective Meeting Skills workshop was:

$$(\$28,487.76 \times 31) \times 0.81 = \$715,327.65$$

Fully Loaded Costs

Program costs included the program fee, which incorporated materials and facilitator costs; travel, lodging, and meals for participants; facilities; participants' time in the workshop (salaries and benefits); and evaluation costs. The needs assessment of $5,000 was also included. However, since the program was intended to go out to the entire 150 managers and supervisors, these costs were prorated over the number of people attending the program, and calculated only for the 72 in the evaluation. Even though the benefits were calculated only for those responding, program costs accounted for all participant costs. The fully loaded costs of the Effective Meeting Skills workshop are shown in Table 14.

Table 14. Costs Used in the ROI Calculation for the Effective Meeting Skills Workshop

Item	Calculation	Cost
Needs Assessment	$5,000 prorated over 150 participants	$2,400
Program Fee	$800 per participant × 72	$57,600
Travel, Lodging, Meals	$245 × 72	$17,640
Facilities	$190 × 6*	$1,140
Participant Time	$219 per day × 1.32 × 2 × 72**	$41,628
Evaluation Costs		$5,000
	Total Costs	**$125,408**

*Facilities cost $190 per day; the workshop required two days and was offered to three groups.
**Participant time includes average salaries of $219 per day multiplied by the benefits factor of 32 percent. Each participant was in the workshop for two days; the cost accounts for all 72 participants.

The return on investing in the Effective Meeting Skills workshop was 470 percent, as shown by the calculation below.

$$BCR = \frac{\$715,327.65}{\$125,408} = 5.7:1$$

$$ROI = \frac{\$715,327.65 - \$125,408}{\$125,408} \times 100 = 470\%$$

The ROI told the division president that for every dollar spent on the workshop, TechnoTel received $4.70 after costs. On the surface, the ROI seemed high in comparison to other investments. But because the division president knew the value of time and knew how much time had been wasted in meetings in the past, the ROI calculation was believable. The evaluation team had been diligent in advising the division president of the evaluation process and keeping him abreast of the findings, thereby enhancing the credibility of the ROI process.

Intangible Benefits
The financial impact to TechnoTel was an important outcome of the evaluation. However, other important outcomes occurred as well. Along with improvement in overall productivity and quality of meetings, employees and their supervisors in TechnoTel were becoming happier in the work setting due to the reduction in wasteful meetings. The groups who had attended the Effective Meeting Skills workshop took the process seriously and had a keen desire to improve their meeting process; therefore, tools were being implemented. This also helped improve customer satisfaction—both external and internal customers. Respondents to the evaluation reported being more accessible and more focused on customer concerns.

An interesting unexpected benefit of the program was that the division president began using the meeting profile worksheet as a tool to manage the cost of his own meetings. He asked that his senior leaders do the same. The tool has become a time management tool throughout this division of TechnoTel.

Communication Strategy

The success of the ROI study at TechnoTel can be attributed to the continuous communication throughout the process. From the outset, the division president was kept informed of the progress with the study. He was involved in the planning stage and data collection. As results at Levels 3 and 4 began rolling in, the evaluation team kept him informed. Once the study was completed and the division president was aware of the results, the senior management team participated in a one-hour briefing. Because there were several new senior managers who were unfamiliar with the evaluation practice at TechnoTel, a full presentation was conducted. The presentation topics included:

- Need for effective meetings
- Program design
- Need for evaluation
- Evaluation methodology
- Evaluation results

At the end of the presentation, each person received a copy of the complete report, as well as a summary copy.

Based on the questions and the response to the presentation, the senior management saw the evaluation process as credible. Even more important, they saw the value of the Effective Meeting Skills workshop and asked that the program be implemented in other areas of TechnoTel.

Lessons Learned

Regardless of the number of evaluation studies conducted, there are always lessons to learn. Because the evaluation team thought there was an understanding of the evaluation process, they did not spend time explaining Questions 8 and 9. Had they done a better job covering those questions on the questionnaire, they might have achieved a greater response rate.

Because evaluation is routine at TechnoTel, the questionnaire administration strategy seemed appropriate. However, with only a 67 percent response rate, there was room for improvement.

Questions For Discussion

1. Was the president justified in asking for a comprehensive evaluation of an effective meetings skills workshop?
2. How could the needs assessment have been improved?
3. What steps could have been taken to ensure a higher response rate, especially for Questions 7, 8, and 9 on the questionnaire?
4. How credible are the time savings data?
5. How would you have approached the evaluation strategy for the Effective Meeting Skills workshop?

CHAPTER 13

Measuring ROI in Business Coaching

Nations Hotel

The learning and development team at the Nations Hotel Corporation was challenged to identify learning needs to help executives find ways to improve efficiency, customer satisfaction, and revenue growth in the company. A key component of the program was the development of a formal, structured coaching program, Coaching for Business Impact. The corporate executives were interested in seeing the actual ROI for the coaching project. This case study provides critical insights into how coaching creates value in an organization including ROI.

Background

Nations Hotel Corporation (NHC) is a large U.S.-based hotel firm with operations in 15 countries. The firm has maintained steady growth to include more than 300 hotels in cities all over the world. NHC enjoys one of the most recognized names in the global lodging industry, with 98 percent brand awareness worldwide and 72 percent overall guest satisfaction.

The hospitality industry is competitive, cyclical, and subject to swings with the economy. Room rentals are price sensitive, and customer satisfaction is extremely important for NHC. Profits are squeezed if operating costs get out of hand. NHC top executives constantly seek ways to improve operational efficiency, customer satisfaction, revenue growth, and retention of high-performing employees. Executives—particularly those in charge of individual properties—are under constant pressure to show improvement in these key measures.

The learning and development function, the Nations Hotel Learning Organization (NHLO), conducted a brief survey of executives to identify learning needs to help them meet some of their particular goals. NHLO was interested in developing customized learning processes including, the possibility of individual coaching sessions. Most of the executives surveyed indicated that they would like to work with a qualified coach to assist them through a variety of challenges and issues. The executives believed that this would be an efficient way to learn, apply, and achieve results. Consequently, NHLO developed a formal, structured coaching program—Coaching for Business Impact (CBI)—and offered it to the executives at the vice president level and above.

As the project was conceived, the senior executive team became interested in showing the value of the coaching project. Although they supported coaching as a method to improve executive performance, they wanted to see the actual ROI. The goal was to evaluate 25 executives, randomly selected (if possible) from the participants in CBI.

The Program

Figure 1 shows the steps in the new coaching program from the beginning to the ultimate outcomes. This program involves 14 discrete elements and processes.

1. *Voluntary participation:* Executives had to volunteer to be part of this project. Voluntary commitment translates into a willing participant who is not only open to changing, improving, and applying what is being learned, but also is also willing to provide the necessary data for evaluating the coaching process. The voluntary nature of the coaching program, however, meant that not all executives who needed coaching would be involved. When compared to mandatory involvement, however, the volunteer effort appeared to be an important ingredient for success. It was envisioned that, as improvements were

Figure 1. Coaching for Business Impact Steps.

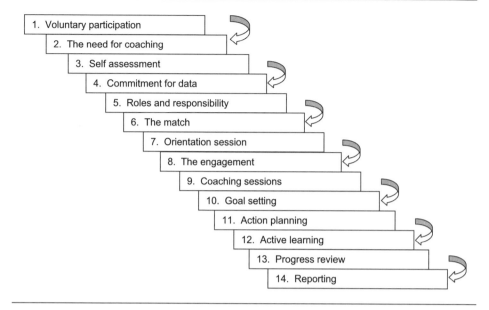

1. Voluntary participation
2. The need for coaching
3. Self assessment
4. Commitment for data
5. Roles and responsibility
6. The match
7. Orientation session
8. The engagement
9. Coaching sessions
10. Goal setting
11. Action planning
12. Active learning
13. Progress review
14. Reporting

realized and executives reflected on the positive perceptions of coaching, other executives would follow suit.

2. *The need for coaching:* An important part of the process was a dialog with the executive to determine if coaching was actually needed. In this step, NHLO staff used a checklist to review the issues, needs, and concerns about the coaching agreement. Along with establishing a need, the checklist revealed key areas where coaching could help. This step ensured that the assistance desired by the executive could actually be provided by the coach.

3. *Self-assessment:* As part of the process, a self-assessment was taken from the individual being coached, his or her immediate manager, and direct reports. This was a typical 360-degree assessment instrument that focused on areas of feedback, communication, openness, trust, and other competencies necessary for success in the competitive hospitality environment.

4. *Commitment for data:* As a precondition, executives had to agree to provide data during coaching and at appropriate times following the engagement. This up-front commitment ensured that data of sufficient quality and quantity could be obtained.

The data made evaluation easier and helped executives see their progress and realize the value of coaching.

5. *Roles and responsibility:* For both the coach and the executive, roles and responsibilities were clearly defined. It was important for the executive to understand that the coach was there to listen, provide feedback, and evaluate. The coach was not there to make decisions for the executive. This clear distinction was important for productive coaching sessions.

6. *The match:* Coaches were provided from a reputable business coaching firm where NHLO had developed a productive relationship. Coach profiles were presented to executives and a tentative selection was made on a priority listing. The respective coach was provided background information on the executive and a match was made. After this match, the coaching process began.

7. *Orientation session:* The executive and coach formally met during an orientation session. Here, the NHLO staff explained the process, requirements, timetable, and other administrative issues. This was a brief session typically conducted in a group; however, it could also be conducted individually.

8. *The engagement:* One of the most important aspects of the process involved making sure that the engagement was connected to a business need. Typical coaching engagements focused on behavioral issues (e.g., an executive's inability to listen to employees). To connect to the business impact, the behavior change must link to a business consequence. In the initial engagement, the coach uncovered the business need by asking a series of questions to examine the consequences of behavior change. This process involved asking "so what?" and "what if?" as the desired behavior changes were described. As the business needs were identified, the measures must be in the categories of productivity, sales, efficiency, direct cost savings, employee retention, and customer satisfaction. The engagement should be connected to corresponding changes in at least three of those measures. Without elevating the engagement to a business need, it would have been difficult to evaluate coaching with this level of analysis.

9. *Coaching sessions:* Individual sessions were conducted at least once a month (usually more often) lasting a minimum of 1 hour (sometimes more), depending on the need and issues at hand. The coach and executive met face to face, if possible. If not, coaching was conducted in a telephone conversation. Routine meetings were necessary to keep the process on track.

10. *Goal setting:* Although individuals could set goals in any area needing improvements, the senior executives chose five priority areas for targeting: sales growth, productivity/operational efficiency, direct cost reduction, retention of key staff members, and customer satisfaction. The executives selected one measure in at least three of these areas. Essentially, they would have three specific goals that would require three action plans, described next.

11. *Action planning:* To drive the desired improvement, the action planning process was utilized. Common in coaching engagements, this process provided an opportunity for the executive to detail specific action steps planned with the team. These steps were designed to drive a particular consequence that was a business impact measure. Figure 2 shows a typical action planning document used in this process. The executive was to complete the action plan during the first two to three coaching sessions, detailing step-by-step what he or she would accomplish to drive a particular improvement. Under the analysis section, Part A, B, and C are completed in the initial development of the plan. The coaches distributed action plan packages that included instructions, blank forms, and completed examples. The coach explained the process in the second coaching session. The action plans could be revised as needed. At least three improvement measures were required out of the five areas targeted with the program. Consequently, at least three action plans had to be developed and implemented.

12. *Active learning:* After the executive developed the specific measures in question and the action plans, several development strategies were discussed and implemented with the help of the coach. The coach actually facilitated the efforts, utilizing any number of typical learning processes, such as reading assignments, self-assessment tools, skill practices, video feedback, journaling, and other techniques. Coaching is

Figure 2. Action Plan Form

Name: _____ Coach _____ Date _____

Impact Objective: _____

Improvement
Measure: _____

Evaluation Period: _____ to _____

Current
Performance: _____

Target
Performance: _____

Action Steps.

1. _____
2. _____
3. _____
4. _____
5. _____
6. _____
7. _____
8. _____

Analysis

A. What is the unit of measure? _____

B. What is the value (cost) of one unit? $ _____

C. How did you arrive at this value?
_____
_____
_____

D. How much did the measure change during the evaluation period? (monthly value)
_____

E. What other factors could have contributed to this improvement?
_____

F. What percent of this change was actually caused by this program? _____ percent

G. What level of confidence do you place on the above information? (100 percent = Certainty and 0 percent = No Confidence) _____ percent

Intangible Benefits: _____

Comments: _____

considered to be an active learning process where the executive experiments, applies, and reflects on the experience. The coach provides input, reaction, assessment, and evaluation.

13. *Progress review:* At monthly sessions, the coach and executive reviewed progress and revised the action plan, if necessary. The important issue was to continue to make adjustments to sustain the process.

14. *Reporting:* After six months in the coaching engagement, the executive reported improvement by completing other parts of the action plan. This includes Part D, E, F, and G and intangible benefits and comments. If the development efforts were quite involved and the measures driven were unlikely to change in the interim, a longer period of time was utilized. For most executives, six months was appropriate.

These elements reflected a results-based project appropriate called "Coaching for Business Impact."

Objectives

An effective ROI study flows from the objectives of the particular project being evaluated. For coaching, it is important to clearly indicate the objectives at different levels. Figure 3 shows the detailed objectives associated with this project. The objectives reflect the four classic levels of evaluation plus a fifth level for ROI. Some of the levels, however, have been adjusted for the coaching environment. With these objectives in mind, it becomes a relatively easy task to measure progress on these objectives.

Planning for Evaluation

Figure 4 shows the completed data collection plan for this project. The plan captures the following techniques and strategies used to collect data for this project:

1. *Objectives:* The objectives are listed as defined in Figure 13-3 and are repeated only in general terms.

2. *Measures:* Additional definition is sometimes needed beyond the specific objectives. The measures used to gauge progress on the objective are defined.

3. *Methods:* This column indicates the specific method used for

Figure 3. Objectives of Business Impact Coaching

Level 1. Reaction Objectives

After participating in this coaching program, the executive will:

1. Perceive coaching to be relevant to the job
2. Perceive coaching to be important to job performance at the present time
3. Perceive coaching to be value added in terms of time and funds invested
4. Rate the coach as effective
5. Recommend this program to other executives

Level 2. Learning Objectives

After completing this coaching program, the executives should improve their understanding of or skills for each of the following:

1. Uncovering individual strengths and weaknesses
2. Translating feedback into action plans
3. Involving team members in projects and goals
4. Communicating effectively
5. Collaborating with colleagues
6. Improving personal effectiveness
7. Enhancing leadership skills

Level 3. Application Objectives

Six months after completing this coaching program, executives should:

1. Complete the action plan
2. Adjust the plan accordingly as needed for changes in the environment

Level 3. Application Objectives (continued)

3. Show improvements on the following items:
   a. uncovering individual strengths and weaknesses
   b. translating feedback into action plans
   c. involving team members in projects and goals
   d. communicating effectively
   e. collaborating with colleagues
   f. improving personal effectiveness
   g. enhancing leadership skills.
4. Identify barriers and enablers

Level 4. Impact Objectives

After completing this coaching program, executives should improve at least three specific measures in the following areas:

1. Sales growth
2. Productivity/operational efficiency
3. Direct cost reduction
4. Retention of key staff members
5. Customer satisfaction

Level 5. ROI Objective

The ROI value should be 25 percent.

Figure 4. Completed Data Collection Plan

Program: ___Coaching for Business Impact___   Responsibility: _____   Date: _____

Level	Objective(s)	Measures/Data	Data Collection Method	Data Sources	Timing	Responsibilities
1	**Reaction/Satisfaction** • Relevance to job • Importance to job success • Value add • Coach's effectiveness • Recommendation to others	• 4 out of 5 on a 1 to 5 rating scale	• Questionnaire	• Executives	• Six months after engagement	• NHLO Staff
2	**Learning** • Uncovering strengths/ weaknesses • Translating feedback into action • Involving team members • Communicating effectively • Collaborating with colleagues • Improving personal effectiveness • Enhancing leadership skills	• 4 out of 5 on a 1 to 5 rating scale	• Questionnaire	• Executives • Coach	• Six months after engagement	• NHLO Staff
3	**Application/Implementation** • Complete and adjust action plan • Identify barriers and enablers • Show improvements in skills	• Checklist for action plan • 4 out of 5 on a 1 to 5 rating scale	• Action Plan • Questionnaire	• Executives • Coach	• Six months after engagement	• NHLO Staff
4	**Business Impact (3 of 5)** • Sales growth • Productivity/efficiency • Direct cost reduction • Retention of key staff members • Customer satisfaction	• Monthly revenue • Varies with location • Direct monetary savings • Voluntary turnover • Customer satisfaction index	• Action Plan	• Executives	• Six months after engagement	• NHLO Staff
5	**ROI** • 25 percent	**Comments:** *Executives are committed to providing data. They fully understand all the data collection issues prior to engaging into the coaching assignment.*				

collecting data at different levels. In this case, action plans and questionnaires are the primary methods.

4. *Sources:* For each data group, sources are identified. For coaches, sources are usually limited to the executive, coach, manager of the executive, and the individual/team reporting to the executive. Although the actual data provided by executives will usually come from the records of the organization, the executive will include the data in the action plan document. Thus, the executive becomes a source of the data to NHLO.

5. *Timing:* The timing refers to the time for collecting specific data items from the beginning of the coaching engagement.

6. *Responsibility:* The responsibility refers to the individual(s) who will actually collect the data.

The data integration plan (Figure 5) shows how the various types of data are collected and integrated to provide an overall evaluation of the program.

Figure 5. Data Integration Plan for Evaluating the Program

Data Category	Executive Questionnaire	Senior Executive Questionnaire	Action Plan	Company Records
Reaction	X			
Learning	X	X		
Application	X	X	X	
Impact			X	X
Costs				X

Figure 6 shows the completed plan for data analysis. This document addresses the key issues needed for a credible analysis of the data and includes the following:

1. *Data items:* The plan shows when business measures will be collected from the one of the five priority areas.

2. *Isolating the effects of coaching:* The method of isolating the effects of coaching on the data is estimation, where the executives actually allocate the proportion of the improvement to the coaching process (more on the consequences of this later). Although there are more credible methods, such as control groups and

Figure 6. The ROI Analysis Plan for Coaching for Business Impact

Program: Coaching for Business Success   Responsibility: _____   Date: _____

Data Items (Usually Level 4)	Methods for Isolating the Effects of the Program	Methods of Converting Data to Monetary Values	Cost Categories	Intangible Benefits	Communication Targets for Final Report	Other Influences/Issues During Application	Comments
• Sales growth	Estimates from executive (Method is the same for all data items)	• Standard Value • Expert input • Executive estimate (Method is the same for all data items)	• Needs assessment • Coaching fees • Travel costs • Executive time • Administrative support • Administrative overhead • Communication expenses • Facilities • Evaluation	• Increased commitment • Reduced stress • Increased job satisfaction • Improved customer service • Enhanced recruiting image • Improved teamwork • Improved communication	• Executives • Senior executives • Sponsors • NHLO staff • Learning & Development Council • Prospective participants for CBI	A variety of other initiatives will influence the impact measure including our Six Sigma process, service excellence program, and our efforts to become a great place to work.	It is extremely important to secure commitment from executives to provide accurate data in a timely manner.
• Productivity/operational efficiency							
• Direct cost reduction							
• Retention of key staff members							
• Customer satisfaction							

trend-line analysis, they are not appropriate for this situation. Although the estimates are subjective, they are developed by those individuals who should know them best (the executives), and the results are adjusted for the error of the estimate.

3. *Converting data to monetary values:* Data is converted using a variety of methods. For most data items, standard values are available. When standard values are not available, the input of an in-house expert is pursued. This expert is typically an individual who collects, assimilates, and reports the data. If neither of these approaches is feasible, the executive estimates the value.

4. *Cost categories:* The standard cost categories included are the typical costs for a coaching assignment.

5. *Communication targets:* Several audiences are included for coaching results, representing the key stakeholder groups: the executive, the executive's immediate manager, the sponsor of the program, and the NHLO staff. Other influences and issues are also detailed in this plan.

Evaluation Results

The careful data collection planning allowed the coaching program to be evaluated at all five levels.

Reaction

Reaction to the coaching program exceeded expectations of the NHLO staff. Comments received for Level 1 evaluation included these:

- "This program was very timely and practical."
- "My coach was very professional."

On a scale of 1 to 5 (1 = unacceptable and 5 = exceptional), the average rating of five items was 4.1, exceeding the objective of 4.0. Table 1 shows the items listed.

Learning

As with any process, the executives indicated enhancement of skills and knowledge in certain areas:

- "I gained much insight into my problems with my team."

- "This is exactly what I needed to get on track. My coach pointed out things I hadn't thought of and we came up with some terrific actions."

Table 1. Executive Reaction to Coaching

Level 1 Evaluation	Rating*
Relevance of Coaching	4.6
Importance of Coaching	4.1
Value of Coaching	3.9
Effectiveness of Coach	3.9
Recommendation to Others	4.2

*Scale 1-5, where: 1 = Unacceptable
5 = Exceptional

Table 2-2 shows seven items with inputs from both the executives and their coaches. For this level, it was considered appropriate to collect the data from both groups, indicating the degree of improvement. The most accurate, and probably most credible, is the input directly from the executive. The coach may not be fully aware of the extent of learning.

Table 2. Learning from Coaching

Measures	Executive Rating*	Coach Rating*
Understanding strengths and weaknesses	3.9	4.2
Translating feedback into action plans	3.7	3.9
Involving team members in projects and goals	4.2	3.7
Communicating effectively	4.1	4.2
Collaborating with colleagues	4.0	4.1
Improving personal effectiveness	4.1	4.4
Enhancing leadership skills	4.2	4.3

*Program value scale 1 to 5.

Application

For coaching to be successful, the executive had to implement the items on the action plans. The most important measure of application was the completion of the action plan steps. Eighty-three percent of the executives reported completion of all three plans. Another 11 percent completed one or two action plans.

Also, executives and the coach provided input on questions about changes in behavior from the use of skills. Here are some comments they offered on the questionnaires:

- "It was so helpful to get a fresh, unique point of view of my action plan. The coaching experience opened my eyes to significant things I was missing."
- "After spending a great deal of time trying to get my coach to understand my dilemma, I felt that more effort went into to this than I expected."
- "We got stuck in a rut on one issue and I couldn't get out. My coach was somewhat distracted and I never felt we were on the same page."

The response rates for questionnaires were 92 percent and 80 percent for executives and coaches, respectively. Table 3 shows a listing of the skills and the rating, using a scale of 1 to 5 where 1 was "no change in the skill" and 5 was "exceptional increase."

Table 3. Application of Coaching

Measures	Executive Rating*	Coach Rating*
Translating feedback into action plans	4.2	3.9
Involving team members in projects and goals	4.1	4.2
Communicating more effectively with the team	4.3	4.1
Collaborating more with the group and others	4.2	4.2
Applying effective leadership skills	4.1	3.9

*Program value scale 1 to 5, where: 1 = No change in skills
5 = Exceptional increase

Barriers and Enablers

With any process, there are barriers and enablers to success. The executives were asked to indicate the specific barriers (obstacles) to the use of what was learned in the coaching sessions. Overall the barriers were weak, almost nonexistent. Also, they were asked to indicate what supported (enablers) the process. The enablers were very strong. Table 4 shows a list of the barriers and enablers.

Table 4. Barriers and Enablers of the Coaching Process.

Barriers	Enablers
• Not enough time	• Coach
• Not relevant	• Action plan
• Not effective when using the skill	• Structure of CBI
• Manager didn't support it	• Support of management

Impact

Specific business impact measures varied with the individual but, for the most part, were in the categories representing the five priority areas. Table 5 shows the listing of the actual data reported in the action plans for the first measure only. The table identifies the executive and the area of improvement, the monetary value, the basis of the improvement, the method of converting the monetary value, the contribution from coaching, the confidence estimate of the contribution, and the adjusted value. Since there are three measures, a total of all three tables are developed. The total for the three is $1,861,158.

Figure 7 shows a completed action plan from one participant, Caroline Dobson (executive number 11). In this example, Caroline reduced annual turnover to 17 percent from 28 percent – an improvement of 11 percent. This represented four turnovers on an annual basis. Using a standard value of 1.3 times base salaries for the cost of one turnover and adding the total base salaries yields a total cost savings of $215,000.

As mentioned earlier, the estimates were used to isolate the benefits of coaching. After the estimates were obtained, the value was adjusted for the confidence of the estimate. Essentially, the executives were asked to list other factors that could have contributed to the improvement and allocate the amount (on a percentage basis) that was directly attributable to coaching. Then, using a scale of 0 percent (no confidence) to 100 percent (total certainty), executives provided the confidence levels for their estimates.

ROI

The costs were fully loaded and included both the direct and indirect costs of coaching. Estimates were used in some cases. Table 6 shows the costs of coaching for all 25 executives in the study.

Table 5. Business Impact from Coaching

Exec Number	Measurement Area	Total Annual Value	Basis	Method for Converting Data	Contribution Factor	Confidence Estimate	Adjusted Value
1	Revenue growth	$ 11,500	Profit margin	Standard value	33%	70%	$ 2,656
2	Retention	175,000	3 turnovers	Standard value	40%	70%	49,000
3	Retention	190,000	2 turnovers	Standard value	60%	80%	91,200
4	Direct cost savings	75,000	From cost statements	Participant estimate	100%	100%	75,000
5	Direct cost savings	21,000	Contract services	Standard value	75%	70%	11,025
6	Direct cost savings	65,000	Staffing costs	Standard value	70%	60%	27,300
7	Retention	150,000	2 turnovers	Standard value	50%	50%	37,500
8	Cost savings	70,000	Security	Standard value	60%	90%	37,800
9	Direct cost savings	9,443	Supply costs	N/A	70%	90%	5,949
10	Efficiency	39,000	Information technology costs	Participant estimate	70%	80%	21,840
11	Retention	215,000	4 turnovers	Standard value	75%	90%	145,125
12	Productivity	13,590	Overtime	Standard value	75%	80%	8,154
13	Retention	73,000	1 turnover	Standard value	50%	80%	29,200
14	Retention	120,000	2 annual turnovers	Standard value	60%	75%	54,000
15	Retention	182,000	4 turnovers	Standard value	40%	85%	61,880
16	Cost savings	25,900	Travel	Standard value	30%	90%	6,993
17	Cost savings	12,320	Administrative support	Standard value	75%	90%	8,316
18	Direct cost savings	18,950	Labor savings	Participant estimate	55%	60%	6,253
19	Revenue growth	103,100	Profit margin	Participant estimate	75%	90%	69,592
20	Revenue	19,500	Profit	Standard value	85%	75%	12,431
21	Revenue	21,230	Profit %	Standard value	80%	70%	18,889
22	Revenue growth	105,780	Profit margin	Standard value	70%	50%	37,023
	TOTAL $1,716,313						**TOTAL $817,126**

2nd Measure Total $649,320
3rd Measure Total $394,712
TOTAL Benefits $1,861,158

Table 6. Costs of Coaching Twent-five Executives

Item	Cost
Needs Assessment/Development	$ 10,000
Coaching Fees	480,000
Travel Costs	53,000
Executive Time	9,200
Administrative Support	14,000
Administrative Overhead	2,000
Telecommunication Expenses	1,500
Facilities (Conference Room)	2,100
Evaluation	8,000
Total	**$ 579,800**

Only a small amount of initial assessment cost was involved, and the development cost was minor, as well, because the coaching firm had developed a similar coaching arrangement previously. The costs for sessions conducted on the phone were estimated, and sometimes a conference room was used instead of the executive offices.

Using the total monetary benefits and total cost of the program, two ROI calculations can be developed. The first is the benefit-cost ratio (BCR), which is the ratio of the monetary benefits divided by the costs:

$$\text{BCR} = \frac{\$1,861,158}{\$579,800} = 3.21{:}1$$

This value suggests that for every dollar invested, $3.21 was generated in benfits. The ROI formula for investments in training, coaching, or any human performance intervention is calculated in the same way as for other types of investments: earnings divided by investment. For this coaching solution, the ROI was calculated thus:

$$\text{ROI } (\%) = \frac{\$1,861,158 - \$579,800}{\$579,800} \times 100 = 221\%$$

In other words, for every dollar invested in the coaching program, the invested dollar was returned and another $2.21 was generated. In this case, the ROI exceeded the 25 percent target.

Figure 7. An Example of an Executive's Completed Action Plan

Name: __Caroline Dobson__   Coach: __Pamela Mills__   Follow-Up Date: __1 September__

Objective: __Improve retention for staff__   Evaluation Period: __January__ to __July__

Improvement
Measure: __Voluntary turnover__

Current
Performance: __28% Annual__

Target
Performance: __15% Annual__

Action Steps		Analysis
1. Meet with team to discuss reasons for turnover – using problem-solving skills.	31 Jan	A. What is the unit of measure? _One voluntary turnover_
2. Review exit interview data with HR – look for trends and patterns.	15 Feb	B. What is the value (cost) of one unit? _Salary x 1.3_ C. How did you arrive at this value? _Standard Value_
3. Counsel with "at-risk" employees to correct problems and explore opportunities for improvement.	1 Mar	D. How much did the measure change during the evaluation period? _11% (annual %) (4 turnovers annually)_
4. Develop individual development plan for high-potential employees.	5 Mar	E. What other factors could have contributed to this improvement? _Growth opportunities, changes in job market_
5. Provide recognition to employees with long tenure.	Routinely	F. What percent of this change was actually caused by this program? _75%_
6. Schedule appreciation dinner for entire team.	31 May	G. What level of confidence do you place on the above information? (100% = Certainty and 0% = No Confidence) _90%_
7. Encourage team leaders to delegate more responsibilities.	31 May	
8. Follow-up with each discussion and discuss improvement or lack of improvement and plan other action.	Routinely	
9. Monitor improvement and provide recognition when appropriate.	11 May	

Intangible Benefits: _Less stress on team, greater job satisfaction_

Comments: _Great Coach – He kept me on track with this issue._

Intangibles

As with any project, there were many intangibles revealed by this analysis. Intangibles were collected on both the follow-up questionnaire and the action plan. Two questions were included on the questionnaire; one involved other benefits from this process and the other asked for comments about the program. Some individuals indicated intangibles when they listed the comments. Also, the action plan contained a place for comments and intangibles. The intangible benefits identified through these data sources included:

- Increased commitment
- Improved teamwork
- Increased job satisfaction
- Improved customer service
- Improved communication

Note that this list includes only measures that were identified as being an intangible benefit by at least four of the 25 executives. In keeping with the conservative nature of the ROI Methodology, it was decided that intangibles identified by only a couple of executives would be considered extreme data items and not credible enough to list as an actual benefit of the program.

Credibility of the ROI Analysis

The critical issue in this study is the credibility of the data. The data were perceived to be very credible by the executives, their immediate managers, and the coaches. Credibility rests on eight major issues:

1. The information for the analysis was provided directly by the executives. They had no reason to be biased in their input.
2. The data was taken directly from the records and could be audited.
3. The data collection process was conservative, with the assumption that an unresponsive individual had realized no improvement. This concept—no data, no improvement—is ultraconservative in regard to data collection. Three executives did not return the completed action plans.
4. The executives did not assign complete credit to this program. Executives isolated only a portion of the data that should be credited directly to this program.

5. The data was adjusted for the potential error of the above estimate.
6. Only the first year's benefits were used in the analysis. Most of the improvements should result in second and third-year benefits.
7. The costs of the program were fully loaded. All direct and indirect costs were included, including the time away from work for the executives.
8. The data revealed a balanced profile of success. Very favorable reaction, learning, and application data were presented along with business impact, ROI, and intangibles.

Collectively, these issues made a convincing case for the CBI program.

Communication Strategy

To communicate appropriately with the target audiences outlined in the ROI analysis plan, three specific documents were produced. The first report was a detailed impact study showing the approach, assumptions, methodology, and results using all the data categories. In addition, barriers and enablers were included, along with conclusions and recommendations. The second report was an eight-page executive summary of the key points, including a one-page overview of the methodology. The third report was a brief, five-page summary of the process and results. These documents were presented to the different groups according to the plan in Figure 8.

Figure 8. NHLO's Plan for Communicating Evaluation Results

Audience	Document
Executives	Brief summary
Managers of executive (senior executives)	Brief summary
Sponsor	Complete study, executive summary
NHLO staff	Complete study
Learning and development council	Complete study, executive summary
Prospective participants	Brief summary

Because this was the first ROI study conducted in this organization, face-to-face meetings were conducted with the sponsor and other interested senior executives. The purpose was to ensure that executive sponsors had a clear understanding of the methodology, the conservative assumptions, and each level of data. The barriers, enablers, conclusions, and recommendations were an important part of the meeting. In the future, after two or three studies have been conducted, this group will receive only a one-page summary of key data items.

A similar meeting was conducted with the learning and development council. The council consisted of advisors to NHLO—usually middle-level executives and managers. Finally, a face-to-face meeting was held with the NHLO staff at which the complete impact study was described and used as a learning tool.

As a result of this communication, the senior executive decided to make only a few minor adjustments in the program and continued to offer CBI to others on a volunteer basis. They were very pleased with the progress and were delighted to have data connecting coaching to the business impact.

Questions For Discussion

1. How did the decision to conduct an ROI study influence the design of the coaching program?
2. Critique the evaluation design and method of data collection.
3. Discuss the importance of getting participants committed to provide quality data.
4. What other strategies for isolating the impact of the coaching program could have been employed here?
5. Discuss the importance of credibility of data in an ROI study.
6. How can the outcomes of coaching be linked to your organization's business objectives?

CHAPTER

Measuring ROI in Leadership Development

Global Car Rental

This case describes how one organization—a leading car rental corporation—implemented a program to improve profitability and efficiency by developing leadership competencies for first-level managers. The learning and development team was asked to identify measures influenced by this program and link these competencies to job performance and business impact. However, the team was faced with a difficulty challenge because it was not given the time, resources, or encouragement to conduct a comprehensive analysis to link the need for leadership development to business needs. Could the participants themselves help with this task?

Background

Global Car Rental (GCR) operates in 27 countries with 27,000 employees. The U.S. division has 13,000 employees and operates in most major cities in the United States. The auto rental business is very competitive, and several major firms have been forced into bankruptcy in the last few years. The industry is price sensitive, and customer service is critical. Operating costs must be managed carefully to remain profitable. Senior executives were exploring a variety of ways to improve GCR, and they perceived that developing leadership competencies for first-level managers would be an excellent way to achieve profitable growth and efficiency.

This case was prepared as a basis for discussion rather than to illustrate either effective or ineffective administrative and management practices. Names of places, organizations, and people have been disguised at the request of the author or organization.

The Need

A recent needs assessment for all functional areas conducted by the learning and development (L&D) staff determined that several leadership competencies were needed for first-level managers. The needs included typical competencies such as problem solving, counseling, motivation, communication, goal setting, and feedback. In addition to developing these competencies, the L&D staff attempted to link the competencies to job performance needs and business needs.

The senior management team, however, did not want the L&D staff to visit all locations to discuss business needs and job performance issues. The senior executives were convinced that leadership skills are needed and that these skills should drive a variety of business measures when applied in the work units. The L&D team was challenged to identify the measures influenced by this particular program. Additionally, top executives were interested in knowing the impact and maybe even ROI for a group of U.S. participants in this program.

This challenge created a dilemma. The L&D staff members realized that for a positive ROI study to be generated, the program should be linked to business needs. They knew, though, that they did not have the time, resources, or the encouragement to conduct a comprehensive analysis linking the need for the leadership development to business needs. The team was faced with the challenge of connecting this program to business impact. They thought that perhaps the participants themselves could help with this task.

Attempting to address the needs, the L&D staff developed a new program, the Leadership Challenge, designed for team leaders, supervisors, and managers who are responsible for those who actually do the work (the first level of management). Program participants were located in rental offices, service centers, call centers, regional offices, and headquarters. Most functional areas were represented, including operations, customer service, service and support, sales, administration, finance and accounting, and information technology. Essentially, this was to be a cross-functional program in the organization.

The Leadership Challenge involved four days of off-site learning with input from the immediate manager who served as a coach for some of the learning processes. Before attending, the program participants had to complete an online pretraining instrument and read a short book. Because few senior executives at GCR had challenged the L&D staff to show the business impact of a program, two groups were evaluated with 36 participants total (i.e., 18 in one group and 18 in the other).

Business Alignment

To link the program to business and job performance needs, prior to attending the program, each manager was asked to identify at least two business measures in the work unit that represent an opportunity for improvement. The measures were available in operating reports, cost statements, or scorecards. The selected measures had to meet an additional two-part test:

1. They had to be under the control of the team when improvements were to be considered.
2. They had to have the potential to be influenced by team members with the manager using the competencies in the program. A description of the program was provided in advance, including a list of objectives and skill sets.

A needs assessment appeared appropriate for the situation, even though there was some concern about whether it could be thorough. The initial needs assessment on competencies uncovered a variety of deficiencies across all the functional units and provided the information necessary for job descriptions, assignments, and key responsibility areas. Although basic, the additional steps taken to connect the program to business impact were appropriate for a business needs analysis and a job performance needs analysis.

Identifying two measures in need of improvement was a simple business needs analysis for the work unit. Restricting the selected measures to only those that could be influenced by the team with the leader using the skills from the program essentially defines a job performance need. (In essence, the individual leader is identifying something that is not currently being done in the work unit that could be done to enhance the business need.) Although more refinement and detail would be preferred, the results of this assessment process should have sufficed for this project.

Objectives
The L&D staff developed the following objectives for the program:
1. Participants will rate the program as relevant to their jobs
2. Participants will rate the program as important to their job success
3. Participants must demonstrate acceptable performance on each major competency
4. Participants will use the competencies with team members on a routine basis
5. Participants and team members will drive improvements in at least two business measures

ROI Appropriateness
With the business and job performance needs analyses complete, this program became a good candidate for the ROI. Without these two steps, it would have been difficult to conduct a successful ROI study. A consideration for conducting the ROI study was identifying the drivers for ROI analyses. In this case, the senior team was challenging the value of leadership development. An ROI study should provide convincing evidence about a major program. Also, this was a highly visible program that merited evaluation at this level because it was strategic and expensive. Consequently, the L&D staff pursued the ROI study, and an ROI objective of 20 percent was established.

ROI Planning

Data Collection Plan
Figure 1 shows the completed data collection plan. Although several data collection methods were possible, the team decided to use a detailed follow-up questionnaire to reflect the progress made with the program. Focus groups, interviews, and observations were considered too expensive or inappropriate. The L&D team explored the possibility of using the 360-degree feedback process to obtain input from team members but elected to wait until the 360-degree program was fully implemented in all units in the organization. Therefore, the questionnaire was deemed the least expensive and least disruptive method.

The questionnaire was sent directly to the participant 3 months after program completion. At the same time, a shorter questionnaire

Figure 1. Data Collection Plan for the Leadership Challenge Program

Purpose of This Evaluation _____

Program: _____   Responsibility: _____   Date: _____

Level	Objective(s)	Measures/Data	Data Collection Method	Data Sources	Timing	Responsibilities
1	**Reaction/Satisfaction** • Participants rate the program as relevant to their jobs. • Participants rate the program as important to their job success	• 4 out of 5 on a 5-point rating scale	• Questionnaire	• Participants	• End of Program	• Facilitator
2	**Learning** • Participants demonstrate acceptable performance on each major competency	• 2 out of 3 on a 3-point scale	• Observation of skill practices • Self-assessment via questionnaire	• Facilitator • Participants	• End of Program • End of Program	• Facilitator • Facilitator
3	**Application/Implementation** • Participants utilize the competencies with team members routinely	• Various measures (ratings, open-ended items, and so forth)	• Questionnaire • Questionnaire	• Participants • Participants' managers	• 3 months	• L&D staff
4	**Business Impact** • Participants and team members drive improvements in at least two business measures	• Various work unit measures	• Questionnaire	• Participants	• 3 months	• L&D staff
5	**ROI** Achieve a 20 percent ROI	Comments:___				

was sent to the participants' immediate manager. Initially, a 6-month follow-up was considered instead of the 3-month follow-up shown on the data collection plan. However, the L&D staff thought that 6 months was too long to wait for results and too long for managers to make the connection between the program and the results.

Questionnaire Topics

Figure 2 shows the email questionnaire used with this group. Important areas explored included application of skills, impact analysis, barriers to application, and enablers. A similar questionnaire that explored the role of the manager in the coaching process was sent to the next level managers without the questions on the impact data.

To achieve a response rate of 81 percent, the L&D team used 12 different techniques:

1. Provide advance communication about the questionnaire
2. Clearly communicate the reason for the questionnaire
3. Indicate who will see the results of the questionnaire
4. Show how the data will be integrated with other data
5. Communicate the time limit for submitting responses
6. Review the questionnaire at the end of the formal session
7. Allow for responses to be anonymous or at least confidential
8. Provide two follow-up reminders, using a different medium each time
9. Have the introduction letter signed by a top executive.
10. Enclose a giveaway item with the questionnaire (pen)
11. Send a summary of results to the target audience
12. Have a third party collect and analyze the data

Another important techniques was to review the questionnaire with participants—question by question—at the end of the four-day workshop to clarify issues, create expectations, and gain commitment to provide data. Third-party collection was achieved by using automated external data collection. Essentially, the data was sent by email to the data collector's server.

Figure 2. Questionnaire for leaders.

FOLLOW-UP QUESTIONNAIRE

Program Name _____ End Date of Program _____

Our records indicate that you participated in the above program. Your participation in this follow-up survey is important to continuously improve this program. Completion of this survey may take 45 to 60 minutes. Thank you in advance for your input.

Currency
1. This survey requires some information to be completed in monetary value. Please indicate the currency you will use to complete the questions requiring monetary value. _____

Program Completion
2. Did you: ❑ complete ❑ partially complete ❑ not complete the program? If you did not complete, go to the final question.

Reaction

	Strongly Disagree				Strongly Agree	Not Applicable
	1	2	3	4	5	
3. I recommended the program to others.	❑	❑	❑	❑	❑	❑
4. The program was a worthwhile investment for my organization.	❑	❑	❑	❑	❑	❑
5. The program was a good use of my time	❑	❑	❑	❑	❑	❑
6. The program was relevant to my work.	❑	❑	❑	❑	❑	❑
7. The program was important to my work.	❑	❑	❑	❑	❑	❑
8. The program provided me with new information.	❑	❑	❑	❑	❑	❑

Learning

	Strongly Disagree				Strongly Agree	Not Applicable
	1	2	3	4	5	
9. I learned new knowledge/skills from this program.	❑	❑	❑	❑	❑	❑
10. I am confident in my ability to apply the knowledge/skills learned in this program.	❑	❑	❑	❑	❑	❑

11. Rate your level of improvement in skill or knowledge derived from the program content. (0% = no improvement; 100% = significant improvement. Check only one.

0%	10%	20%	30%	40%	50%	60%	70%	80%	90%	100%
❑	❑	❑	❑	❑	❑	❑	❑	❑	❑	❑

Figure 2. Questionnaire for leaders *(continued)*

Application

	None				Very Much	Not Applicable
	1	2	3	4	5	
12. To what extent did you apply the knowledge/skills learned during the program?	❑	❑	❑	❑	❑	❑

	Infrequently (unacceptable)			Frequently (exceptional)		Not Applicable
	1	2	3	4	5	
13. How frequently did you apply the knowledge/skills learned during the program?	❑	❑	❑	❑	❑	❑

	Low				High	Not Applicable
	1	2	3	4	5	
14. What is your level of effectiveness with the knowledge/skills learned during the program?	❑	❑	❑	❑	❑	❑

	Low				High	Not Applicable
	1	2	3	4	5	
15. Rate the effectiveness of the coach.	❑	❑	❑	❑	❑	❑

	Not Critical				Very Critical	Not Applicable
	1	2	3	4	5	
16. How critical is applying the content of this program to your job success?	❑	❑	❑	❑	❑	❑

	Not Well				Very Well	Not Applicable
	1	2	3	4	5	
17. To what extent did you stay on schedule with your planned actions?	❑	❑	❑	❑	❑	❑

18. What percent of your total work time did you spend on tasks that require the knowledge/skills presented in this program? Check only one.

0%	10%	20%	30%	40%	50%	60%	70%	80%	90%	100%
❑	❑	❑	❑	❑	❑	❑	❑	❑	❑	❑

Barriers/Enablers To Application

19. Which of the following deterred or prevented you from applying the knowledge/skills learned in the program? (Check all that apply).

No opportunity to use the skills ❑

Lack of management support ❑

Lack of support from colleagues and peers ❑

Insufficient knowledge and understanding ❑

Lack of confidence to apply knowledge/skills ❑

Systems and processes within organization will not support ❑
application of knowledge/skills

Other ❑

20. If you selected "other" above, please describe here. _____

21. Which of the following supported you in applying knowledge/skills learned in the program? (Check all that apply).

Opportunity to use the skills ❑

Management support ❑

Support from colleagues and peers ❑

Sufficient knowledge and understanding ❑

Confidence to apply knowledge/skills ❑

Systems and processes within organization will support ❑
application of knowledge/skills

Other ❑

22. If you selected "other" above, please describe here. _____

Results – 1st Measure

23. Please define the first measure you selected and its unit for measurement. For example, if you selected "sales," your unit of measure may be "one closed sale."

24. For this measure, what is the monetary value of improvement for one unit of this measure? For example, the value of a closed sale is sales value times the profit margin ($10,000 x 20% = $2,000). Although this step is difficult, please make every effort to estimate the value of a unit. Put the value in the currency you selected, round to nearest whole value, and enter numbers only (for example, $2,000.25 should be entered as $2,000).

Figure 2. Questionnaire for leaders *(continued)*

25. Please state your basis for the value of the unit of improvement you indicated above. In the closed sale example, a standard value, profit margin, is used, so "standard value" is entered here.

_____

26. For the measure listed as most directly linked to the program, how much has this measure improved in performance? If not readily available, please estimate. If you selected "sales," show the actual increase in sales (for example, four closed sales per month, enter the number 4 here). You can input a number with up to one decimal point. Indicate the frequency base for the measure.

_____ ❏ daily   ❏ weekly   ❏ monthly   ❏ quarterly

Return On Investment – 1st Measure

27. What is the annual value of improvement in the measure you selected above? Multiply the increase (Question 26) by the frequency (Question 26) times the unit of value (Question 24). For example, if you selected "sales," multiply the sales increase by the frequency to arrive at the annum value (for example, four sales per month x 12 x $2,000=$96,000). Although this step is difficult, please make every effort to estimate the value. Put the value in the currency you selected, round to nearest whole value, enter numbers only (for example, $96,000.50 should be entered as $96,000).

_____

28. List the other factors that could have influenced these results. _____

_____

29. Recognizing that the other factors could have influenced this annual value of improvement, please estimate the percentage of improvement that is attributable to the program. Express as a percentage. For example, if only 60% of the sales increase is attributable to the program, enter 60 here.

_____%

30. What confidence do you place in the estimates you have provided in the questions above? 0% means no confidence, and 100% is certainty. Round to nearest whole value, and enter a number only (for example, 37.5% should be entered as 38).

_____%

Results – 2nd Measure

31. Please define the second measure you selected and its unit for measurement. For example, if you selected "sales," your unit of measure may be "one closed sale."

_____

32. For this measure, what is the monetary value of improvement for one unit of this measure? For example, the value of a closed sale is sales value times the profit margin ($10,000 x 20% = $2,000). Although this step is difficult, please make every effort to estimate the value of a unit. Put the value in the currency you selected, round to nearest whole value, and enter numbers only (for example, $2,000.25 should be entered as $2,000).

_____

33. Please state your basis for the value of the unit of improvement you indicated above. In the closed sale example, a standard value, profit margin, is used, so "standard value" is entered here.

_____

34. For the measure listed as most directly linked to the program, how much has this measure improved in performance? If not readily available, please estimate. If you selected "sales," show the actual increase in sales (for example, four closed sales per month, enter the number 4 here). You can enter a number with up to one decimal point. Indicate the frequency base for the measure. _____

   ❑ daily   ❑ weekly   ❑ monthly   ❑ quarterly

Return On Investment- 2nd Measure

35. What is the annual value of improvement in the measure you selected above? Multiply the increase (Question 34) by the frequency (Question 34) times the unit of value (Question 32). For example, if you selected "sales," multiply the sales increase by the frequency to arrive at the annum value (for example, four sales per month x 12 x $2,000=$96,000). Although this step is difficult, please make every effort to estimate the value. Put the value in the currency you selected, round to nearest whole value, and enter numbers only (for example, $96,000.25 should be entered as $96,000).

   _____

36. List the other factors that could have influenced these results. _____
   _____

37. Recognizing that the other factors could have influenced this annual value of improvement, please estimate the percentage of improvement that is attributable to the program. Express as a percentage. For example, if only 60% of the sales increase is attributable to the program, enter 60 here.
   _____%

38. What confidence do you place in the estimates you have provided in the questions above? 0% means no confidence, and 100% is certainty. Round to the nearest whole value, and enter a number only (for example, 37.5% should be entered as 38%).
   _____%

39. What other benefits have been realized from this program? _____
   _____

40. Please estimate your direct costs of travel and lodging for your participation in this program. Put the value in the currency you selected, round to nearest whole value, and enter numbers only (for example, $10,000.49 should be entered as $10,000).
   _____

41. Please state your basis for the travel and lodging cost estimate above. _____
   _____

Feedback

42. How can we improve the training to make it more relevant to your job?
   _____
   _____
   _____
   _____

Thank you for taking the time to complete this survey!

ROI Analysis Plan

The completed ROI analysis plan is shown in Figure 3. This plan details the specific issues that must be addressed and the particular techniques selected to complete the ROI analysis.

Method of Isolation

The method the L&D team used to isolate the effects of the program proved to be a challenge. Because the managers represented different functional areas, there was no finite set of measures that could be linked to the program for each participant. Essentially, each manager could have a different set of measures as he or she focused on specific business needs in the work unit. Consequently, the use of a control group was not feasible. In addition, the trend-line analysis and forecasting methods proved to be inappropriate for the same reason.

Therefore, the evaluation team had to collect estimations directly from participants on the questionnaire. Question 29 isolated the effects of this program using an estimate. Question 30 adjusted for the error of the estimate. The challenge was ensuring that participants understood this issue and were committed to provide data for the isolation.

Converting Data to Monetary Value

The participants provided estimates for converting their selected measures to monetary values. In the planning, the L&D team assumed that there were only a few feasible approaches for participants to place monetary value on measures. Because there was little agenda time to discuss this issue, the L&D staff had to rely on easy-to-obtain data using three options. The good news was that in GCR, as with many other organizations, standard values have been developed for the measures that matter and they were the first option. If a measure is something that the company wants to increase, such as productivity or sales, someone already will have placed a value on that measure to show the contribution of the improvement. If it is a measure the company wants to reduce, such as turnover, accidents, or absenteeism, someone has more than likely placed a monetary value to show the impact of these critical measures. Consequently, the participants were asked to use standard values if they were available.

If these were not available, as a second option participants could

Figure 3. The ROI analysis plan

Program: _____ Responsibility: _____ Date: _____

Data Items (Usually Level 4)	Methods for Isolating the Effects of the Program/Process	Methods of Converting Data to Monetary Values	Cost Categories	Intangible Benefits	Communication Targets for Final Report	Other Influences/ Issues During Application	Comments
• Varies, depending on measures selected	• Participant estimate	• Standard value • Expert value • Participant estimate	• Needs assessment (prorated) • Program development (prorated) • Facilitation fees • Promotional materials • Facilitation and coordination • Meals and refreshments • Facilities • Participants' salaries and benefits for time away from work • Managers' salaries and benefits for time involved in program • Cost of overhead • Evaluation costs	• Job satisfaction for first-level managers • Job satisfaction for team members • Improved teamwork • Improved communication	• Participants (first-level managers) • Participants' managers • Senior executives • L&D staff • Prospective participants • L&D council members	• Several process improvement initiatives are going on during this program implementation	• Must gain commitment to provide data • A high response rate is needed

call on an internal expert who knew more about that particular measure. In many cases, this person was an individual from the department furnishing a particular report because the data came directly from the operating reports. Essentially this was expert input. If no standard was available or experts identified, the last option was for the participants to estimate the value. Because this was a measure that mattered to the participant, he or she should have some perception about the value of improving it.

The actual amount was entered on Question 24. Then, Question 25 provided the basis for showing the details for how that value was developed. Question 25 is critical. If omitted, the business impact measure was removed from the analysis under the guiding principle of not using an unsupported claim in the analysis. Incidentally, the participants were informed about this principle as the questionnaire was reviewed with them at the end of the workshop.

Costs

The costs for the program were typical—analysis, design, development, and delivery components—and represented the fully loaded costs containing both direct and indirect categories.

Other Issues

The L&D team anticipated some intangible benefits and, consequently, added a question to identify improvements in these intangible benefits (Question 39). To ensure that all the key stakeholders were identified, the evaluation team decided which groups should receive the information in the impact study. Six specific groups were targeted for communication. The remainder of the ROI analysis plan listed other issues about the study.

Results

Twenty-nine questionnaires were returned for an 81 percent response rate. Participants provided a rich database indicating success at each level of evaluation.

Reaction

Table 1 shows the reaction data obtained from the follow-up questionnaire. Although some initial reaction was collected at the end of the workshop using a standard reaction questionnaire, the team decided to collect and present to the senior team the reaction obtained in the follow-up. Each of the reaction measures exceeded the goal of a 4.0 rating, except for the issue about the amount of new information, which was slightly less than the desired level.

Table 1. Reaction data from participants.

Issue	Rating*
Recommended to others	4.2
Worthwhile investment	4.1
Good use of time	4.6
Relevant to my work	4.3
Important to my work	4.1
Provided me with new information	3.9

*Rating scale: 1 = Strongly disagree; 5 = Strongly agree

Learning

Although several skill practices and self-assessments were taken during the workshop to measure learning, the team decided to present the learning data directly from the follow-up questionnaire. As shown in Table 2, the learning measures met or exceeded expectations in terms of the amount of new skills and knowledge and confidence in using them. Also, the average skill or knowledge improvement was 48 percent (Question 11).

Table 2. Learning Data from Participants

Issue	Rating*
Learned new knowledge/skills	4.3
Confident in my ability to apply new knowledge/skills	4.1

*Rating: 1 = Strongly Disagree; 5 = Strongly Agree

Application

Table 3 shows application data obtained in the follow-up questionnaire. The applications exceeded expectations, and the effectiveness of the coach rating was a particular highlight. The percentage of time spent on tasks requiring the use of the acquired knowledge/skills averaged 43 percent (Question 18). The participants' managers received the questionnaire primarily about the coaching component, and they reported success. They routinely coached the participants when requested and frequently reinforced the use of the skills.

Table 3. Application Data from Participants

Issue	Rating*
Extent of use of knowledge/skills	4.3
Frequency of application of knowledge/skills	3.8
Effectiveness with using knowledge/skills	4.3
Effectiveness of coach	4.7
Criticalness to job	4.2
Stay on Schedule	4.1

*Rating:1 = Lowest; 5 = Highest

Barriers and Enablers

Much to the surprise of the staff, the barriers were minimal and the enablers were strong. The program enjoyed good management support and was tailored to the job environment. Therefore, few barriers prevented the transfer of learning, and the enablers were built into the program. Tables 4 shows the barriers and enablers.

Business Impact

Business impact data (Level 4) is shown in table 14-5. This table shows specific improvements identified directly from the questionnaire, by participant number, for the first 15 participants. To save space, the remaining 14 participants are included as a total. Usually, each participant provided improvements on two measures. The total for the second measure is shown at the bottom of Table 5.

The top row of Table 5 reveals the linkage between the questions on the questionnaire and the columns in this table. The total annual improvement for each measure is reported first. Incidentally, the specific measure was identified and could be reported as well, but to reduce confusion only the measure categories were reported. The

Table 4. Top Five Barriers and Enablers Identified by Participants

Barrier	Frequency
No Opportunity to Use Skills	14%
Lack of Support from Colleagues and Peers	14%
Insufficient Knowledge and Understanding	10%
Lack of Management Support	7%
Lack of Confidence to Apply Learning	3%

Enablers	Frequency
Management Support	55%
Opportunity to Use Skills	52%
Confidence to Apply Learning	38%
Support from Colleagues and Peers	34%
Sufficient Knowledge and Understanding	34%

heading "Converting Data to Monetary Value" shows the extent to which the three options were used to convert data to monetary value. Most participants selected "Standard" because standard values were readily available. The column of "Other Factors" indicates the number of other factors that contributed to the results. In most cases several factors were present. No more than four other factors were identified in any section. In a few cases, there were no other factors. In summary, the standard values were used 71 percent of the time, and other factors were identified 85 percent of the time.

ROI Analysis

The total cost of the program, using a fully loaded analysis, is shown in Table 6. The needs assessment was prorated over 4 years, based upon the anticipated life cycle of the project. A thousand managers in the United States would attend this program in the four-year time period before another needs assessment was conducted. Program development was prorated over three years assuming that the delivery could change significantly in that time frame. The remainder of the costs were directly charged and included the delivery expenses, the salaries for the participants (the first level man-

Table 5 Business Impact Calculations

Participant Number	Annual Improvement (Q27)*	Measure (Q23)*	Converting Data to Monetary Value (Q25)*	Contribution from Program (Q29)*	Other Factors (Q28)*	Confidence Estimate (Q30)*	Adjusted Value[†]
1	$ 13,100	Sales	Standard	60%	3	80%	$ 6,288
3	41,200	Productivity	Expert	75%	1	95%	29,355
4	5,300	Sales	Standard	80%	1	90%	3,816
6	7,210	Cost	N/A	70%	2	70%	3,533
9	4,215	Efficiency	Standard	40%	3	75%	1,265
10	17,500	Quality	Expert	35%	4	60%	3,675
12	11,500	Time	Standard	60%	2	80%	5,520
14	3,948	Time	Standard	70%	1	80%	2,212
15	14,725	Sales	Standard	40%	3	70%	4,123
17	6,673	Efficiency	Estimate	50%	3	60%	2,002
18	12,140	Costs	N/A	100%	0	100%	12,140
19	17,850	Sales	Standard	60%	2	70%	7,497
21	13,920	Sales	Standard	50%	3	80%	5,568
22	15,362	Cost	N/A	40%	4	90%	5,530
23	18,923	Sales	Standard	60%	1	75%	8,515
						Total for the items above	$ 101,039
						Total for the next 14 items	$ 84,398
						Total for 2nd measure	$ 143,764
						Total Benefits	$ 329,201

* Question numbers in Figure 2 Questionnaire.
† Total Monetary Benefits = Q27 x Q29 x Q30.

agers), as well as their managers (second level). The training and education overhead was allocated using a figure of $312 per day of training.

Table 6. Summary of Fully Loaded Costs

Cost of Item	Cost
Needs assessment (prorated over 4 years)	$ 900
Program development (prorated over 3 years)	2,000
Program materials ($120/participant)	4,320
Travel, meals, and Lodging ($1,600/participant)	57,600
Facilitation and coordination ($4,000/day)	32,000
Facilities and refreshments ($890/day)	7,120
Participants salaries (plus benefits) for time and program	37,218
Manager salaries (plus benefits) for time involved in program	12,096
Training and education overhead (allocated)	2,500
ROI evaluation costs	5,000
Total for 36 participants	$ 160,754

The BCR was calculated as follows:

$$\text{BCR} = \frac{\text{Total Benefits}}{\text{Total Costs}} = \frac{\$329,201}{\$160,754} = 2.05$$

The ROI was calculated as follows:

$$\text{ROI} = \frac{\text{Net Total Benefits}}{\text{Total Costs}} = \frac{\$329,201 - \$160,754}{\$160,754} \times 100 = 105\%$$

Major Issues

The data were perceived to be credible by both the L&D staff and senior management group. Credibility rests on seven major issues:

1. The information for the analysis was provided directly from the new managers. The managers had no reason to be biased in their input.
2. The data was provided anonymously because no one had to provide his or her name on the questionnaire. Anonymity

helped eliminate the possibility of bias.

3. The data collection process was conservative under the assumption that an unresponsive individual has realized no improvement. This concept—no data, no improvement—is an ultraconservative approach to data collection.

4. The L&D staff did not assign complete credit to this program. The participants isolated a portion of the data that should be credited directly to this program.

5. The data was adjusted for the potential error of the estimate. Estimates were used to isolate the effects of the program.

6. Only the first year of benefits were used in the analysis. Most of the improvement should result in second- and third-year benefits.

7. The costs of the program were fully loaded. All direct and indirect costs were included, including the time away from work for the participants and managers.

The data represents a balanced profile of success. Very favorable reaction, learning, and application data was presented along with business impact, ROI, and intangibles. Collectively, these issues made a convincing case for the program.

Communication Strategy

To communicate appropriately with the target audiences outlined in the ROI analysis plan, the L&D team produced three specific documents. The first report was a detailed impact study showing the approach, assumptions, methodology, and results using all six data categories. In addition, barriers and enablers were included in the study, along with conclusions and recommendations. The second report was an eight-page executive summary of the key points, including a one-page overview of the methodology. The third report was a brief, five-page summary of the process and results. These documents were presented to the different groups according to the plan presented in Figure 4.

Because this was the first ROI study conducted in this organization, face-to-face meetings were conducted with the executives. The purpose was to ensure that executives understood the methodology, the conservative assumptions, and each level of data. The barriers, enablers, conclusions, and recommendations were an important part

Figure 4. Distribution plan for Leadership Challenge evaluation reports

Audience	Document
Participants	Brief summary
Managers of participants	Brief summary
Senior executives	Complete study, executive summary
L&D staff	Complete study
L&D Council	Complete study, executive summary
Prospective participants	Brief summary

of the meeting. In the future, after two or three studies have been conducted, this group will receive only a one-page summary of key data items. A similar meeting was conducted with the L&D council. The council members were advisors to the L&D department who are usually middle- and upper-level executives and managers. Finally, a face-to-face meeting was held with the learning and development staff where the complete impact study was described and used as a learning tool.

Lessons Learned

This case study shows how the evaluation process can be accomplished with minimal resources. The approach shifted much of the responsibility for evaluation to the participants as they collected data, isolated the effects of the program, and converted the data to monetary values—the three most critical steps in the ROI process. The results were easily communicated to various target groups through three specific documents. L&D staff and senior management perceived the data to be credible. The ROI was positive, and the program showed important connections with business results.

Discussion Questions

1. Is this approach credible? Explain.
2. Is the ROI value realistic?
3. What types of programs would be appropriate for this approach?
4. What additions or revisions could be made to the evaluation strategies provided?
5. What evaluation strategies other than the questionnaire could be used in this situation?

CHAPTER 15

Measuring ROI in Leadership Development

Linear Network Systems

This program represents a comprehensive leadership development initiative for first-level managers in a technical environment. The payoffs for the program included productivity, defined as the percent of on time production, voluntary turnover, and absenteeism. The program is very data rich and the analysis follows all of the issues around the ROI Methodology, including forecasting. The study is arranged in parts which makes it easier for self study.

PART A

Background

Linear Network Systems (LNS) is an important supplier to the telecom industry, producing a variety of network equipment. A publicly held company, LNS has been operating for more than 15 years with manufacturing and support facilities scattered throughout the USA and Canada. The company has been very successful and stable.

Although LNS has been a very profitable company, it recently experienced competitive cost and quality pressures, that caused some deterioration in sales. Although several factors are related to the decline, senior management is concerned about the ability of the first-level management team to lead today's workforce. The President of LNS, asked the Human Resource Development

This case was prepared to serve as a basis for discussion rather than an illustration of either effective or ineffective administrative and management practices. All names, dates, places, and organizations have been disguised at the request of the author or organization.

Manager, Pam O'Kelly, to provide appropriate training.

For several months, LNS has been attempting to develop these team leaders. Several team-building sessions had been conducted. The president felt that the leaders were experiencing some difficulty in making the transition to leadership and that they needed to develop leadership skills to motivate team members to improve productivity.

Situation

O'Kelly contacted a consulting firm to inquire about potential leadership training. The principal consultant suggested that a needs assessment be conducted to determine specific training needs and also to determine if other issues need to be addressed. LNS officials reluctantly agreed to a needs assessment. They were convinced that training was needed and wanted the "standard leadership training" program. After some convincing, the consultant conducted the needs assessment using four methods:

1. Reviewing operational performance documents
2. Interviewing a sample of first-level managers and middle managers
3. Observing a small sample of first level managers on the job
4. Administering a questionnaire to all first- and second-level managers

The assessment identified a lack of skills and a need for significant leadership training. Most of the skills focused on understanding and motivating employees, setting goals, and providing feedback.

The Program

A six-module, 24-hour training program was proposed for one plant as a pilot group. All first- level operating and support managers would be trained at the same time. The program would be conducted in six four-hour segments scattered over a one-month period. Between sessions, participants would be requested to apply the new skills so that there would be transfer of training to the job. Initially, the program was planned to focus on the following areas:

- Understanding employee needs
- Motivating employees for improved performance
- Counseling employees

- Solving problems with employees
- Providing appropriate leadership behavior
- Inspiring teamwork

The program was labeled "Leadership for Improved Performance" and was planned for all 16 supervisors in the pilot plant. A follow-up evaluation was planned several months after the training was completed. If the program were effective, LNS would offer it throughout their organization.

Discussion Questions

1. How important is the needs assessment for this situation? Is the resistance to a needs assessment typical? At what levels should the needs assessment be conducted?
2. At what levels should this program be evaluated?
3. Should the objectives of the program be modified? If so, how?

PART B

Needs Assessment

An improper or inadequate needs assessment may result in a program designed to address skills that are not needed or are already in place. The needs assessment was conducted at Level 4 (business needs), Level 3 (job performance needs), and Level 2 (skill and knowledge needs). Without a multiple level needs assessment, it would be more difficult to evaluate the program designed to change job behavior (Level 3) and drive business impact improvement (Level 4). Thus, the needs assessment became a very critical issue for identifying performance deficiencies at all three levels and was an important component in LNS's plan to develop first-level managers.

Business Performance Measures

The needs assessment identified several business performance measures where improvement was needed, all related to inadequate leadership skills. These included the following data items:

- Productivity (measured by the percentage of shipments met)
- Employee turnover
- Absenteeism

There was some skepticism among senior management that pro-ductivity could be enhanced through leadership training, although most of the first-level managers agreed that they could boost produc-tivity with improved teamwork. Employee turnover was high and, although there were many factors that influenced turnover, most managers felt that turnover was a variable under their control. Finally, absenteeism was extremely high, particularly on second shifts and on Mondays and Fridays.

LNS had developed an adequate measurement system, which mon-itored, among other variables, productivity, turnover, and absen-teeism measures by the production unit. Each first-level manager received absenteeism and turnover data monthly, and productivity measures were available weekly for the production departments. Support departments can significantly influence the measures by providing excellent support and assistance.

Top management approved the leadership program proposal, including the structure and timing.

Evaluation Levels

Because LNS management was interested in the accountability of training, and the consulting firm was eager to show results of train-ing, both parties were anxious to conduct an ROI evaluation for this project. ROI data can be very convincing for marketing a program to other groups. With this approach, business impact data would be col-lected, converted to monetary values, and compared to the program cost to develop the ROI (Level 5). In addition, Levels 1, 2, and 3 data would be collected to measure reaction, learning, and application. Thus, all five levels of evaluation were pursued.

There was another important reason for evaluating this program at all five levels. Because this program is linked to key organizational measures, a success would show a direct linkage to the company's bottom-line. A significant payoff to the company would clearly show management that leadership training is a high impact process and that it can make a difference by improving important business per-formance measures.

Objectives

Because Levels 3 and 4 data must be collected, it is essential that specific objectives be measurable and directly related to the Level 3 and 4 data obtained from the needs assessment. Therefore, program objectives were revised to include the following. After attending this program, participants should:

- Be able to describe and identify applications for two motivational models
- Be able to describe and identify applications for two leadership models
- Set measurable performance goals each month for each employee
- Apply performance feedback skills each day with each employee.
- Reduce employee turnover from an average annual rate of 29 to 25 percent in four months
- Reduce absenteeism from a weekly average of 5 to 3 percent in four months
- Increase productivity by 2 percentage points in 4 months

The specific targets were difficult to develop and required the complete cooperation of the plant manager and the department heads.

Discussion Questions

1. What is your reaction to these objectives? Do you think this program could influence each measure?
2. What are the recommended post-program data collection methods
3. Complete the data collection plan for evaluation (See Figure 1).

PART C

Data Collection Plan

The consultant and the HRD Manager decided that the action planning process would be utilized in the follow-up evaluation. First-level managers should know how to develop action plans and their managers should be able to provide assistance and support with the process. The action plan would show how the newly acquired skills are applied to improve measures such as productivity, turnover, and absenteeism. A portion of the program allowed for a discussion of

Figure 1. Evaluation plan: data collection

Data Collection Plan

Program: Leadership for Improved Performance   **Responsibility:** _____   **Date:** _____

Level	Objective(s)	Measures/Data	Data Collection Method	Data Sources	Timing	Responsibilities
1	Reaction/Satisfaction					
2	Learning					
3	Application/Implementation					
4	Business Impact					
5	ROI					

Comments: _____

action plans, and the program facilitator was required to approve the action plan verifying that it meets basic requirements. A model action plan would be provided to help ensure that supervisors understand the process.

After discussions with management, it was felt that within four months supervisors should be able to apply leadership skills to achieve measurable results. Although a six-month time frame was recommended, senior management indicated that they might want to proceed with the program in other plants before six months and therefore preferred a three-month period. Four months was a compromise.

Because all of the action plans involve different time frames, each participant was asked to provide a progress report in four months, or in some cases, the completed project. This would provide a snapshot of the performance improvement within that time-frame.

Although the action plan, by design, collected Levels 3 and 4 data, a follow-up questionnaire was planned to gain more evidence of on-the-job behavior change (Level 3). Responsibilities for data collection at Levels 1 and 2 usually rest with the facilitator and that was the case here. The Area Training Coordinator was assigned the responsibility for collecting the questionnaire data (Level 3) and monitoring performance (Level 4). The data collection plan is presented as Figure 2.

Isolating the Effects of Training

One of the most important challenges facing program evaluators is determining the specific technique that isolates the effects of the training program, recognizing that other factors may influence outcome measures at the same time the program is being conducted. This is one of the most important issues (usually raised by management) when they want to know exactly how much of the results are related specifically to the program.

Discussion Questions

1. What method(s) should be used to isolate the effects of training?
2. Should more than one technique be used to isolate the effects of training? Please explain.

Figure 2. Evaluation plan: data collection

Data Collection Plan

Program: Leadership for Improved Performance   **Responsibility:** _____   **Date:** _____

Level	Objective(s)	Measures/Data	Data Collection Method	Data Sources	Timing	Responsibilities
1	**Reaction/Satisfaction** • Positive reaction • Identify planned actions	• Average rating of at least 4.2 on 5.0 scale on quality, usefulness and achievement of program objectives • 100% submit planned actions	• Standard feedback questionnaire	• Participants	• End of program	• Facilitator
2	**Learning/Skills** • Knowledge on motivational models • Knowledge on leadership models • Skills for motivating employees • Knowledge/skills on providing counseling • Knowledge/skills on measuring employee performance • Problem solving skills • Knowledge/skills on teamwork • Leadership behavior skills	• Demonstrated ability to provide employee feedback/motivating/ problem solving/ leadership skills • Scale of 1 to 5 on assessment of knowledge	• Skill practice • Facilitator assessment • Participant assessment	• Participants • Facilitator • Participants	• During program	• Facilitator
3	**Application and Implementation** • Extent of skill use • Frequency of skill use • Success with skill use • Setting performance goals • Complete all steps of action plan	• Scale of 1 to 5 on assessment of application • The number of steps completed on action plan	• Follow-up questionnaire • Action plan	• Participants • Participants	• 4 months after program • 4 months after program	• Area Training Coordinator
4	**Business Impact** • Reduce employee turnover • Reduce employee absenteeism • Increase productivity	• Voluntary turnover - 29% to 25% • Unplanned absenteeism - 5% to 3% • Percentage of shipments met - improve by 2%	• Action plan	• Participants	• 4 months after program	• Area Training Coordinator
5	**ROI** • 25 percent					

Comments: _____

PART D

Isolating the Effects of Training

In discussions with management and participants in the training program, two factors were identified which could have an influence on each of the business performance measures, in addition to the training program. First, the implementation of the total quality management program placed emphasis on improving all three measures in this case. Quality was defined in a broad sense, including being at work (absenteeism), remaining with the company (turnover), and ensuring that customer shipments were on time (productivity).

The second factor was the various team-building activities that were initiated as LNS attempted to move to a team-based structure. First level managers were encouraged to use employee input, conduct meetings with employees, and to take action to improve productivity. If successful, team building should increase productivity and reduce turnover and absenteeism.

Because it was important to determine the precise impact of the training program, it was necessary to isolate the effects of training from the other two factors. One of the most effective approaches is the use of a control group arrangement in which one group receives training and another similarly situated group does not receive training. LNS explored the control group arrangement in this setting. Initially it appeared to be an excellent opportunity to use this plant location as a pilot group and select another similar plant as a control group. However, no other plant had the same product line, same type of processes, same workforce characteristics, and same environmental conditions, all important variables to reflect performance. Thus, the control group arrangement was not considered a feasible approach.

The approach utilized to isolate the effects of training was participants' estimates. Participants would be asked to indicate how much of their improvement was linked directly to this training. Participants provided the information in a portion of the action plan. Each participant was presented with a six-month average of the data prior to training to compare with post-training data. After training, managers regularly receive reports for each of the items as part of their operating data.

Converting Data to Monetary Values

The next task in setting up the ROI process is to select the technique to convert data to monetary values. The challenge facing the evaluation team is to determine the most credible and accurate techniques for placing values on each of the Business Impact (Level 4) data items.

Discussion Questions

1. What is the most appropriate technique to assign a value to productivity?
2. What is the most logical way to convert employee turnover to a monetary value?
3. What is the most appropriate method to place a monetary value on an absence?
4. For other potential improvement measures, what range of potential techniques can be used to convert data to monetary values?

PART E

Converting Data to Monetary Values

As part of the next step in the ROI process, LNS's data are converted to monetary values. The value of improved productivity was a standard value developed by engineering and production control. Each 1 percent of improvement in productivity would save the plant $21,000, annually.

The company had no detailed historical records on turnover costs, although the company expected these costs to be significant when considering the cost of employment, recruiting, training, and lost productivity. The consultant provided information from external studies, which showed that turnover can cost one times the annual pay of the employees (100 percent of annual direct compensated). Annual wages of non-supervisory employees averaged $31,000. Management thought that a figure of one times the annual pay would be too high for the cost of turnover since the training period was relatively short, recruiting costs were normally quite low, and exit costs were not very significant. After discussing this with senior management, the compromise figure of $24,800 for the cost of turnover (80 percent of annual direct compensated). This appeared to be a very conservative estimate. Sixteen first-level managers were trained in this program, and they supervised a total of 385 employees.

The consultant located previous studies about the cost of absenteeism in a similar manufacturing sector, which showed a range of $89–$210 per absence with an average of $180. Brief estimates taken in the training session, with input from the 16 managers, yielded an average cost of $98. This was considered the most credible value because it was developed with the focus group process, using estimates from participants (supervisors) and adjusted for error. LNS employees worked an average of 228 days per year.

Costs

The consultant also decided to include all direct costs of participant materials as well as the participants' salaries. Because the consulting firm provided standard material for the new program, development costs were insignificant. Although the first-level managers were not replaced while they were in training, the salaries and benefits of managers were included for the time during the training sessions. The average salary of the first level managers was $47,500. The employee benefits factor was 39 percent of salaries. A total of three days were consumed in the program. The total charge for the program from the consulting firm was $51,000, including customization time, facilitation, and needs assessment. The charge for course materials was $185 per participant; miscellaneous refreshments and food was $195 per participant; the use of the conference room was estimated to be $200 per 1/2 day session, although LNS does not routinely capture and report this as a part of training. The consultant estimated the additional cost of the evaluation to be $10,000.

Discussion Questions

1. What major cost categories should always be included in the analysis?
2. What is the total cost for the program?
3. Should any other costs be included? Please explain.

PART F

Costs

The costs to train 16 supervisors are:

Needs Assessment, Program Development, Facilitation	$51,000
Supplies and Materials ($185 X 16)	2,960
Food ($195 X 16)	3,120
Facilities (6 X 200)	1,200
Evaluation	10,000
Salaries and Benefits, for the time away from routine work ($548 X 1.39 X 16)	12,188
Total	**$ 80,468**

The facilitation charge from the supplier, which totaled $51,000, includes the costs for needs assessment, program development, and facilitation. If the program had been developed internally, these three charges would have to be developed separately. The daily salary was developed by dividing average salary ($47,500) by the total number of week days worked (52 X 5 = 260). To obtain the total salaries and benefits cost for the three-day workshop, this number is multiplied by 3, adjusted upward by the benefits factor of 39 percent (This is equivalent to multiplying the average salary by 1.39). The total for each participant is multiplied by 16 to obtain the salaries and benefits for the group.

Follow-Up

Because management was interested in knowing the results of the program as soon as possible, a four-month evaluation period was used. Data for six months prior to and four months after the program are presented in Figures 3, 4, and 5, showing the productivity, turnover, and absenteeism values for the plant. The training was conducted during a one-month period and no improvements were expected during that month. Consequently, the one-month training period was excluded from the analysis. As Figure 3 shows, productivity was enhanced after the implementation of training. According to the records of the production control department, the average percent of on-time production for six months prior to training was 92 percent. A value of 95 percent was used as post-training performance, which is the average of months three and four. Averaging the two monthly values avoids a spike in the values. The plant's annual turnover rates averaged 29.5 percent for the six months prior to training and are presented in Figure 4. Turnover was calculated monthly and was reported as an annualized value for comparison, (i.e., a 2 percent monthly turnover was reflected as a 24 percent annual turnover rate on the report). The average for months three and four yields a value of 24.7 percent. The monthly absenteeism

Figure 3. Productivity

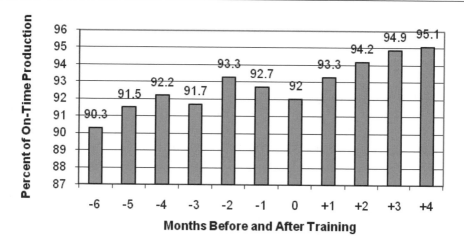

Figure 4. Turnover

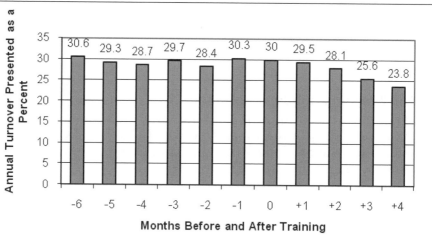

Figure 5. Absenteeism

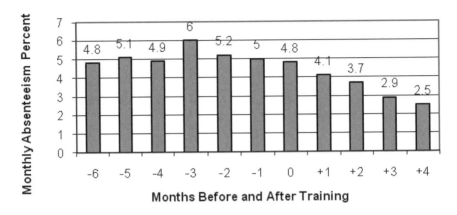

rates are shown in Figure 5. The absenteeism rate for the six months prior to training averaged 5.2 percent and was considered much too high by management. This figure includes only unexpected and unplanned absences. The average for months three and four yields a value of 2.7 percent.

In addition to action plans, supervisors completed a brief questionnaire where they estimated how much of the improvement in performance was related to each of the three factors influencing the output variables. The results are presented in Table 1.

Four of the supervisors submitted action plans focusing on measures other than productivity, turnover, or absenteeism. Three improvement areas were identified: time savings, efficiency, and direct cost savings. Table 2 shows a summary of these additional benefits.

Discussion Questions

1. Using the data in the case, complete Table 15-3 below.
2. What are the total benefits expected from the program using improvements in productivity, turnover, absenteeism, and the additional benefits?
3. What are the benefit/cost ratio and the ROI for the program?

Table 1. Contribution of Various Factors

	Training Program	TQM	Team Building	Total
Productivity (% of Schedule)	32%	49%	19%	100%
Turnover (Annualized)	72%	7%	21%	100%
Absenteeism (% Absence)	76%	4%	20%	100%

Table 2. Additional Benefits

Supervisor	Annual Improvement Value	Basis for Value	Isolation Factor	Confidence	Adjusted Value
#3	$36,000	Improvement in efficiency of group. $3,000/month x 12 (group estimate)	50%	85%	$15,300
#8	$24,000	Time savings: Improvement in customer response time (8 hours to 6 hours). Estimated value: $2,000/month	55%	60%	$ 7,920
#10	$ 8,090	Time savings: Team project completed 10 days ahead of schedule. Annual salaries of $210,500 = $809/day x 10 days	45%	90%	$ 3,279
#15	$14,900	Direct cost savings	60%	90%	$ 7,830

Table 3. Improvement in Primary Measure

	Pre-Training 6 Months Average	Post-Training, Months 3 and 4 Average	Pre-Post Differences	Participant's Estimate of Impact of Training	Unit Value	Annual Impact of Training (Estimates)
Productivity (% of Schedule)					$	$
Turnover (Annualized)					$	$
Absenteeism (% Absence)					$	$

PART G

The tabulations of the benefits for the program for the primary measures are shown in Table 4, 5, and 6.

Table 4. Annual Values for the Primary Measures

	Pre-training, 6 Month Average	Post-training Months 3 and 4 Average	Pre–Post Differences	Participant's Estimate of Impact of Training	Unit Value	Annual Impact of Training (Estimates)
Productivity (% of Schedule)	92%	95%	3%	.96% (3% X 32%)	$21,000 for 1%	$20,160
Turnover (Annualized)	29.5%	24.7%	4.8%	3.46% (4.8% X 72%)	$24,800 for each turnover	$330,360
Absenteeism (% Absence)	5.2%	2.7%	2.5%	1.9% (2.5% X 76%)	$98 for each absence	$163,446

Calculations

Productivity:
Savings = .96 X $21,000 = $20,160

Turnover:
Change in number leaving in a year = 385 X 3.46% = 13.3
Savings = 13.3 X $24,800 = $330,360

Absenteeism:
Change in absences (Incidents) = 385 x 228 x 1.9% = 1668
Savings = 1668 X $98 $163,446

Table 5.Summary of Primary Monetary Values

Measures	Benefits
Increase in Productivity	$20,160
Reduction in Employee Turnover	$330,360
Reduction in Absenteeism	$163,446
Total	$513,966

Table 6. Summary of Other Monetary Values

Measures	Benefits
Efficiency	$15,300
Time Savings (participant 1)	$7,920
Time Savings (participant 2)	$3,279
Direct Cost Savings	$7,830
Total	$34,329

ROI and BCR Calculations

Total Benefits: $513,966 + $34,329 = $548,295

$$BCR = \frac{\$548,295}{\$80,468} = 6.81$$

$$ROI\ (\%) = \frac{\$548,295 - \$80,468}{\$80,468} \times 100 = 581\%$$

Discussion Questions

1. Are these numbers lower or higher than you expected? Comment.
2. How do you think these estimates would compare with the values at six months after the program is conducted? One year?
3. How could the ROI process be improved?
4. What are the potential intangible benefits from this program?

PART H

ROI Analysis

The values presented in this study were much higher than management anticipated. In discussions held before implementation, the senior management team (president, director of manufacturing, and plant manager) agreed that for the program to be successful, the payoff would have to be in productivity. This senior management group even suggested that absenteeism and turnover be considered intangible data and reported as additional improvements without a conversion to monetary values. Thus, in early discussions, absenteeism and turnover, although linked directly to the skills training, were considered to be potentially low impact variables. If the original suggestion had been followed, the program would have generated a negative ROI. An important lesson was learned. Behaviorally driven Level 4 data, although considered to be soft in nature, can have a tremendous impact in the organization. And in this situation, the impact would have been considerably enhanced if more appropriate values were used for the monetary conversion of absenteeism and turnover. (Instead, lower, more conservative values were used).

An important issue evolved concerning the projection of output data six months to one year after the program. It was clear that the output was moving in the right direction and it appeared that further improvement was in store. While it is tempting to assume the variables will continue to improve, in reality, other variables usually enter the analysis and a deterioration of the output variables may be realized, unless additional training or other interventions are implemented. This is what happened in this case. Each data item continued to improve for the six months. Absenteeism tapered off and then increased slightly, turnover remained fairly constant, while productivity continued to improve, perhaps driven by the TQM and team building sessions.

As part of the evaluation process, the evaluation team (consultant, facilitators, HRD manager, and department heads) explored ways in which the process could be improved. The team discussed several issues. First, because the control group strategy most accurately isolates the effects of training, the team thought it would have been better to initiate this program in a plant that could be compared to another location in a control group arrangement. This strategy will often develop more confidence in the process and will build a more convincing case for a high impact ROI.

A second issue was the needs assessment. The team thought it was important to have sufficient evidence of a direct connection between the Level 4 business impact measures and the planned training program. However, some team members wanted to see more evidence of how this was accomplished so that they would be more convinced about the direct linkage.

The third issue was the early follow-up. The consultants wanted to wait six months to capture the improvement, although management insisted on making a decision in four months. Perhaps a compromising solution is to capture data at four months, make the decision based on the apparent high impact level, and continue to capture data for another two months and develop an ROI impact study with six months of data, which would then be communicated to the target audience.

The fourth issue involved the apparent lack of a comprehensive evaluation at Level 3. Some team members wanted a more comprehensive assessment of actual behavior changes, which would convince them that the supervisors were actually operating differently. While this is an important issue, it was a trade-off process. A comprehensive Level 3 evaluation is time consuming and costly. When a Level 4 evaluation was planned with a specific technique to isolate the effects of training, other team members felt that a more comprehensive Level 3 was unnecessary.

Overall, the evaluation team perceived this to be an excellent ROI analysis. The process was credible with an acceptable level of accuracy.

Intangible Benefits

Other potential intangible benefits were identified including improved job satisfaction of the first-level managers, improved overall job satisfaction, reduction in stress for supervisors, and an increase in the bonus for supervisors (bonus pay is linked to productivity). While these items were considered to be important benefits of the program, they were not measured because of the additional effort required for monitoring and analysis. When intangible benefits are important and influential to the target audience, they should be monitored and analyzed in a more comprehensive way.

Interestingly, the management group initially proposed absenteeism and turnover measures as intangible benefits. If this suggestion had been followed, the improvements in absenteeism and turnover would have been presented as intangible benefits, resulting in a negative ROI. The team learned a valuable lesson. There should be an attempt to convert each intangible measure that is monitored and isolated. If the conversion process becomes unmanageable, inaccurate, or not very credible, then a data item is listed as an intangible benefit and reported without any further analysis. (Guiding Principle #11).

Discussion Questions

1. Although the ROI analysis plan is usually completed prior to pursuing the evaluation process, please take a few minutes to complete the plan shown in Figure 6.
2. Could the ROI forecast be developed on a pre-program basis? Please explain.
3. Is a forecast with reaction data possible? Please explain.
4. Would an ROI forecast with Level 2 or 3 data be possible? Please explain.
5. How should the results of this study be communicated? Please explain.

Figure 6. ROI Analysis Plan

Program: _Leadership for Improved Performance_   Responsibility: _____   Date: _____

Data Items (Usually Level 4)	Methods for Isolating the Effects of the Program/Process	Methods of Converting Data to Monetary Values	Cost Categories	Intangible Benefits	Communication Targets for Final Report	Other Influences/ Issues During Application	Comments

PART I

ROI Analysis Plan

Figure 7 shows the ROI analysis plan for the leadership development program. Each decision and strategy outlined in the various parts of this case is reflected on this form. This document is a decision-making tool for ROI analysis and is used to make specific plans for the analysis to be complete. It is completed before beginning the evaluation process.

Preprogram Forcast

A preprogram forecast could have been conducted, based on estimated improvements of the three business impact measures. A group of experts, most knowledgable about these measures and the work context, would estimate the improvement that would be achieved with the implementation of the Leadership Program. Although the numbers may not be accurate, they would provide some insight into the value of the program, particularly when the ROI percent is calculated.

Level 1 ROI Forecast

Although it was not attempted in this case, it is possible and perhaps instructive to develop a Level 1 ROI forecast. With this process, a series of potential impact questions could be asked where participants anticipate potential changes and estimate the particular impact of changes for each of the three variables (productivity, turnover, and absenteeism). Estimates could be provided on other measures that may be driven by the program. First year values could be developed, along with a confidence percentage obtained from participants reflecting their level of certainty with the process. The data could be adjusted with this confidence level to provide a forecast of the benefit and the calculation of the ROI. Although this ROI value is subjective and often inflated, this analysis would provide some insight into the relationship between the projections at the end of the program and the actual performance four months later. Also, it may actually enhance the results because participants who make projections of performance may be motivated to meet those projections.

Figure 7. ROI Analysis Plan

Date:_____

Data Items (Usually Level 4)	Methods for Isolating the Effects of the Program	Methods of Converting Data	Cost Categories	Intangible Benefits	Communication Targets	Other Influences/ Issues
Productivity % of Shipments Met	• Participant Estimates	• Direct Conversion - Company Standard Value	• Program Fee from Consulting Company • Program Materials • Food and Refreshments • Facilities • Evaluation Costs • Salaries and Benefits of Participants	• Improved Team Leader Job Satisfaction • Improved Employee Job Satisfaction • Stress Reduction • Increase in Bonus Pay	• Participants • Managers of Participants • Senior Management • HRD and HR Staff • Other Plant Managers • Potential Clients	• Team building was in process • Total Quality Management program has been launched • Management support is good • Management is very anxious to see results
Turnover (Quits and Discharges)	• Participant Estimates	• External Studies • Senior Management Estimate				
Absenteeism	• Participant Estimates	• External Studies • Participant Estimate				

Measuring ROI in Leadership Development **317**

Levels 2 and 3 ROI Forecast

At LNS, it was impossible to capture data for a Level 2 ROI forecast. For this forecast to be possible, a validated instrument must be developed to measure the performance of first-level managers in the program and have it correlated with subsequent on-the-job performance. This was not feasible in this situation.

A Level 3 ROI forecast was not considered because of the concern over the subjective assessments that must be made converting Level 3 data to monetary values. Also, the client was very bottom-line oriented and preferred to discuss performance in terms of Level 4 measures (productivity, turnover, absenteeism, etc.). While management recognized that skills must be acquired and behavior must be changed, they were less interested in discussing the extent to which changes have occurred and the value of the change. Thus, a Level 3 ROI forecast would have provided little value for the client.

Communication of Results

Communication of results from an ROI impact study is crucial to the ROI Methodology. Three documents were created: a detailed impact study, an executive summary, and brief summary, with a little more detail than the executive summary. Although there can be many target audiences, six audiences received the study results at LNS:

1. The participants (first-level managers) were provided a summary of the study results revealing what they had accomplished, collectively. The brief summary of the impact study showed how the ROI was developed.
2. The managers of the participants (middle-level managers) received a summary of the study with an appropriate explanation. These department heads for the various production and support departments were aware of the ROI impact study and were anticipating the results.
3. Senior management received executive summaries and copies of the detailed study. At LNS, this group included the president, director of manufacturing (for all plants), and the plant manager. In addition, this group received a briefing on the study results and discussed how it was developed along with its interpretation. This step is important to ensure that there is a

complete understanding of the ROI Methodology.

4. The HRD and HR staff received copies of the complete study so that they could understand how the ROI Methodology is applied to this type of program. This ROI study was part of an ongoing effort to build skills and develop strategies to increase accountability of HR programs.

5. Plant managers for the other locations received copies of the executive summary to show what can be accomplished with this type of training. Essentially, this communication served as an internal marketing tool to convince others that leadership development can improve their plants.

6. Potential clients for the consulting firm received brief summary copies of the study. This target group was unique to the consulting firm. With permission of the company, the study summary was used by the consulting firm to convince other prospective clients that leadership development can produce high impact. The name of the organization was disguised and sensitive data was slightly altered to protect the identity of the company.

Collectively, these six target audiences received information on the ROI impact study, ensuring that all important audiences understand the results and the process.

Discussion Questions

1. How can the results of this study be used to generate additional funding for measurement and evaluation?
2. How should the ROI Methodology be transferred internally in terms of responsibilities and skills?
3. How should management support for ROI be enhanced?
4. What other steps should be taken to implement the ROI Methodology at LNS?

PART J

Implementation Issues

A variety of implementation issues emerged at LNS:

- The HRD staff at LNS used the results of this study to make a request for additional funding for measurement and evaluation in the future. In essence, the plan is to use the savings generated from the studies to drive additional funding for measurement and evaluation.
- One individual was appointed as coordinator for measurement and evaluation and was asked to lead the process. Appointing a champion and a leader to implement the ROI Methodology ensures that the process works properly, is executed timely, and is supported appropriately.
- To ensure that the study can be replicated, the internal leader participated in all phases of ROI Implementation. The consulting firm worked closely with this individual to ensure that each step of the ROI Methodology was understood and could be applied in other situations.
- To help accomplish the transfer of capability, the consulting firm organized additional training for the evaluation leader to develop skills in the ROI Methodology and provide additional practice with ROI calculations.
- To help improve management support, a 2½-hour briefing was scheduled with the management team (department managers and above) at the next quarterly meeting to discuss the results of this study, and the potential opportunity for significant returns from training. This program also underscored the manager's responsibility to make training effective in the company.
- Specific targets were set where a few programs were identified for planned ROI calculations. This provided some guidance for the HRD director to focus on high priority programs.
- A policy statement was developed to capture the basic requirements for measurement and evaluation. This document described the responsibilities for all stakeholders, outlined how ROI studies would be conducted, and indicated how the results would be communicated.

Collectively, these seven actions provided adequate support to implement the ROI Methodology internally and make it a routine activity at LNS.